Principles
of Salvation

San Diego Christian College
Library
Santee, CA

252
F514p

Principles of Salvation

Charles G. Finney

Compiled and Edited by Louis Gifford Parkhurst, Jr.

BETHANY HOUSE PUBLISHERS

MINNEAPOLIS, MINNESOTA 55438

A Division of Bethany Fellowship, Inc.

Copyright © 1989
Louis Gifford Parkhurst, Jr.
All Rights Reserved

Published by Bethany House Publishers
A Division of Bethany Fellowship, Inc.
6820 Auto Club Road, Minneapolis, Minnesota 55438

Printed in the United States of America

Library of Congress Cataloging-in-Publication Data

Finney, Charles Grandison, 1792–1875.
    Principles of salvation / Charles G. Finney ; compiled and edited by
Louis Gifford Parkhurst, Jr.
       p. cm.
    Sermons originally published 1839–1891.
    Bibliography: p.
    1. Evangelistic sermons. 2. Sermons, American. I. Parkhurst, Louis
Gifford, 1946–   .   II. Title.
BV3797.F525P76   1989
252'.3—dc20   89–14961
ISBN 1-55661-032-7   CIP

DEDICATION

This collection of Charles G. Finney's sermons on salvation are dedicated to the congregation of Christ Community Church in Oklahoma City, Oklahoma. To a people who are committed to the truth, who stand for the truth, and who desire that others come to the truth, who speak the truth in love and love one another.

CHARLES G. FINNEY was one of America's foremost evangelists. Over half a million people were converted under his ministry in an age that offered neither amplifiers nor mass communication as tools. Harvard Professor Perry Miller affirmed that "Finney led America out of the eighteenth century." As a theologian, he is best known for his *Revival Lectures* and his *Systematic Theology.*

LOUIS GIFFORD PARKHURST, JR., is pastor of Christ Community Church in Oklahoma City, Oklahoma. He garnered a B.A. and an M.A. from the University of Oklahoma and an M.Div. degree from Princeton Theological Seminary. He is married and the father of two children. This is his fourteenth volume of the works of Charles G. Finney for Bethany House Publishers.

CONTENTS

BOOKS IN THIS SERIES

OTHER BOOKS BY FINNEY

PREFACE

Principles of Salvation is the promised companion to *Principles of Faith*. It will stand alone as Finney's most definitive treatment of the process and the assurance of salvation. Combined, these two books contain more than forty sermons dealing with these two major Christian themes.

Previously, some have read Finney out of context concerning faith and salvation; some have harshly judged him—and a few others have become legalistic professing Christians. I hope the sermons in these two books will solve some of these problems. Since Finney began his *Systematic Theology* (which is really volume two; he never completed volume one) with a discussion of moral law, some have misjudged him with regard to salvation. I hope *Principles of Faith* and *Principles of Salvation* will be a good starting point for those who wish to study his *Systematic Theology*.

Finney's words are true to Scripture and reason. His words are true to the way God created us with a mind, will, and body; true to what we have become as fallen, sinful creatures. His words are true concerning what we can become by the grace of God through a saving faith in Jesus Christ. Because his words are true and suited to the purposes of God, God the Holy Spirit can anoint his words, bring them home to us, save us, and save others through us. I pray that you will be blessed through these two books, and be prepared to bless others.

With Love in the Risen Lamb,
L. G. Parkhurst, Jr.

PART 1

Christ or the Crowd

"If any man will come after me, let him deny himself, and take up his cross daily, and follow me" (Luke 9:23).

1

ON FOLLOWING CHRIST*

"Jesus saith unto him, If I will that he tarry till I come, what is that to thee? Follow thou me" (John 21:22).

Jesus Christ spoke these words to Peter, having warned him previously that in his later years Peter would have his liberty restrained—and ultimately glorify God through martyrdom. A question arose in the mind of Peter, who was more curious than wise, about how things would be for his fellow disciple John. "Lord, and what shall this man do?" he inquired. Gently rebuking this idle inquisitiveness, Jesus replied, "If I will that he tarry till I come, what is that to thee? Follow thou me."

Jesus' reply hints at a principle with a broad practical application. Assuming this principle is for us at the present day, what is Jesus saying to *us*?

Suppose Jesus himself stood before you at this moment. You wait eagerly as He prepares to speak. You see the halo of glory around His head. You note the blending of meekness and majesty that identifies Him most fully as the Son of God. Your whole soul is moved within you to catch every word He may utter. Oh, what an earnest expectation! If He were to speak, you would hear even the ticking of your clock more plainly than you do now. If you did not happen to catch every word distinctly, you would turn to someone and ask, "What did He say? What was that?"

He speaks to you in a tone positive, yet commanding. What is this command? Remember, if it is the Lord Jesus Christ, He has the *right* to command. Who else in earth or heaven has this right more absolutely than He? It is of the utmost importance to know what He com-

*Sermons on the Way of Salvation, 358–371.

mands us to do. Whatever it is, it vitally affects our well-being both to know and to do it. Words from one so benevolent must be for our good. Certainly, He never spoke unless it was for the good of those to whom He spoke.

Jesus must speak for the general good; for the Great King and Lord of all never overlooks what pertains to the general good. Moreover, He must be safe to obey. Indeed, how can it be otherwise? Did anyone ever obey Him and find it unsafe?

Of course it must be our duty to obey Him. How shall Christ ever command us, if we are not solemnly bound to obey Him? Also, it must be *possible* for us to obey. Did Christ ever enjoin us otherwise? Could He possibly do a thing so unreasonable?

All these points must be assumed and admitted. How can we—even for a moment—doubt any one of them?

This, then, is the state of the case. What, now, should be the attitude of our mind? Manifestly this: *Let Him speak. I will surely listen and obey. What does He say? Every word He says, I know, will be infinitely good. Let me catch every intimation of His will.* "The judgments of the Lord are true and righteous altogether. More to be desired are they than gold, yea, than much fine gold: sweeter also than honey and the honeycomb" (Ps. 19:10-11).

Or will you turn away and say, "I don't care what He says"? Would you not rather say this: *Let Him say what He will, it is all good, and I will surely hear and obey it*? If this is your attitude toward Him, then you are ready to examine what He says.

Observe, He gives you something to be done, and more to the point, something to be done *by yourself*. To you it does not matter just now what others may do, or what God's providence may allot to them. *What is that to thee?* It has always been the temptation of the human heart to look at the duties of others rather than one's own. You must resist and put down this temptation. Christ has work for *you* to do, and it becomes you to address yourself earnestly to it. Observe, also, that it is to be done *now*. He gives you no furlough, not even to go home and bid farewell to those of your house. There can be no excuse for delay.

What does He require? He says, *"Follow thou Me."* What does this mean? Must I leave my home? Must I abandon my business? Am I to follow Him all over the land? We can see plainly that when Jesus dwelt in human flesh among men, He called certain of them to follow Him as His servants and disciples. They were to attend Him in all His journeys, to go where He went and stop where He stopped. They were to aid Him in His missionary work.

Now, Christ is no longer here in human flesh. Following Him cannot have precisely the same physical sense. Yet now, no less than then, it implies that you obey His revealed will and do the things that please

Him. You must imitate His example and follow His instructions. By various methods, He still makes His will known and you are to follow wherever He leads. You must accept Him as the Captain of your salvation and allow His laws to control all your life. He comes to save you from your sins. He comes to save you from the ruin that unforgiven sin must bring. You must accept Him as such a Savior. This is a part of following Him.

The Implications of Obedience

Following Jesus Christ implies confidence in Him who commands. With confidence, you commit yourself fully to obey Him and trust all consequences of your actions to His disposal. There can be no hearty, cheerful obedience without this implicit confidence.

Following Him implies a willingness to be saved by Him. You must be willing to be *saved from all sin*. You cannot reserve a favorite indulgence. You recoil from all sin and set yourself earnestly to withstand every sort of temptation.

When you decide to follow Christ, you commit yourself to follow Him through evil or good report, whatever the effect may be on your reputation. You are ready to make sacrifices for Christ, rejoicing to be counted worthy to suffer shame for His name.

A common fault is to admit what Christ requires, yet shy from doing it. Some say, "I go, sir," but go not. Such a person does not follow Christ, who requires *immediate* action. He has work for you to do *today*, and He demands that you commit yourself to full obedience.

Why Follow Him?

Suppose Jesus Christ were personally to announce to you, "Follow thou me." Would you ask to know *why*? You could very soon assign some weighty reasons. Your own mind would suggest them. And do you know any reasons why you should *not* follow Him? I presume it is settled in every mind why you should obey His command, here and now, without one moment's delay. Can you think of any reason why you should not obey His command? Do you doubt at all whether this is your duty? Can you think of any reason why it is not? Then it must be your duty and you ought to do it. The matter should lie in your mind: *If this is my duty, of course I must do it at once. Doing my duty is the business of my life.*

You owe it to Jesus Christ to follow Him. If you are a student, make His ideals and goals your own. Imagine a young man intent on serving Christ. You ask him why he goes to college. He answers, "Because I will be better prepared to teach men about Jesus Christ." While in class he entreats his teachers, "Give me an education. Give me all the discipline of mind and heart you can, so I may be better able to teach and preach Jesus Christ. Tell me all you know of Him. Pray for me that God may teach my heart the whole gospel." In this way a Christian student follows Christ.

Do you not owe this to Him? Can you deny this? Have you any right to live for yourself? If you could gain some good for the moment, could you think it *right* to have your own way and disown Christ? What if you were to gain the whole world and lose your own soul? You owe it to yourself not to neglect this command of grace.

You owe it to your friends to follow Christ, friends who have done much for you and whom you love, friends over whom you exert a precious influence. For their sakes you ought to know Christ, that you may lead them to follow Him also. You owe it to your father and mother. Are they praying souls? Due to the sympathy they feel for you and to the strong desire they have for your salvation, you should follow Christ. If they have never prayed, it is time they did, and time that you should lead them to Christ.

You owe it to the whole world. Millions do not know Jesus; some of these you might teach so that they shall not die without having known Him.

One more thought as to yourself. The weight of your decision, whether or not you obey this precept, will shape what you will be for all eternity. What you do in this matter will have its fruits on your destiny long after the sun and stars have faded away. You may choose to live in such a manner that, when you die, men shall say, "There goes from earth one nuisance, and hell has more sin in it now than it ever had before."

Jesus is the only path of peace. If you would have peace, you must seek and find it in Him. Thousands have found it. But none has ever found it anywhere else.

Jesus Christ says to you, "Follow thou Me." Will you set yourself to find some excuse? What are your excuses?

Do you say, "There are so many opinions among men, I do not know what to do"? Ah! but you *do know*. It is only a pitiful pretense when you say you don't know enough to purely go on in duty and please God. No opinions of men need stumble you if you simply follow Christ.

You talk about the various opinions among Christian sects. But, differ much as they may in lesser matters, on the great things of salvation, Bible-believing churches all agree. They all agree essentially that to follow Christ in confidence and simple love is the whole of duty of man and will ensure God's approval. Follow this simple direction and all will be well with you.

But some will say, "I believe all will be saved." You do, indeed! Will all become like Christ before they die? Do all in fact become holy in this world? Christ is in heaven. How can you go there unless you first become like Him in heart and in life?

All will be saved? The question is forced on my mind: *What is this belief—that all men will be saved—good for?* People plead this belief as their excuse for not following Christ. They say, "No need to trouble ourselves with following Christ, since everyone will be all right at last anyhow." Can this belief make men holy and happy? Some will answer, "It makes me happy for the present, and that is the most I care for." But does it make you *holy*? Does it beget true Christian self-denial and impartial benevolence? A faith and practice that make you happy without being holy is but a sham. Indeed, it cannot fail of being utterly mischievous, for it lures and pleases without the least advance toward saving your soul. It only leaves you the more a slave of sin and Satan.

But you say, "It makes me so miserable to believe that any will be forever lost!" What of it? What if it does make you feel unhappy? It may make you unhappy to see your guilty friend sent to the penitentiary or the gallows now. But such a doom may be nonetheless deserved even if it does hurt your feelings.

How can there be any other way of final happiness except through real holiness? The fountain of all happiness must lie in your own soul. If your soul is renewed to holiness and made unselfish, loving, forgiving, humble—then you will be happy of course. But you cannot be truly happy without such a character.

Some may say, "I don't believe in the necessity of a change of heart." Yet, *you do*. You are altogether mistaken, if you suppose you don't believe in the necessity of a change of heart. There cannot be such a person in all Christendom, a person who knows that by nature his heart is not right with God, yet does not think that he must become right with God before he can enjoy God's presence in heaven.

Is there one whose conscience does not testify that, before conversion, his heart is alienated from God? Do you not know that you are unlike God in spirit, and that you must be changed so as to become like God before you can enjoy Him? What? A sinner, knowing himself to be a sinner, believes he can be happy in God's presence without a radical moral change? Impossible! Everyone knows that the sinner, out of sympathy with God, must be changed before he can enjoy God's presence and love. Everyone, unchanged by God's grace, knows himself to be a sinner, and not holy by nature.

A case in point to show the force of truth on even hardened hearts came recently to my knowledge. A Christian lady, visiting one of the towns in Canada, was called on by a gentleman of high standing in society who had always lived a prayerless, ungodly life. A man of strong will and nerves, professedly a skeptic, he yet told the lady that he would do anything she said in order to become a Christian. "Well, then," she said, "kneel down here, and cry out, 'God, be merciful to me, a sinner.'"

"What?" he replied, "when I don't believe myself a sinner?"

"You need not excuse yourself on that ground," she said, "for *you know you are a sinner.*"

Having passed his word of honor to a lady, he could not draw back, and therefore kneeled and repeated the proposed words. Arising, he was told, "Do so again, and say the same words."

"I don't believe myself a sinner," he said again, raising the old objection.

She made the same answer as before, and a second time he repeated the words of that prayer. The same things were said and the same things were done, the third time, and then, hardened as he was, his heart felt the force of those words, and he began to cry in earnest, "God, be merciful to me, a sinner!" His heart broke and he prayed till mercy came!

So often, when people say they don't believe this and that, they *do believe it* so far as conviction is concerned. They *know the truth*, with respect to their own guilt.

Perhaps you plead, "I must attend to other duties first; my studies or my business." No, my friend; no other duties must stop you from following Jesus. This is the greatest duty, and ought to be the first.

Hear what the Savior said on this very point. He said to one man, "Follow Me!" and he answered, "Lord, suffer me first to go and bury my father" (Matt. 8:21). This is a strong case, and is placed on record for our instruction because it is strong. It may seem to you very unnatural that Jesus would call anyone away from a duty so obvious and so urgent in every human heart. Yet, what did He say? He gave no heed to this plea, but answered, "Let the dead bury their dead." Not even the last rites of burial must be allowed to stand before obedience to Christ's call.

No doubt Christ saw a tendency in this man to plead off, and therefore He saw the necessity of meeting it promptly. Suppose the man had said, "Yes, Lord, I am ready. My father lies unburied, but I am ready—if Thou callest me—to follow Thee even now." It is at least supposable, if not probable, that Jesus would have answered, "Yes; I will go with thee to that funeral. Let us lay the dead solemnly in their last bed, and then go to our preaching."

Another man replied to His call, saying, "Lord, I will follow thee; but let me first go and bid them farewell which are at home at my house." To him, Jesus replied, "No man, having put his hand to the plow, and looking back, is fit for the kingdom of God" (Luke 9:61–62).

Thus Christ teaches that no duty must prevent your giving up your heart to follow Him. You must make up your mind fully to this life-business, immerse yourself in it. Anything less than this is an offense to God.

Do you say, "I must study"? You must first make up your mind to serve Christ in whatever you do, or else study is an unacceptable duty. When Jesus says to you, "My son, give me your heart," He wants your heart, and nothing else. He does not wish to be put off by some other duty. When He says, "Follow Me," He demands an explicit answer—a "yes" or a "no." He cannot accept any evasiveness.

You are now called to follow Christ with the understanding that if you give yourself to Him, He will give himself to you. Think of that. Would it not be a blessed thing to have Christ give himself to you, to be your eternal Friend, to be your portion and joy forever?

Suppose Jesus were to pass nearby, calling to one after another by name to follow Him. When He came near you, would you think in your heart, *I certainly hope He will call me*? Or can it be you would think, *I hope He will not call me*? Can it be you *could* think that? Would you not rather think, *Oh, is it possible He will pass me by? How awful! Can it be? And if so, shall I never see Him passing by so near, again*?

Oh sinner, Jesus *is* now passing by *so near*. Arise and speak to Him, for He calls to you. And you must decide now whether or not you will follow Him—and your decision will decide your eternity!

Don't concern yourself with what others will think. Don't say, as Peter did, "Lord, what shall this man do?" This is an old but clever device of your adversary: turning your mind to think about others. If you are wise, you will think only about yourself in this matter.

There is great comfort in reaching the point where you say, "I will follow Him anywhere. Let others do as they please. I will serve Christ." When you come to this point wholeheartedly, you will find it is a most precious decision.

You are now called to take a step here today that will decide all your future being. Is it not better that you take this step *confidently*?

Suppose I should now say, "Come, separate yourselves according to the decision you make. All you who will follow Christ, rise and come to Him *now*." What will *you* do? Will you refuse, saying, "I will not follow Christ yet. I have goals of my own to accomplish first. I will not be His servant now." Is this your decision? Are you willing that it be put on record? *It will go on record anyhow, whether you want it or not.*

Some of you may say, "I will not decide just now. I did not begin the day expecting to make so great a decision at this time." Indeed! Did you not expect to hear a gospel sermon today? And did you not know that every gospel sermon contains, in fact, a call to repent and follow Jesus?

But now will you turn and say, "Lord, I can't understand why I should follow You"? Don't say that, for you *can* understand it. And you can decide this question today.

"But," some young men worry, "if I should go after Him, I am afraid I shall have to give up some of my own plans for my life. I might have to give up my intended profession, or be barred from some lucrative business that pays better than following Christ."

Then you can go and tell these things to your Savior. Tell Him you cannot trust Him to provide for your worldly interests. You are also afraid He would send you to preach the kingdom of God, and pay you poorly for your services. No doubt He will excuse you from His service here—and from entering into the joy of your Lord hereafter besides!

There is a young man who says, "I can't follow Christ now, because I cannot leave my dear Christian mother." Then go upon your knees and spread out your excuse before the Lord. Say to Him, "My good mother gave me the best Christian instruction and her constant prayers. She did everything she could to make me Your servant. But now that You are calling me to follow You, I find I cannot go and preach your love to a dying world. For she cannot spare me and I cannot leave her." Indeed, you cannot afford not to. Though your pious mother thinks her claim is above that of the Savior, you both must make your choice.

2

A PUBLIC PROFESSION OF CHRIST*

All people are, or ought to be, interested in knowing what is implied by making a public profession of faith in Christ. There are several sound reasons for making such a profession, though some in their pride try to argue away its necessity.

The Implications of a Public Profession

A public profession of Christ is a public affirmation of hearty confidence in the facts revealed in the gospel of Jesus Christ, together with all things that are recorded of Him in the Bible. Certainly, this is implied in making a public profession of Christian faith. We must acknowledge publicly our submission and consecration to Him, whereby we surrender everything up to Him as the only Savior of the world.

A public profession is a public vow of cooperation with Him in His great work—that of bringing about the salvation of men. It implies a public renunciation of a self-seeking spirit, a public profession of self-denial, in that we no longer live for ourselves. It is a profession of universal devotion to God.

A public profession also implies dependence on Him in all areas of life. Further, it implies a confession of sin and the admission that we cannot begin to save ourselves by our own righteousness. A public profession admits the impossibility of being saved through the Law; and is a public declaration of the fact that Christ has provided the only possible way by which a person can be saved. All professions of Christ, therefore, bear testimony of confidence in the truths of the

*From *The Penny Pulpit*, an address delivered on Friday evening, March 28, 1851, after the admission of a number of new members to the fellowship of the church at the Tabernacle, Moorfields. Originally, the sermon had no specific scriptural text.

gospel, of submission to Christ, and of dependence on His authority.

A public profession is also a public renunciation of the spirit of the world. A person cannot be in love with both the world and Christ. It is an oath of allegiance to Christ, a public affirmation that He is your God and Savior.

When a person professes faith in Christ, he professes to be a representative of Christ. By making a public profession of Christian faith, he professes that he has received the Spirit of Christ and intends to exhibit it to the world. By professing Christianity, he says to the world, "I will illustrate by my life, temper, spirit, and actions, the essence of Christianity." Nothing less than these things is implied in making a public profession of Christianity.

Purposes of a Public Profession

Surely a public profession involves no more than simple honesty. The fact is, to not confess these things is to utterly betray God and Christ, deceiving your own soul and the world at large. The facts of the gospel being perceived, they cannot with any show of reason be denied; to acknowledge them is but a simple act of honesty.

Christians are not their own, they are bought with a price (1 Cor. 6:19–20); therefore, in honesty they should publicly acknowledge this. In short, it is a simple matter of honesty that everyone to whom the gospel is preached—everyone who has heard of Christ and His nature, His love for men, and His atonement on their behalf—should at once acknowledge that these things are so, avowing their confidence in them, their sympathy with them, their dependance on them, and their submission to them. No individual has a right to call himself an honest person unless he openly acknowledges that these facts are as true as heaven itself.

A public profession of Christianity is essential to self-respect. No person who understands the essence of Christianity will be able to rest until he can publicly profess it. He cannot have any solid self-respect until that time. He must be ashamed of himself.

A gentleman once told me that before he became a professing Christian, the minister whose preaching he attended used to deliver an annual sermon in which he would explain to the members of his congregation the conditions that must be met in order to participate at the communion table. Of those present, the minister observed, a few had celebrated the ordinance once that year, some twice, and a great many not at all.

"When these facts were brought out," said the gentleman, "I said to myself, 'Why, our minister takes notice of those who are absent from the communion table,' and I became so ashamed of myself that I frequently stayed away altogether. How could it be that I could go to a Christian church, hear the word of God, mingle with the congregation, and with God's people, *and never publicly avow my attachment to Christ, never avow my belief in the Bible and in the gospel?*"

A public profession is also essential to true peace of mind, because if a person does not profess what he knows to be the truth, he violates the law of his own conscience.

Such a profession is owed to Christ by everyone who knows that Christ tasted death "for every man" (Heb. 2:9). Christ has become the Advocate for every person who submits to His will and acknowledges his obligations to Him. A great many sinners seem to forget that they receive their daily bread from heaven because of what Christ has done for them. Everything they have in this world, every drop of water with which they cool their tongue, is granted because Christ appeared on their behalf and gave himself to die for them. God would never bless the wicked of this world as He does, if Christ had not undertaken His mediatorial work. Everyone, then, whether saint or sinner, is bound to acknowledge his indebtedness to Christ, and that publicly, before all people.

A circumstance will illustrate this. A man who had lived all his life hearing the message of the gospel became uneasy that he had never given his heart to Christ, although he knew of its truth. He had a dream in which he and his brother were journeying to a certain place. A messenger from heaven met them and said, "As you travel along you will come to a place where the road forks, one branch to the right and the other to the left. At that spot you must separate. You will be told which road you must each take. The one who takes the road to the right will go to heaven, while he that takes the one to the left must go to hell!"

The man became greatly agitated as they walked along, until they came to the roads of which the heavenly messenger had told him. He was told that he must take the road to the left. Filled with the greatest consternation, he turned to pursue the path assigned to him. As he was about to part from his brother, he said, "Well, farewell brother, you are going to heaven, for you have been a very good man, but I am going to hell! I shall not see you any more, but I want you to tell the Lord Jesus Christ that I am greatly obliged to Him for all the favors I have received at His hands, for all the good He has done me, and for all the good He would have done had I been willing. Though I shall never reach heaven to see the Lord Jesus to tell him these things myself, I want you to carry this message to Him: that I am greatly obliged for all that He has done for me, and even for what He now appoints. I have nothing to accuse Him of, although I have failed to get to heaven, for it is my own fault!"

With this he burst out into loud weeping, and awoke, and then realized, in a manner most clear and bright, his own real relation to Christ. The dream had prepared his mind—probably the Holy Spirit was concerned in it—for a full reception of the truth, breaking his heart all to pieces so he immediately surrendered himself to Christ.

Now notice, although he knew he was going to hell, he recognized that he had received a great many favors from God on account of Christ, and that, therefore, he owed a deep debt of gratitude and obligation to Him. And so he told his brother to thank Him for those favors that he had received at His hands.

Now I suppose some who profess to know Christ have not even done so much as that. Did you ever send such a message to Christ, or thank Him yourself for His favors toward you?

It is right and reasonable that you should publicly acknowledge Christ, and thus show that you regard yourself as being under very great and lasting obligation to Him. You owe it to yourself to make this acknowledgement. You owe it to those who are related to you, and you owe it to those who are under your influence. You cannot live without exerting some influence, and therefore it is your duty to publicly profess Christ, that the people you affect might gain the full benefit of your example. Think, if you are a parent, what an influence you have upon your children. Almost everything will depend upon the example that you set them.

You owe it to the Church of God. The Church has been praying for you, and doubtless, you are indebted to them for the blessings of spiritual life. If you read your Bible, you will find that the prayers of God's people are continually pointed to as the grounds by which God spares sinners. It is to the Church that they owe the means of grace, and a great many of the blessings which they enjoy. You owe it to the Church, therefore, to make a public profession of faith in Christ.

You owe a public profession to the world at large, because the world bears a vital interest in this matter. Do not hesitate. You have a right to take the credit for all that you might do to save the world when you do your duty in this manner.

The gospel of Christ expressly commands people to profess the name of Christ before the universe. This is one of the plainest commands in the whole Bible. By doing this one guards his heart against sin. Who does not see the importance of this? A mind should as much as possible be closed against sin and temptation. A public profession guards the person who makes it. It protects the mind from those influences that might lead it away.

This principle is perfectly illustrated in the Bible by the institution of marriage. Parties who wish to live together must recognize the great importance of committing themselves to each other by a public act. To go about it in any other way leaves them much more exposed to temptation. What a safeguard it is that the wife can stand forth as a married woman, against being addressed by other men, and the same with the husband. So it is with those who publicly commit themselves to Christ. The world hears the proclamation that it can no longer expect the endorsement of the one committed, for once a person is committed to Christ, the door is closed against the world and sin.

The individual's public profession induces Christ to watch over him, enabling that person to persevere in a holy life by His grace. For example, when an individual considers himself a Christian, and yet makes no public profession of Christ, what honor does he bring to Christ? What inducement is there for Christ to watch over him? When people see that he lives a consistently moral life, if he makes no profession of Christ, they ascribe all the credit of his conduct to his natural goodness—not to grace. The world will give all the credit to the man, and not to Christ, to whom the credit really belongs.

Now what has Christ to do with a person such as this? He does not honor Christ. Why then should Christ continue to watch over him? Why should such a person's candle remain lit if it is always kept under a bushel? When a person acknowledges his dependance on Christ, he presents an inducement for Christ to continue to give him grace.

A man who throws himself upon the grace of Christ engages and ensures for himself the protection of an Almighty arm. Look at Peter in the ship. When he saw Christ walking on the water, Peter said, "If it be thou, bid me come unto thee on the water"; and as soon as the Lord said "Come" he did not hesitate, but cast himself upon the protection of Christ. And did He let Peter sink? Oh no, Christ did not let him sink when he had fully committed himself (Matt. 14:28). So when an individual, from right motives, makes public his attachment to Christ, he may depend upon being preserved. Christ will never forsake him.

And so, with all humility, let he who is willing speak these things with confidence: "O Lord Jesus, I have committed myself to serve Thee before the world as a living example of Thy grace. Now shall the light that is in me become darkened? Will You withhold Thy grace from me, so that I crucify Thee afresh, putting Thee to open shame? May it never be, Lord." Do you not think that this would be a convincing argument in the eyes of Christ? Yes, this ought to persuade Him if the words are spoken in good faith.

Another reason why we ought to make a public profession of faith is that it allows us to be channels by which His covenant blessings flow to His people. If we want these blessings, we must comply with God's order.

Those who make a public profession of Christian faith take a special interest in the problems and concerns of the whole Church body. It is not true that people who belong to different denominations make up so many different churches. The fact is, they are all branches of the same church—the Church of God—if they are real Christians. They may differ in certain forms and in minor things, but if they are truly Christian, they are one in heart.

Every genuine disciple of Christ sustains an intimate relation to the entire Church. The Head of the Church is in heaven, and there also are the charter members; yet those who remain below are of the same spirit as those who are made perfect in heaven. Every visible member of Christ, then, brings himself by his public profession under the watchful care, the sympathy and prayers of the entire Church of God. Understand, I am not speaking of mere pew-sitters, and there have always been plenty of these in every age, but of the Church in whatever denomination it is found.

Another reason for making a public profession is this: when individuals become entirely honest with themselves and with God, they are able to rest again, for they have peace with God. They then have fellowship with the Father and with the Son, and they cease to shrink away from public responsibility.

Why Some Neglect This Duty

Someone might say, "I am not a Christian." Well, is that a good excuse for not doing your duty? It is only to replace one sin with another. Why are you not a Christian? Suppose a person should try to justify himself for having committed some horrible crime by pleading that he was very wicked and loved sin. That, certainly, would not be regarded as a good excuse! No! It will not do to plead that you are not a Christian, expecting that such a plea will excuse you, for it only aggravates your guilt.

Another might say, "I do not make a profession because I fear I will disgrace Christ and His cause." Is that a good reason? Is it the real one? I fear there must be some mistake in that. Do you love and fear Him so much that you abstain from making a profession lest you should dishonor Him or His cause? *But do you not dishonor Him by your denial?* Indeed! How is it then that you are not afraid to sin by denying Christ, which you do by refusing to acknowledge Him?

"Ah!" says another, "I am afraid of such a responsibility." You fear the responsibility of professing Christ? Well, do you not fear the heavier responsibility of denying Him? Is there no responsibility in taking part with His enemies and refusing to obey His commands? Yes, indeed, there is a solemn, awful responsibility.

Another might say, "It is such a solemn thing if what you have said is actually implied in making a profession." Yes, it is. But it is also a solemn thing *not* to make such a profession, refusing to do it when Christ requires it—and reason, conscience and the entire universe demand it.

Still others shirk because, "I can as well be saved without it." What does this mean, *As well be saved without it*? Is it then a mere question of loss and gain with you? Is the whole point simply to be saved no matter what? Do you care nothing about your relationship to Christ? Nothing about obeying His commands, just so you gain salvation at last? Is that all you care about? But what can you mean by that, "I can as well be saved without it." Can you be saved by disobeying Christ as readily as by obeying Him? You refuse to acknowledge Him, and yet expect Him to save you? What does Christ himself say? "He that is ashamed of Me before men, of him will I be ashamed before My Father and the holy angels."

Now I suppose it is true that those who have no opportunity to avow and acknowledge Christ before others may be saved without it; but if people neglect to perform their duty after the chance is provided to carry it out, they will not be excused. To say that people can be saved without publicly acknowledging Christ when they have had every opportunity to do it is the same as saying that they can just as easily be saved while sinning. What is sin but a neglect of duty? Can a man live and die in sin and yet be a Christian?

Oh, say some, but this is only one sin. Well, suppose it is. But if you deliberately live in it you live in sin, for if you indulge in any form of iniquity you do not renounce any sin from your heart.

Can you recognize God's authority in anything if you do not submit to it in everything? What does the Bible say? "For whosoever shall keep the whole law, and yet offend in one point, he is guilty of all" (James 2:10). There is a great mistake on this subject. A great many suppose that they can neglect this duty, acknowledging their Lord only privately, and still get to heaven as if they had complied with it. You who think so are entirely mistaken, for if you neglect acknowledged duty, you live in known sin—and how can you be saved if you live in sin? It is impossible!

Consider this as well: a public profession of faith is the only way to receive an assurance of acceptance with God. For how can you expect to realize His promises without a public committal of yourself to Christ? Faith inherits the promises, unbelief does not.

The fact is, many persons are waiting for evidences that they are accepted by God, but are unwilling to obey Him. Further, a great many who have had a clear hope in Christ have put off making a public profession for so long that they have grieved the Holy Spirit and brought darkness over their own minds. The path was once clear, but they neglected it, and now they will in all probability die in that darkness, or be obliged to make a public profession of faith before God will restore the light they seek. I have known a great many cases where people waited for light, but did not obtain it till they had made up their minds to obey God; and when they had done this light came.

Some say, "I do not want to publicly commit myself." Now this excuse, though it may be the truth of the matter, reveals a heart that is not right before God. For if your heart were right, you would not hesitate for an instant to commit yourself before the world. Nay! you would be anxious to as publicly as possible attach yourself to Christ.

Another reason that some people give is that such a profession will subject them to scrutiny. "People will watch me to see how I live." Ah! and why do you shrink from that? "If I do not make a public profession, less will be expected of me." Is that a good reason why you should not make a public profession? Would you be called to do any more than what *ought* to be expected of you?

"But it will subject me to persecution." And is that a good reason? Did Christ shrink from coming to rescue you because it would subject Him to persecution? He was persecuted for your sake—can you not afford to bear any persecution for Him? Surely it is enough that the servant be *as* His Lord, and the disciple *as* His Master?

If Christ had avoided accomplishing your salvation for fear of being persecuted, where would you be now? But He did not withhold His cheek from those who struck him, or from those that plucked off the hair of his beard. He was maligned, slandered and murdered for your sake—how then can you begin to compare your lot with His?

Some people, I am ashamed to say, do not speak out because they are afraid that if they make a public profession of faith, they would be expected to support the institutions of the gospel. And is that a good reason why you should not align yourself with the cause of Christ, because by doing so you would be expected to do your part in this great work? O shame, that anyone should ever have such a thought! Whose are you? To whom belongs all your possessions? Can you afford to not be a Christian? Afford it! And could Christ afford to die for you? Suppose He had said, when He found what your salvation would cost Him, "I cannot afford it." Where would you and I be today if Christ had said this?

Another says, "It will subject me to greater restraint than I like. I shall not be able to go to such and such places. I sometimes like to visit certain places that are no place for Christians. Now I can occasionally indulge myself; but if I made a public profession such a course would injure my reputation as a Christian—and thereby, the cause of

Christ." Then you do not like the restraints that Christ would impose upon you? Well, how do you expect to secure heaven when you have continued to indulge your sinful desires—desires that are inconsistent with the Christian character? And yet you hope to be saved. Friend, do not deceive yourself, I beg of you!

Some fear they will be sorry if they publicly profess Christ. What will make you sorry? Do you think that if you make a public profession, and then live as you ought to live, that you will be sorry? What some people actually mean by this excuse is this: "I wish to be out of the church of God because I shall not like to live such a life as will be demanded of me." Now, if you feel thus, it is a plain proof that you have not committed your soul to Christ.

Another laments, "There are so many denominations and churches, I do not know which to join!" If you cannot make up your mind, ask Christ to give you some light. Is there nowhere that you can find Christian sympathy and fellowship? There must be such a place! There are those who have prayed for you, and earnestly besought the Lord to distill upon you the dew of His heavenly grace, and if you seek you will find them.

Still others say that it is a dreadful thing to make a false profession. So it is, but it is an equally dreadful thing to make no profession at all.

"Oh, but I can live a Christian life without it." Well, suppose you could? As I have already mentioned, this would only deny Christ, refusing Him His proper due. For unless such a profession is rendered, a man takes for himself the praise for his consistent walk, though it is really the effect of the water of grace that Christ has distilled upon his heart. By this, human nature is exalted and Christ is robbed. When the communion table is spread, and he does not partake, he says to the world: "See how I control myself. You see I have no need of Christ. See how good I am. I do not need the grace of Christ!" But it is false! You cannot be a Christian and make no profession of Christ!

The Implications of Not Making a Public Profession

Refusing to publicly profess Christ is a public denial and rejection of Christ of the most emphatic kind. It is a denial of the Life! It is a denial of dependence on Him, of obligation to Him not in words only, but in deeds! It is a profession that you have no part nor lot in Him.

It is a denial of the truth in relation to Christ, a public acknowledgment of unbelief, or unfaithfulness, which is unbelief. It is a public proclamation that in your view the Christian faith is a delusion, and Christ an imposter! Perhaps you do not say this outright, or at least do not intend to say it. Perhaps you never realized that not making a public profession implied these things, but it is true nevertheless.

Not to make a profession of Christ is a public avowal of sympathy for the other side. I know that many are not aware of what it means to stand aloof from a profession of Christ, and it is for this reason that I state these things, that they who hear me may no longer be ignorant of them.

Such silence is a public profession of unrepentance as well as unbelief. Everyone makes some public profession. Do not suppose that because you do not make a public profession in favor of Christ that you can remain neutral, for your refusal is a public declaration against Him. His friends are on one side, and His enemies on the other, and you must belong to one party or the other. If you are not committed to Him, you voluntarily subject yourself to the doom of the enemies of Christ.

Christians should watch over each other with paternal love, looking for good and not for evil. I have sometimes witnessed a spirit the very opposite of this. I have seen older church people watching for the mistakes of younger Christians. Oh, I trust it will not be so in your church! Set yourself to be a brother or sister in deed. Fathers sympathize with the youth!

New Christians should always remember to voluntarily place themselves in such a position as to draw the eyes of the world upon them, and of the church. They are continually observed by men and angels alike. Let them remember this! Do not be deterred from witnessing for Christ because of the great responsibility it involves. Christ has said, "My grace is sufficient for thee"; therefore they should not hesitate to put themselves in the position that Christ requires. He will give strength equal to the task.

Let those young Christians who have entered into fellowship, and those who will do so at the next opportunity, identify themselves fully with the people of God. They must always manifest sympathy with every good work, and everything that belongs to God's cause. Once they have publicly attested to it, let it possess their heart. Let all their actions witness that their profession is not an empty one!

3

BOUND TO KNOW YOUR TRUE CHARACTER*

"Examine yourselves, whether ye be in the faith; prove your own selves" (2 Corinthians 13:5).

According to the text, what does God require of you? He requires you to understand your own heart. You must take the proper steps to prove your real character as you appear in the sight of God, who does not seek to test your strength or knowledge, but your moral character. You should thoroughly test your character so you can understand yourself as you really are. The text implies that you should know what God thinks of you. Does He consider you a saint or sinner? God gives you a positive command to ascertain your own true character, to know whether you are an heir of heaven or hell.

If for no reason but your own peace of mind, you must fulfill this requirement. If you are uncertain as to your real character, you cannot have a settled peace of mind. You may be apathetic, more or less completely and perfectly, but apathy is very different from peace of mind. And very few people who continue to hear the gospel can remain indifferent for any length of time. You will not be able to suppress all of your uneasy and uncertain feelings concerning your true character and destiny. I am not speaking of hypocrites, who have seared their consciences, or of scoffers who have driven away God's Spirit and may be given up as lost. But the others must have this question settled in order to enjoy peace of mind.

Knowing your true character is essential to Christian honesty. If you are not truly settled in your mind as to your own character, then you are hardly honest with regard to religion. If you profess to be a

---

*Lectures to Professing Christians, 191–210.

Christian, when you do not honestly believe yourself to be a saint, you are half a hypocrite at heart. For this reason, when you pray you are always in doubt whether your prayers are heard as prayers coming from a child of God.

To be effective for the cause of Christ, you must judge accurately your own character. If you must always agitate this question in your mind, "Am I a Christian?"; if you must always anxiously look at your own estate and be doubtful about how you stand, it will be a great hindrance to your usefulness. If when you speak to sinners you are uncertain as to whether or not you yourself are saved, then you cannot exhort with the same confidence and simplicity that comes from knowing your own feet are on a solid rock.

Some think saints should always be in the dark to retain their humility. As if it would make a child of God proud to know that he is a child of God. But knowing that you are a child of God is one of the most weighty considerations in the universe to keep you from dishonoring Him. When you are in an anxious state of mind, you can have but little faith and your usefulness cannot be extensive until the question is settled.

Every requirement of God is practical. Some believe that the question of whether you are a saint or a sinner can never be settled in this world. I am amazed at the number of people who behave as if it were a virtue to have doubts concerning whether or not they are Christians. For hundreds of years it has been popular to look with suspicion upon any Christian who is not filled with such doubts. Some have considered "certainty" as an absolute sign that a person knows nothing of the awful condition of his own heart.

One of the universal questions put to candidates for admission to the Church has been, "Have you any doubts of your good estate?" And if the candidate answers, "O yes, I have great doubts," then all is well. His doubts evidence that he is spiritual, humble and has a deep acquaintance with his own heart. But if he has no doubts, it is apparent to them that he knows little of his own heart and is most probably a hypocrite. In the face of all this opinion, I maintain that the duty enjoined in the text is a practical duty. All Christians can put themselves to such a proof as to know themselves, and have a satisfactory assurance of their real character.

That people *can* know their true character is evident from the command in the text: "Examine yourselves, whether ye be in the faith; prove your own selves." Could God require you to examine yourself and prove yourself and see what is your true character, if He knew it was impossible for you ever to ascertain it?

The conscience is our best possible medium of proof, for it gives the most accurate assessment of our character, and settles the great question: *What is our state before God?* We may have, and ought to have, the same kind of assurance of our state before God as we have of our existence; and that is, consciousness. We cannot rest until we have such evidence; to obtain it we need but to notice what consciousness constantly testifies to our hearts. Then we can settle the question of our spiritual condition as certainly as we can know of our own existence.

God gives us so many opportunities to act on what is in our heart that nothing but negligence can prevent our coming to a decision on the matter. If people were shut up in dungeons, with no opportunity to act, no chance of being influenced by circumstances and no way to develop the state of their hearts, they would not be very much to blame for not knowing themselves.

But God has placed us in the circumstances in which we find ourselves in this life on purpose to test us. He does this in order that we may know what is in our hearts: whether we will keep His commandments or not. Our circumstances must produce an impression on our minds and lead us to feel and act in some way. This affords opportunities of self-knowledge, when we see how we are inclined to act in such diversified circumstances.

We are qualified to test our own true characters because we have a perfect standard by which to judge them: the Law of God. We know exactly what it contains, and therefore it is an infallible and invariable rule by which to judge ourselves. We can bring our feelings and actions to this rule, compare them by this standard, and know exactly their true character in the sight of God, for God himself tries them by the same standard.

Nothing but dishonesty can possibly lead us to self-deception. The individual who is self-deceived is not only careless and negligent, but decidedly dishonest, or he would not deceive himself. He must be prejudiced by pride and blinded by self-will, or he could not help but know that he is not what he professes to be. The circumstances that call forth the exercises of his mind to reveal the true condition of his heart are so many and so various that it must be willful blindness if he is deceived.

Or he might be ignorant, if he never had any opportunities to act on his conscience, or if circumstances did not call forth his feelings. A person who has never seen a beggar might not be able to say how he would treat one. But place him where he meets beggars every day, and he must be either willfully blind or dishonest if he does not know the temper of his heart toward a beggar.

How to Examine Yourself

You cannot do your duty by waiting for evidence of your salvation to come to you. But many do so, waiting for certain feelings to come.

Perhaps they pray about it—perhaps very earnestly—and then wait for the feelings to come that will prove to them their good estate before God.

Many times they will not do any work of God until they get this evidence. They will sit and wait in vain expectation for the Spirit of God to come and lift them out of this sloth while they remain thus passive and stupid. They may wait till doomsday and never get evidence they are saints in this manner.

The true state of your heart before God cannot be revealed by trying to force your feelings into giving evidence of salvation. The human mind is designed so that it will never feel by *trying* to feel. You may try as hard as you please to feel in a particular way, but that is totally absurd, because when you do that there is nothing before the mind to produce emotion or feeling. *Feelings are always produced when the mind is intensely fixed on some object.*

When the mind is not fixed upon the object, but on direct attempts to put forth feeling, no feelings will be produced. You may as well shut your eyes and attempt to see. In a dark room there is no object to awaken the sense of sight, and you may *exert* yourself and strain your eyes and try to see, but you will see nothing. When the mind's attention is taken up with looking inward and attempting to examine the nature of the present emotion, that emotion ceases to exist at once, because the attention is no longer fixed on the object that causes the emotion.

If you hold your hand before a lamp, it casts a shadow. But if you take the lamp away, there is no shadow. Light must produce a shadow. Certainly, if the mind is turned away from the object that awakens emotion, then the emotion ceases to exist. The mind must be fixed on the object, not on the emotion, or no emotion will surface, no witness in the spirit.

You will never get evidence of your true character by spending time lamenting the state of your heart. Some people spend their time complaining, "Oh, I don't feel. I can't feel. My heart is so hard." What are they doing? Nothing but mourning and crying because they don't feel. Perhaps they are trying to work themselves up into feeling! Surely that is just as reasonable as trying to fly. While they are mourning and thinking about their hard hearts, and doing nothing to change their condition, they are the ridicule of the devil.

Suppose a man should shut himself away from a furnace and then go about complaining about how cold he is. The children would laugh at him. All his groaning will not change the matter, if he has shut himself out from the means of warmth.

What, then, must you do? If you wish to test the true state of your heart with regard to any object, you must fix your attention on that object. You place yourself in the midst of objects to test the state of your eyes, or in the midst of sounds if you wish to test the perfectness of your ears. And the more you shut out other objects that excite the other senses, and the more strongly you fasten your minds on just one, the more perfectly you test the keenness of your vision or your hearing. A multiplicity of objects is liable to distract the mind.

When we attend to any object calculated to awaken feeling, it is impossible not to feel. The mind is so constituted that it cannot help but feel. It is not necessary to stop and ask, "Do I feel?" Suppose you put your hand near a fire. Do you need to stop and ask the question, "Do I really feel the sensation of warmth?" You know, of course, that you do feel. If you pass your hand rapidly by a lamp, the shadow may be so slight as not to be noticed, but is nonetheless real; and if you paid attention closely enough, you would know it.

Where the impression is slight, a greater effort is required to bring it to your consciousness. So the passing feeling of the mind may be so slight as not to occupy your thoughts, and thus may escape your notice, but it is nonetheless real. But hold your hand over a fire a minute, and the feeling will force itself upon your notice, whatever your other occupations are.

If the mind is fixed on an object calculated to excite emotions of any kind, it is impossible not to feel those emotions to a degree. And if the mind is intently fixed, it is impossible not to feel the emotions in such a degree as to be conscious of the existence of those feelings. These principles will show you how you are to prove your character and know the real state of your feelings toward any object. Fix your attention on the object till your emotions are so excited that you become conscious of what they are.

I will specify another thing that ought to be borne in mind: be certain that the things on which your mind is fixed, on which you wish to test the state of your heart, are realities. There is a great deal of imaginary religion in the world, which people practice, mistaking it for real. They have high feelings. Their minds are excited and their feelings correspond with the object of their contemplation. But here is the source of the delusion: the object is imaginary. The feeling is not false or imaginary, but the object is a fiction.

A person may form a notion of God, or of Jesus Christ, or of salvation, that is altogether aside from the truth. His *feelings* concerning these imaginations are the same as they would be if he had true Christianity. And so, he is deluded. How men view sin is undoubtedly a great source of the false hopes and professions in the world.

How Do You View Sin?

God requires you to know the state of your mind toward sin. Sin—not your own particular sins, but sin itself—is an outrage committed against God. But the true state of your heart is not revealed simply by finding in your mind a strong feeling against sin. *All* intelligent beings feel a disapproval of sin when viewed without reference to their own selfish gratification.

The devil, no doubt, feels a disapproval of certain sins. He no more feels approval for others' sin—when viewed abstractly—than does Gabriel. He blames sinners and condemns their conduct. Whenever he has no selfish reason for being pleased at what they do, he abhors it. You will often find that wicked people have a strong abhorrence of sin. There is not a wicked man on earth who would not condemn and abhor sin in the abstract, especially those sins committed by others that directly affect his own well-being.

The mind was created so that sin is universally, naturally, and necessarily abhorrent to reason and to conscience. Every power of the mind revolts at sin. A man takes pleasure in those who commit iniquity only when he has some selfish reason for wishing them to commit it. No rational being approves of sin, as sin.

However, there is a striking difference between the inbred disapprobation of sin, in the abstract, and the emphatic detestation and opposition to sin that is founded on love to God. An illustration will help. It is one thing for a youth to feel that a certain act is wrong, and quite another thing to view it as an injury to his father. In the second instance there is something that is added to his former conviction. He is not only indignant because the act is wrong, but his love to his father produces a feeling of *grief* that is peculiar. So the individual who loves God feels not only a strong disapproval of sin, as wrong, but a feeling of grief mingled with indignation when he views it as committed against God.

If, then, you want to know how you feel toward sin, ask yourself how you feel when you move around among sinners and see them break God's law? When you hear them swear profanely, or see them break the Sabbath, or get drunk, how do you feel? Do you feel as the Psalmist did when he wrote, "I beheld the transgressors, and was grieved; because they kept not Thy word" (Ps. 119:158)? So he says, "Horror hath taken hold upon me because of the wicked that forsake thy law" (Ps. 119:53).

You ought to test the state of your heart toward your own sins as well. Recall your conduct in former times, and see whether you condemn and loathe the transgressions you find in your behavior, as an affectionate child would when he remembers how he has disobeyed a beloved parent.

It is one thing to feel a strong conviction that your former conduct was wicked. It is quite another thing to grieve over it because it was a sin against God. Probably there are few Christians who have not looked back upon their former conduct toward their parents with deep misgiving, and thought how a beloved father and an affectionate mother have been disobeyed and wronged; and who have not felt, in addition to a strong disapproval of their conduct, a deep emotion of grief that threatened to vent itself in weeping, and perhaps did gush forth in irrepressible tears. Now this is true repentance toward a parent. And repentance toward God is the same thing, and if it is genuine, it will correspond in degree to the intensity of attention with which the mind is fixed on the subject, God.

Test your feelings toward unrepentant sinners. Go among them and converse with them on the subject of their souls. Warn them, see what they say, and how they feel, and get at the real state of their hearts, and then you will know how you feel toward the impenitent.

Do not shut yourself up in your closet and try to imagine an unrepentant sinner. You may merely bring up a picture in the imagination that will affect your sympathies and make you weep and pray. But go. Bring your heart in contact with the living reality of a sinner; reason with him and exhort him. Find out his excuses, his obstinacy, his insincerity. Pray with him if you can. You cannot do this without arousing emotions in your mind. If you are a Christian, it will awaken such mingled emotions of grief, compassion and indignation, as Jesus Christ feels, that you will have no room to doubt the state of your heart on this subject.

You must prove the state of your mind toward God. Fix your thoughts intently on Him. And do not set yourself down to imagine a God after your own foolish heart, but take the Bible and learn from it the true nature of God. Do not fancy a shape or appearance, or imagine how He looks. But fix your mind on the Bible's description of how He feels, what He does, and what He says. You will not be able to help but feel. Here you will detect the real state of your heart, which you cannot mistake.

Test your feelings toward Christ. You are bound to know whether you love the Lord Jesus Christ or not. Recall to your memory the circumstances of His life, and see whether they are realities to your mind. Think about His miracles, His sufferings, His lovely character, His death, His resurrection, His ascension, His intercession now at the right hand of the throne of God. Do you believe all these? Are they realities to your mind? What are your feelings in view of them?

When you think of His willingness to save, His ability to save, His atoning death, His power, if these things are realities to you, you will have feelings of which you will be conscious, and concern of which there will be no mistake.

What are your feelings toward the saints? If you wish to test your heart on this point, whether you love the saints, do not let your thoughts run to the ends of the earth, but fix your mind on the saints by you and see whether you love them, whether you desire their sanctification, whether you really long to have them grow in grace, whether you can bear them in your heart to the throne of grace in faith, and ask God to bestow blessings on them.

How do you feel in regard to revivals? If you wish to know the state of your feelings toward revivals, then read about them, think of them, fix your mind on them, and you cannot but have feelings that will show plainly the state of your heart. The same is true of the heathen, of slaves, of drunkards, of the Bible, of any object of pious regard. The only way to know the state of your heart is to fix your mind on the reality of those things till you feel so intensely that there is no mistaking the nature of your feelings.

Should you find a difficulty in attending to any of these objects sufficiently to produce feeling, it will be for one of two reasons: either your mind is taken up with some other part of Christianity, so you cannot fix your attention to the specified object, or your thoughts wander with the fool's eyes to the ends of the earth. The former is sometimes the case.

I have known some Christians to be very much distressed because they did not feel so intensely as they think they ought on some subjects (e.g., their own sins). A person's mind may be so much taken up with anxiety and labor and prayer for sinners, that it requires an effort to think enough about his own soul to feel deeply. And when he goes on his knees to pray about his own sins, that sinner with whom he has been talking comes right up before his mind and he can hardly pray for himself. He should not count this against himself.

If the reason you do not feel on one subject concerning the kingdom of God is because your feelings are so engrossed over another of equal importance, this is not wrong. But if your thoughts run all over the world, and that is the reason you do not feel deeply enough to know what is your true character, if your mind will neither concentrate on the Bible nor fasten on any object concerning God and His work, lay a strong hand on yourself, and fix your thoughts with a death-grasp, till you do feel.

You can command your thoughts. God has put the control of your mind in your own hands. And in this way, you can control your own feelings by turning your attention upon the object you wish to feel about. Bring yourself, then, powerfully and resolutely to that point. Give it not over till you fasten your mind to the subject, till the deep fountains of feeling break in your mind, and you know what the state of your heart is, and understand your real character in the sight of God.

Let me remind you that doing God's work is indispensable to self-examination. An individual can never know the true state of his heart unless he is active in the duties of Christianity. Shut up in his closet he never can tell how he feels toward objects that are without, and he never can ascertain his feelings toward them until he goes out and acts.

How can he know his real feeling toward sinners if he never brings his mind in contact with sinners? He goes into his closet, and his imagination may make him feel, but it is a deceitful feeling because it is not grounded in reality. If you wish to test the reality of your feelings toward sinners, go out and warn sinners, and then the reality of your feelings will manifest themselves.

Unless people judge their hearts by the reality of things, they are constantly subject to delusion. Imagine a person shut up in a cloister, shut out from the world of reality and living in a world of imagination. He becomes a perfect creature of imagination. So it is in Christianity with those who do not bring their mind in contact with realities. Such people think they love mankind, and yet do them no good. They imagine they abhor sin, and yet do nothing to destroy it.

How many people deceive themselves by an excitement of the imagination about missions, for instance. How common it is for people to get up a great deal of feeling, and hold prayer meetings for missions, who really do nothing to save souls. Women will spend a whole day at a prayer meeting to pray for the conversion of the world, while their unrepentant house-keeper in the kitchen is not spoken to all day, and perhaps not in a month, concerning her soul. People will lead a public meeting, and talk about feeling for the heathen, but make no direct effort to reach sinners around them. This is all a figment of the imagination.

There is no reality in such a religion as that. If they had real love of God, and love of souls, and real piety, the pictures drawn by the imagination about the distant heathen would not create so much more feeling than the reality around them.

Do not excuse them by saying that their attention is not turned toward sinners around them. They hear the profane oaths, and see the Sabbath-breaking and other vices as a naked reality before their eyes every day. And if these produce no feeling, they pretend in vain that they feel as God requires for sinners in heathen lands or anywhere else.

Nay, take a certain individual, as full of compassion for the heathen as he imagines, and place him among the heathen. Transport him to the Friendly Islands or elsewhere, away from the fictions of imagination, into the cold and naked reality of heathenism. All his deep feelings will vanish. He may write letters home about the abominations of the heathen, and all that, but his concern for their souls will disappear.

You hear people talk with feeling about the heathen, who have never converted a soul at home. Rely upon it, that is all imagination. If they do not promote revivals at home, where they understand the language and have direct access to their neighbors, much less can they be depended on to promote the real work of Christianity on heathen ground.

The churches ought to understand this, and keep it in mind in selecting men to go on foreign missions. They ought to know that if the naked reality at home does not excite a person to action, the devil would only laugh at a million such missionaries.

The same delusion often manifests itself in regard to revivals. There are some who are a great friend to revivals—that is, the revivals of former days, or of revivals in the abstract, or distant revivals, or revivals that are yet to come. But as to any present revival, they remain aloof and doubtful.

One such man can read about revivals in President Edwards' day, or in Scotland, or in Wales, and be greatly excited and delighted. He can pray, "O Lord, revive thy work; O Lord, let us have such revivals, let us have a Pentecost season, when thousands shall be converted in a day." But get him into the reality of things, and he will never see a revival in which he can take any interest or feel a compulsion to respond. He is friendly to the fictitious imaginings of his own mind. He can create a state of things that will excite his feelings, but no naked reality ever brings him out to cooperate in actually promoting a revival.

In the days of our Savior, the people said—and no doubt really believed—that they abhorred the doings of those who persecuted the prophets. They said, "If we had been in the days of our fathers, we would not have been partakers with them of the blood of the prophets." No doubt they wondered that people could be so wicked as to do such things. But they had never seen a prophet. They were moved simply by their imagination. And as soon as the Lord Jesus Christ appeared, the greatest of prophets, on whom all the prophecies centered, they rejected Him, and finally put Him to death, with as much cold-hearted cruelty as ever their fathers had killed a prophet. "Fill ye up," says our Savior, ". . . the measure of your fathers . . . that upon you may come all the righteous blood shed upon the earth" (Matt. 23:32, 35).

People have always fallen in love with the fictions of their own imaginations, and over such they have stumbled into hell. Look at the universalist. He imagines a God who will save everybody, regardless of their estate before Him, and believes in a heaven that will accommodate everybody. He learns to love the god he has made, and the heaven he has imagined, and perhaps will even weep with love. His feelings are often deep, but they are delusive, because they are excited by fiction, not by truth.

Christianity consists in love, in feeling and doing right or good. If you wish to have great piety, do not think of cultivating it in a way that never caused piety to grow; that is, by retiring into a cloister, and withdrawing from contact with mankind. If the Lord Jesus Christ had supposed such circumstances to be favorable to piety, He would have directed so. But He knew better. He has therefore appointed circumstances as they are, so that His people may have a thousand objects of benevolence, a thousand opportunities to do good. And if they go out of themselves and turn their hearts upon these things, they cannot fail to grow in piety and to have their evidences increasing and satisfactory.

In only one department of self-examination can we consistently shut ourselves up in the closet: that is when we want to examine the motives of our past conduct. In such cases it is often necessary to abstract our thoughts and keep other things from our minds, and turn our minds back and look at things we have done, and the motives underlying these actions. To do this effectively, it is often necessary to resort to retirement, fasting, and prayer. Sometimes it is impossible to wake up a lively recollection of what we wish to examine without calling in the laws of association to our aid. We attempt to call up past scenes, and all seems confusion and darkness, until we strike upon some associated idea that gradually brings the whole scene fresh before us.

Suppose I am to be called as a witness in court concerning a transaction. I can sometimes gain a lively recollection of what took place only by going to the place, and all the circumstances come flooding back, as if it happened only yesterday. In the same manner, we may find that as we re-examine some part of our history, that no shutting ourselves up will bring it back, no protracted meditation or fasting or prayer. Nothing brings back the feelings we are trying to recall until we throw ourselves into some circumstances that will wake up the associated ideas and thus bring back the feelings we formerly had.

Suppose a minister wished to look back and see how he felt and the spirit with which he had preached years ago. He wished to know how much real piety there was in his labors. He might recall a great deal in his closet on his knees by the aid of the Spirit of God. But this revelation would come back much more effectively if he went to the place and preached there again. The exact attitude in which his mind was before may recur to him and stand in strong reality before his mind.

As you examine yourself, be careful not to expect to find your mind operating in all the Christian graces at once. This is contrary to the nature of the mind. It is enough if you are able to focus on the subject that is before your mind. If your feelings are not what they should be concerning that subject, that is another thing. But if you find that your emotions at the time are right, do not get troubled because you are presently not feeling something about another topic. The mind is so constituted that it can only have one train of emotions at a time.

From this you see why people often do not feel more than they do. They are thinking on something not calculated to produce feeling. They feel, but not on the right subjects. People always feel on some subjects. The reason they do not feel deeply on Christian subjects is because their attention is not deeply fixed on such subjects.

Do you see why there is such a strange diversity in the meditations of real Christians? There are some Christians whose feelings, when they have any feeling, are always of the happy kind. There are others whose feelings are always of a sad and distressing kind. They are in almost constant agony for sinners. The reason is that their thoughts are directed to different objects. One class are always thinking of the class of objects calculated to make them happy. The other class are thinking of the state of the church, or the state of sinners, and become weighed down as with a burden, as if a mountain were on their shoulders. Both may be Christian, and both classes of feelings are right, in view of the objects at which they look.

The Apostle Paul had continual heaviness and sorrow of heart on account of his brethren. No doubt this was right and proper, for his brethren, who had rejected the Savior, were often the object of his thoughts. The dreadful wrath that they had brought upon themselves, the doom that hung over them, was constantly before his mind. How could he be otherwise than sad?

Observe the influence of these two classes of feelings in the usefulness of individuals. Show me a very joyful and happy Christian, and he is not generally a very useful Christian. Generally, such are so taken up with enjoying the sweets of Christianity that they do but little to win souls to Christ. There are those ministers who preach a great deal on such happy topics as these, making their pious hearers very contented. Such ministers are seldom instrumental in converting sinners, however much they may have refreshed, edified and gratified saints.

On the other hand, you will find men who are habitually filled with a deep agony of soul over the state of sinners. These men will be largely instrumental in converting men. The reason is plain. Both types of ministers preach the truth—both preach the gospel, in different proportions—and the feelings awakened correspond with the views they preached. The difference is that one comforted the saints, the other converted sinners.

You may see a class of professing Christians who are always happy. They are lovely companions, but they are very seldom engaged in pulling sinners out of the fire. You find others always full of agony for sinners, looking at their state and longing to have souls converted. Instead of enjoying the bit of heaven on earth they might find here, they follow the example of the Son of God when He was on earth, groaning in His spirit and spending all night in prayer. The real revival spirit is a spirit of agonizing desires that prays for sinners.

Do you see how you may account for your own feelings at different times? People often wonder why they feel as they do. The answer is plain. Your feelings are directly affected by your thoughts. You direct your attention to those objects that are calculated to produce those feelings.

Do you see why some people's feelings are so variable? It is because their thoughts are unsteady. If they would fix their thoughts, they would regulate their feelings.

Do you see the way to produce a desired state of feeling in your own mind, and to produce any desired state of feeling in the minds of others? Focus your attention on a subject that is calculated to produce those feelings before your mind, and confine them there, and the feelings will not fail to follow.

There are multitudes of pious persons who dishonor Christianity by their doubts. They talk incessantly of their doubts, and they embrace a hasty conviction that they have no faith. If they were to fix their minds on other subjects—on Christ, for instance—or go out and seek sinners and try to bring them to repentance, instead of dwelling on their doubts, they would feel strongly enough to strengthen every wavering conviction.

Remember, you are not to wait till you feel right before you do this. Perhaps some things I have said have not been rightly understood. I said you could do nothing for God unless you felt right. Do not therefore suppose that you are to sit still and do nothing till you are satisfied that you feel right about it. But place yourself in circumstances to make you feel right, and go to work.

On the one hand, to bustle about without any feeling is no way, and on the other hand, to shut yourself up in your closet and wait for feeling to come is no way. Be sure to remain active. You never will feel right otherwise. Then keep your mind always under the influence of those objects that are calculated to create and keep alive Christian feelings.

4

TRUE AND FALSE REPENTANCE*

"For godly sorrow worketh repentance to salvation not to be repented of: but the sorrow of the world worketh death" (2 Corinthians 7:10).

In chapter seven of Second Corinthians, the apostle refers to an epistle that he had formerly written to the church at Corinth, addressing them on a certain subject in which they were greatly to blame. He speaks here of the effect that he had in bringing them to true repentance. They sorrowed after a godly sort. This was the evidence that their repentance was genuine.

"For behold this selfsame thing, that ye sorrowed after a godly sort, what carefulness it wrought in you, yea, what clearing of yourselves, yea, what indignation, yea, what fear, yea what vehement desire, yea, what zeal, yea, what revenge! In all things ye have approved yourselves to be clear in this matter" (v. 11).

In the verse above he speaks of two kinds of sorrow for sin, one working repentance unto salvation, the other working death. He alludes to what is generally understood as two kinds of repentance: true and false repentance.

It is high time for people who profess to be Christians to be taught to discriminate much more than they do in regard to the nature and character of the various practices of Christianity. If this were done, the Church would not be so overrun with false and unprofitable church members.

Recently, I have been frequently led to examine the reason why there is so much shallow Christianity. I have sought to know the foundation of the difficulty. The Bible is not false, so why do multitudes suppose themselves to be Christians when they are not? Why are so many deceived? Why do so many, who are still unrepentant sinners,

*Lectures to Professing Christians, 155–174.

get the idea that they have repented? Doubtless, there is a lack of discriminating instruction concerning true and false repentance.

True Repentance

True repentance requires a change of opinion respecting the *nature* of sin. This change of opinion is followed by a corresponding change of feeling toward sin, for feeling is the result of thought. When this change of opinion produces a corresponding change of feeling, if the opinion is right and the feeling corresponds, this is true repentance. Of course, the new opinion must be the right one; that is, the repentant's opinion regarding sin must be the same as God's. Godly sorrow, such as God requires, springs from such views of sin as God holds.

To one who truly repents, sin looks like a very different thing from what it did before repentance. Instead of being desirable or fascinating, sin now looks the very opposite: most odious and detestable. A truly repentant sinner will be astonished that he could ever have desired sin.

Unrepentant sinners may look at sin and see that it will ruin them, knowing God will punish them for it, but the sin itself appears desirable to them. If their sin could end in happiness, they never would think of abandoning it. But it is different for the repentant sinner, who sees his former conduct as perfectly shameful. He looks back upon it, exclaiming, "How hateful, how detestable, how worthy of hell, such and such a thing was in me."

True repentance involves a change of opinion with regard to the *character* of sin and its *relation* to God. Sinners do not see why God threatens sin with such terrible punishment. They love it so much themselves that they cannot see why God should find it worthy of everlasting punishment. At the time conviction is strongly upon them, they see it differently. In that moment, they see it in the same light that a Christian does. But the difference is this: the unrepentant only want a corresponding change of feeling to become Christians. They now agree that sin's relation to God is such that it deserves eternal death, but they do not change their actions as a result. This is the case with the devils and wicked spirits in hell.

Mark this! A change of opinion respecting sin is indispensable to true repentance and it always precedes it. The heart never goes out to God in true repentance without a previous change of opinion concerning the nature of sin. There may be a change of opinion without repentance, but no genuine repentance without a change of opinion.

True repentance demands a change of opinion regarding the *infectious nature or tendency* of sin. Before the sinner repents, he thinks it utterly incredible that sin should have such tendencies as to deserve everlasting death. He may be fully changed, of course, as to his opinions on this point without repentance; but it is impossible for a person to truly repent without seeing sin as ruinous to himself and everybody else, for time and eternity. He must recognize that sin is at variance with all that is lovely and happy in the universe. He must see that sin by its very nature is injurious to himself and everybody else, and that there is no remedy for it except universal abstinence from it. The devil knows it to be so. Possibly, you are an unrepentant sinner and know this to be so as well.

True repentance involves a change of opinion with regard to the *penalty* of sin. The word *repentance* implies a change in the sinner's state of mind. The person who sins carelessly is almost devoid of right ideas, as far as this life is concerned, with regard to the penalty of sin. Even if he admits, in theory, that sin deserves eternal death, he does not really believe it. For if he believed it, it would be impossible for him to remain a careless sinner because we always live what we believe.

He is deceived, if he supposes that he honestly holds the opinion that sin deserves the wrath of God forever. But the truly awakened and convicted sinner has no more doubt of this than he has of the existence of God. He sees clearly that sin deserves everlasting punishment from God. He knows that this is a simple matter of fact, *and believes in his heart that he himself is subject to the truth of it.*

In true repentance, a corresponding change of feeling is produced that touches the four aspects of sin: the nature of it, its relations, its tendencies, and its penalties. The individual who truly repents not only confesses sin as detestable and vile and worthy of abhorrence, but he really abhors it and hates it in his heart. A person may acknowledge sin as hurtful and abominable, while his heart loves it, desires it, and clings to it. But when he truly repents, he most heartily renounces it.

He feels how sin affects his relation to God, causing the horror of utter separation from Him. This is the source of those gushings of sorrow in which Christians sometimes break out when contemplating sin. The Christian views it as to its nature and simply feels abhorrence. But when he views it in relation to God, he weeps. The fountains of his sorrow gush forth and he wants to get right down on his face and pour out a flood of tears over his sins.

The individual who truly repents does not close his eyes to the tendencies of sin. When this happens a vehement desire awakens in him to stop sin, to save people from their sins, and to roll back the tide of death. It sets his heart on fire and he goes to praying, laboring, and pulling sinners out of the fire with all his might, to save them from the awful bonds of sin. When the Christian sets his mind on this, he will do anything in his power to make people give up their sins. It is just as if he saw all the people taking poison, so he lifts up his voice to warn them to *beware*.

He is convinced of the penalty of sin. Intellectually, he has the conviction that sin deserves everlasting punishment, and in his heart he feels that it would be right, reasonable, and just for God to condemn him to eternal death. And so, far from finding fault with the sentence of the law that condemns him, he thinks it the wonder of heaven, a wonder of wonders, that God can forgive him. Instead of thinking it hard, severe, or unkind of God that incorrigible sinners are sent to hell, he is full of adoring wonder that he is not sent there himself, and that this whole guilty world has not long since been hurled down to endless burnings.

It is the last thing in the world he would think to complain of, that all sinners are not saved. But oh, it is a wonder of mercy that all the world is not damned. And when he thinks of such a sinner as himself being saved, he feels a sense of gratitude that he never knew anything of until he became a Christian.

The Fruits of Genuine Repentance

I wish to show you the works of true repentance, to make it so plain to your mind that you can know without a doubt whether you have repented or not. If your repentance is genuine, there is in your mind a conscious change of views and feelings in regard to sin. You are just as conscious of this as you are of a change of views on any other subject. Now, can you say this? Do you know that on this point there has been a change in you, and that old things are done away and all things have become new?

Where repentance is genuine, the disposition to repeat sin is gone. If you have truly repented, you do not now love sin. Now, you do not abstain from sin through fear of punishment, but because you hate it. Is this true of *you*? Do you know that your disposition to commit sin is gone? Look at the sins you used to practice when you were unrepentant. How do they appear to you? Do they look pleasant? Would you really love to practice them again if you dared? If you do, if you still have the disposition to sin, you are only convicted of sin. Your *opinion* of sin may be changed, but if the love of that sin remains, as your soul lives, you are still an unrepentant sinner.

Genuine repentance works a reformation of conduct. I take this idea to be chiefly intended in the Scriptures, where it says "Godly sorrow worketh repentance." Godly sorrow produces a reformation of conduct. Otherwise it is a repetition of the same idea—or saying— that repentance produces repentance. Whereas, I suppose the apostle was speaking of such a change of mind as produces a change of conduct as well, ending in salvation. Now, let me ask you, are you really reformed? Have you forsaken your sins? Or, are you practicing sin still? If so, you are still a sinner. However much you may have changed your mind, if you have not changed your conduct, made an actual reformation, you have not made a godly repentance, or such as God approves.

Repentance, when true and genuine, leads to confession and restitution. The thief has not repented while he keeps the money he stole. He may have conviction of sin, but he has not repented of sin. If he had, he would go and give back the money. If you have cheated anyone, and do not restore what you have taken unjustly; or if you have injured anyone, and do not set about rectifying the wrong you have done (as far as in you lies) you have not truly repented.

True repentance is a permanent change of character and conduct. The text speaks of repentance unto salvation "not to be repented of." What else does the apostle mean by that expression but this, that true repentance is a change so deep and fundamental that the man never changes back again?

People often quote it as if it read, repentance that does not need to be repented of. But that is not what he says. *It is not to be repented of.* In other words, repentance that will not be repented of is so thorough that there is no going back. The love of sin is truly abandoned. It is "unto salvation." It goes right on, until he reaches the very gates of heaven. The reason it ends in salvation is because the repentance is such as will not be repented of.

Do you see why the doctrine of the Perseverance of the Saints is true, and what it means? True repentance is such a thorough change of feelings that the person who repents so abhors sin that he will naturally persevere and not go and take back all his repentance and return to sin again.

False Repentance

False, or spurious, repentance is said to be "worldly" or the "sorrow of the world." False repentance is sorrow for sin arising from worldly considerations and motives connected with the present life—or at most respects only a person's "own happiness" in a future world with no regard to the true nature of sin.

False repentance is not founded on the change of opinion that is essential to true repentance. The change is not fundamental, nor does it consider the four aspects of sin. A person may see the evil consequences of sin with a worldly point of view, and it may fill him with consternation. He may see that his sin will greatly affect his character or endanger his life; that if some of his concealed conduct should be found out, he would be disgraced. This may fill him with fear and distress. It is very common for people to have this kind of worldly sorrow when some worldly consideration is at the bottom of it all.

False repentance is founded in selfishness. It may be simply a strong feeling of regret, that he has done as he has, because he sees the evil consequences of it, because it makes him miserable or exposes him to the wrath of God, or injures his family or his friends, or because it produces some injury to himself in time or in eternity. All this is pure selfishness. He may feel a biting conscience and a consuming remorse without true repentance. It may be grounded in fear—deep and dreadful fear—of the wrath of God and the pains of hell, and yet be purely selfish. All the while there may be no such thing as a hearty abhorrence of sin, nor will his heart understand or feel the conviction regarding the infinite evil of sin.

Evidence of False Repentance

False or spurious repentance leaves the feelings unchanged. It leaves the disposition to sin in the heart unbroken and unsubdued. The feelings regarding the nature of sin are not changed enough, and the individual still feels a desire for sin. He abstains from it, not from abhorrence of it, but from dread of the consequences of it.

False repentance works death. It leads to the concealment of sin, to hypocrisy. The person who has exercised true repentance is willing to have it known that he has repented. He is willing to have it known that he was a sinner. He who has only false repentance resorts to excuses and lying to cover his sins, and is ashamed of his repentance. When he is called to account at the anxious seat, he will cover up his sins with a thousand apologies and excuses, trying to smooth them over and extenuate their enormity.

If he speaks of his past conduct, he always does it in the softest and most favorable terms. You see a constant disposition to cover up his sin. This repentance leads to death. It makes him commit a new sin to cover the old. Instead of an open-hearted breaking forth of sensibility and frankness, you see a palavering, smooth-tongued, half-hearted mincing out of something that is intended to answer the purpose of a confession, and yet it confesses nothing.

How is it with you? Are you ashamed to have any person talk with you about your sins? Then your sorrow is only a worldly sorrow, and works death. Sinners often avoid conversation about their sins, yet they call themselves anxious inquirers, expecting to become Christians in that way.

The same kind of sorrow is found in hell. No doubt all those wretched inhabitants of the pit wish to get away from the eye of God. No such sorrow is found among the saints in heaven. Their sorrow is open, full and hearty. Such sorrow is not inconsistent with true happiness. The saints are full of happiness, and yet full of deep, undisguised and gushing sorrow for sin. But worldly sorrow is ashamed of itself, is mean and miserable, and works death.

False repentance produces only a partial reformation of conduct. The reformation that is produced by worldly sorrow extends only to those things of which the individual has been strongly convicted. The heart is not changed. You will see him avoid only those cardinal sins, those blatant sins, of which he has been warned.

If a young convert is deceived, you will find that there is only a partial change in his conduct. He is reformed in certain respects, but there are many wrong things that he continues to practice. Instead of being tremblingly sensitive with regard to temptation, and quick to detect sin in everything that is contrary to the spirit of the gospel, he will be, perhaps, strict and quick-sighted in regard to certain things, but loose in his conduct and lax in his views on other points—and very far from manifesting a Christian spirit in regard to all sin.

Ordinarily, the transformation produced by false sorrow is temporary even in those things that are changed. The individual continually lapses into his old sins, for the disposition to sin is not gone. It is only checked and restrained by fear, and as soon as he has a hope and is in the church and gets bolstered up so that his fears are allayed, you will see him gradually wearing back, returning to his old sins.

This was the difficulty with the house of Israel, and that is what made them constantly return to their idolatry and to other sins. They had only worldly sorrow. You see it now everywhere in the church. Individuals are reformed for a time, and taken into the church, then relapse into their old sins. They love to call it "getting cold in religion" and "backsliding," and the like, but the truth is, they continue to love sin. When the occasion presents itself, they return to it as the sow that was washed returns to wallowing in the mire, because she was always a sow.

Understand thoroughly the foundation of all those fits and starts in religion that you see so much of. People are awakened and convicted, and by and by they get hope and settle down in false security—and then away they go. Perhaps they may remain on their guard enough that they will not be turned out of the church, but the foundations of sins are not broken up, and they soon return to their old ways. The woman that was absorbed in vanity loves it still, and gradually returns to her ribbons and baubles. The man who loved money loves it yet, and soon slides back into his old ways, and dives into business, pursuing the world as eagerly and devotedly as he did before he joined the church.

Go through all the departments of society, and if you find thorough conversions, you will find that their most besetting sins before conversion are farthest from them now. The real convert is least likely to fall into his old besetting sin, because he abhors it most. But if he is deceived and worldly-minded, he always tends to go back into the same sins. The woman that loves dress comes out again in all her glory, and dashes as she used to do. The fountain of sin was not broken up. They have not purged out iniquity from their heart, but retained it in their heart all the time.

False repentance is a forced reformation. The reformation produced by a false repentance is not only partial and temporary, but is also forced and constrained. The reformation of the truly repentant is from the heart. He no longer has a disposition to sin. In him the Bible promise is fulfilled. He actually finds that wisdom's ways "are ways of pleasantness, and all her paths are peace" (Prov. 3:17).

He experiences that the Savior's yoke is easy and His burden is light. He has felt that God's commandments are not grievous but joyous. *More to be desired are they than gold, yea, than much fine gold: sweeter also than honey and the honeycomb* (Ps. 19:10).

But this spurious kind of repentance is very different. It is a legal repentance, the result of fear and not of love; a selfish repentance, anything but a free, voluntary, hearty change from sin to obedience. You will find, if you have this kind of repentance, that you are conscious that you do not abstain from sin by choice, but from other considerations: the forbidding of conscience, or the fear you shall lose your soul, your hope, or your character—rather than from abhorrence of sin or love to duty.

Such persons always need to be persuaded to do their duty with an express passage of scripture, or else they will apologize for sin, evading duty, and think there is no great harm in doing it. The reason is, they love their sins, and if there is not some express command of God that they dare not fly in the face of, they will practice them. Not so with true repentance. If a thing seems contrary to the great law of love, the person who has true repentance will abhor it, and avoid it whether he has an express command of God for it or not.

Show me such a person, and I tell you he won't need an express command to make him give up drinking or making or vending strong drink. He sees it is contrary to the great law of impartial benevolence, and he truly abhors it, and would no more do it than he would blaspheme God, steal, or commit any other abomination.

So the man who has true repentance does not need a "thus saith the Lord" to keep him from oppressing his fellow man, because he would not do anything wrong. How certainly men would abhor anything of the kind, if they had truly repented of sin.

Spurious repentance leads to self-righteousness. The individual who has this repentance may know that Jesus Christ is the only savior of sinners, and may profess to believe on Him and to rely on Him alone for salvation. But in the end, he is actually placing ten times more reliance on his reformation than on Jesus Christ for his salvation. And if he would watch his own heart, he would know it is so. He may say he expects salvation by Christ, but in fact he is dwelling more on the changes he has seen, and his hope is founded more on that, than on the atonement of Christ. He is really patching up a righteousness of his own.

False repentance leads to false security. The individual supposes that the worldly sorrow he has had is true repentance, and he trusts the next life to it. It is a curious fact that so far as I have been able to get at the state of mind of this class of persons, they seem to take it for granted that Christ will save them because they have been sorry for their sins, although they are not conscious that they have ever felt any resting in Christ. They felt sorrow, and then they got relief and felt better, and now they expect to be saved by Christ, when their very consciousness will teach them that they have never felt a hearty reliance on Christ at all.

False repentance hardens the heart. The individual who has this kind of sorrow becomes harder in heart in proportion to the number of times that he feels such sorrow. If he has strong emotions of conviction, and his heart does not break up and flow out, the fountains of feeling are more and more dried up, and his heart becomes more and more difficult to reach. On the other hand, every time you bring the truth to bear upon a Christian, one who has truly repented, so as to break him down before God, he becomes more and more mellow, and more easily affected, excited, melted, and broken down under God's blessed word, so long as he lives—and to all eternity. His heart gets into the habit of going along with the convictions of his understanding, and he becomes as teachable as a little child.

Here is the grand distinction. Let churches, or individual members, who have only this worldly repentance, pass through a revival, and get woken up, and bustle about, and then grow cold again. Let this be repeated and you find them more and more difficult to be roused, till by and by, they become as hard as a millstone, and nothing can ever rally them to a revival again.

Directly over against this are those churches and individuals who have truly repented. Let them go through successive revivals, and they will grow more and more mellow and tender, until they get to such a state that if they hear the trumpet blow for a revival, they kindle and glow instantly, and are ready for the work.

This distinction is as broad as between light and darkness. It is everywhere observable among the churches and church members. You see the principle illustrated in sinners, who pass through repeated revivals; by and by, they will scoff and rail at all religion, and although the heavens hang with clouds of mercy over their heads, they heed it not, but reject it. It is so in churches and members; if they have not true repentance, every fresh excitement hardens the heart and renders them more difficult to be reached by the truth.

False repentance scars the conscience. Such persons are liable at first to become distressed whenever the truth is flashed upon their mind. They may not have so much conviction as the real Christian. But the real Christian is filled with peace at the very time that his tears are flowing from conviction of sin. And each repeated season of conviction makes him more and more watchful, tender, and careful, till his conscience becomes, like the apple of his eye, so tender that the very appearance of evil will offend it. But the other kind of sorrow, which does not lead to hearty renunciation of sin, leaves the heart harder than before, and by and by, it sears the conscience as with a hot iron. This sorrow works death.

False repentance rejects Jesus Christ as the ground of hope. Depending on reformation and sorrow, or anything else, it leads to no such reliance on Jesus Christ that the love of Christ will constrain him to labor all his days for Christ. This kind of repentance is sure to be repented of.

By and by you will find such persons becoming ashamed of the deep feelings that they had. They do not want to speak of them, and if they talk of them it is always lightly and coldly. They perhaps bustle about in time of revival, and appear to participate as much as anybody, and very likely were among the most fervent in everything that was done. But now the revival is over, and you find them opposed to new measures, changing back to their old ways, and ashamed of their zeal. They, in fact, repent of their repentance.

Such persons, after they have joined the church, will be ashamed of having come to the anxious seat. When the height of revival has gone by, they will begin to talk against being too excitable, and the necessity of getting into a more sober and traditional way in the expressions of their faith. Here is the reason—they had a repentance of which they afterward repented.

You sometimes find persons who profess to be converted in a revival, turning against the very measures, means, and doctrines to which they profess to have been converted. Not so with the true Christian. He is never ashamed of this repentance. The last thing he would ever think of being ashamed of is the excitement or feeling he felt in a revival.

One reason why there is so much spasmodic religion in the church is because people have mistaken conviction for conversion, the sorrow of the world for that godly sorrow that works repentance unto salvation, not to be repented of. I am convinced, after years of observation, that is also the true reason for the present deplorable state of the church all over the land.

See why sinners under conviction feel as if it were a great sacrifice to become Christians? They think it a great trial to give up their ungodly companions as well as their sins. Whereas, if they had true repentance, they would not think it any cross to give up their sins.

I recollect how I *used* to feel when I first saw young persons becoming Christians and joining the church. I thought it was a good thing on the whole to have religion, because they would save their souls and get to heaven. But for the time, it seemed to be a very sorrowful thing. I never dreamed then that these young people could be really happy in the present.

I believe it is very common for persons who know that Christianity is good in general terms, and good to have in the end, to think they cannot be happy in it. This is all due to a mistake respecting the true nature of repentance. They do not understand that true repentance leads to an abhorrence of those things that were formerly loved. Sinners do not see that when their young friends become true Christians, they feel an abhorrence for their balls, parties, sinful amusements, and follies, because the love for these things is crucified.

I once knew a young lady who was converted to God. Her father was a very proud and worldly man. She used to be very fond of dress, and the dancing school, and balls. After her conversion, her father would force her to go to the dancing school. He used to go along with her, and force her to stand up and dance. She would go there and weep, and sometimes when she was standing up on the floor to dance, her feelings of abhorrence and sorrow would so come over her that she would turn away and burst into tears.

Here you see the cause of all that. She had truly repented of these things, with a repentance not to be repented of. Oh, how many associations such a scene recalled to her, what sorrow and compassion she felt for her former companions, what abhorrence of their giddy mirth, and how she longed to be in the prayer-meeting. How could she be happier in the prayer meeting, you ask? Such a question comes from the impenitent, or those who have experienced only worldly sorrow.

And what is the matter with those professing Christians who think it a cross to be very strict in practice? Such persons are always apologizing for their sins, and excusing certain practices that are not consistent with strict Christianity. It shows that they love sin still, and will go as far as they dare in it. If they were true Christians, they would abhor it, run from it, and would feel it to be a cross to be dragged back to it.

Do you see why some do not know what it is to enjoy Christianity? They are not cheerful and happy in their faith; they are grieved because they have to break off from so many things they love, or because they have to give so much money. They are in the fire all the time. Instead of rejoicing in every opportunity of self-denial, and rejoicing in the plainest and most cutting exhibitions of truth, it is a great trial to them to be told their duty, when it crosses their inclinations and habits. The plain truth distresses them. Why? Because they do not love to do duty. If they did, every ray of light that broke in upon their minds from heaven, pointing out their duty, would be welcomed, and satisfy them more and more.

Those persons who feel cramped and distressed because the truth presses them, if their hearts do not yield to this truth, they are no Christians. *Hypocrite* is the name of all such professors of the faith. If you find that they are distressed like anxious sinners, and that they become increasingly distressed the more you point out their sins, be sure they have never truly repented of their sins nor given themselves up to belong to God.

For this reason many professed converts, who have had very deep experiences at the time of their conversion, later apostatize. At first, they had deep convictions and great distress of mind; afterward they felt relieved of their burdens of sin, and their joy was very great. They were amazingly happy for a season, but by and by their enthusiasm declines, and then they apostatize.

Some, who do not discriminate properly between true and false repentance, and who think there cannot be such "deep" experiences without divine power, call these cases "falling from grace," but the truth is, they went out from us because they were not of us. They never had that repentance that kills and annihilates the disposition to sin.

Do you see why backsliders are so miserable? Perhaps you will infer that I suppose all true Christians are perfect, simply because their disposition to sin is broken up and changed. That is not so. There is a radical difference between a backslidden Christian and a hypocrite who has gone back on his profession. The hypocrite loves the world, and enjoys sin when he returns to it. He may have some fears and some remorse, and some misgivings about the loss of his reputation; but after all he enjoys sin.

Not so with the backslidden Christian. He loses his first love, then he falls prey to temptation, and so he goes into sin. But he does not love it; indeed, he is miserable, for sin is always bitter to him. He feels unhappy and away from home. Though he does not experience the presence of the Spirit of God, and does not feel the love of God in exercise to keep him from sin, still he does not love sin. He feels that he is a wretch. He is as different from the hypocrite as can be.

Such a man, when he leaves the love of God, may be delivered over to Satan for a time, for the destruction of the flesh, that the spirit may be saved. But he can never again enjoy sin as he used to, or delight himself as he once could in the pleasures of the world. Never again can he drink in iniquity like water. So long as he continues to wander, he is wretched. If you are such a one, you know it only too well.

Do you see why convicted sinners are afraid to pledge themselves to give up their sins? They tell you they dare not promise to do it, because they are afraid they shall not keep the promise. There you have the reason. They love sin. The drunkard knows he loves rum, and though he may be constrained to keep his promise and abstain from it, yet his appetite still craves it. And so with the convicted sinner. He feels that he loves sin, that the hold of sin has never been broken off, and he dares not promise.

See why some professed Christians are so much opposed to pledges? It is for the same reason. They love their sins so well, they know their hearts will plead for indulgence, and they are afraid to promise to give them up. Hence many who profess faith think they are Christians, but refuse to join the church. The secret reason is, they feel that their heart is still going after sin, and they dare not come under the obligations of the church covenant. They do not want to be subject to the discipline of the church, in case they should sin. This person knows he is a hypocrite.

Those sinners who have worldly sorrow do not see where the difficulty lies, and that is why they are not converted. Their intellectual views of sin may be such that if their hearts corresponded, they would be Christians. And perhaps they are thinking that this is true repentance. But if they were truly willing to give up sin, and all sin, they would not hesitate to pledge themselves to it, and to have all the world know that they had done it.

If you are such a person, I ask you now to come forward, and take these seats.* If you are willing to give up sin, you are willing to promise to do it, and willing to have it known that you have done it, well and good. But if you resist conviction when your understanding has enlightened you to your duty, if your heart still goes forth after your sins—tremble, sinner, at the prospect before you. All your convictions will avail you nothing. They will only sink you deeper in hell for having resisted them.

If you are willing to give up your sins, you can come forward. But

---

*I believe it is helpful to see how Finney issued an "Altar Call" in the following verses. People were invited forward to the "Anxious Bench" for further instruction. As you remember from his sermon on a public profession of Christ, a public profession of faith and a renunciation of sin is an essential aspect of beginning the Christian walk.

if you still love your sins, and want to retain them, you can keep your seats. And now, shall we go and tell God in prayer that these sinners are unwilling to give up their sins, that though they are convinced they are wrong, they love their idols, and after them they will go? The Lord have mercy on them, for they are in a fearful case.

5

TRUE AND FALSE CONVERSION*

"Behold, all ye that kindle a fire, that compass yourselves about with sparks: walk in the light of your fire, and in the sparks that ye have kindled. This shall ye have of my hand; ye shall lie down in sorrow" (Isaiah 50:11).

It is clear from these words in the chapter that the prophet was addressing those who professed to be religious, and who flattered themselves that they were in a state of salvation. But, in fact, their hope was a fire of their own kindling, and sparks created by themselves.

Before I proceed with the subject of the nature of true and false conversion, let me warn you that it will be of no use unless you will be honest in applying it to yourself. If you mean to profit by the discourse, you must resolve to apply it faithfully to yourself, just as scrupulously as if you thought you were now going to the solemn judgment. If you will do this, I hope to be able to lead you to discover your true state, and if you are now deceived, direct you in the true path to salvation. If you will not do this, I shall preach—and you will hear—in vain.

The Natural State of Man Is Pure Selfishness

Prior to his conversion, the natural man has no impartial benevolence. Selfishness is regarding one's own happiness supremely, and seeking one's own good because it is his own. The selfish person places his own happiness above other interests of greater value, such as the glory of God and the good of the universe. This is evident from many considerations.

Lectures to Professing Christians, 211–231.

All mankind is selfish, and all the dealings of mankind are conducted on this principle. If someone overlooked this, and undertook to deal with mankind as if these things were not so, as if in his natural state man possesses disinterested benevolence, he would be working in vain.

The Character of the Converted Person Is Benevolent

A converted individual is benevolent, and not supremely selfish. Benevolence is loving the happiness of others, or choosing the happiness of others over one's own. Benevolence is a compound word that properly signifies good will, or choosing the happiness of others. This is God's state of mind. We are told that God is love; that is, He is benevolent. Benevolence comprises His whole character. All His moral attributes are only so many facets of benevolence. An individual who is converted is in this respect like God.

I do not mean that no one is converted unless he is purely and perfectly benevolent as God is; but that in the balance of his mind, his prevailing choice is benevolent. He sincerely seeks the good of others for its own sake. And, by disinterested benevolence I do not mean that a person feels no interest in the object of his goodwill. What I mean is that a person seeks the happiness of others for its own sake, and not for how it reflects on himself, or how it promotes his own happiness. He chooses to do good because he rejoices in the happiness of others and desires their happiness for its own sake.

God is purely and disinterestedly benevolent. He does not make His creatures happy for the sake of promoting His own happiness, but because He loves their happiness and chooses it for its own sake. Not that He does not feel happy in promoting the happiness of His creatures, but that He does not do it for the sake of His own gratification. The person who is disinterested in this sense of the word feels happy in doing good. If he did not love to do good, and enjoy doing good, it would not be virtue in him.

Benevolence is a facet of holiness. It is what the law of God requires: "Thou shalt love the Lord thy God with all thy heart, and with all thy soul, and with all thy strength, and with all thy mind; and thy neighbor as thyself" (Luke 10:27). Just as certainly as the converted man yields obedience to the law of God, and just as certainly as he is like God, he is benevolent. Seeking the happiness of others—and not his own happiness—as his supreme end is the leading feature of his character.

Conversion Is a Change From Selfishness to Benevolence

True conversion demands a change in the final goal, and not merely a change in the means of attaining that goal. It is not true that the converted and the unconverted differ only in the means they use, while both are aiming at the same end. It is not true that Gabriel and Satan are pursuing the same end—their own happiness—only pursuing a different way. Gabriel does not obey God for the sake of promoting his own happiness.

A person may change his means, and yet have the same end, his own happiness. He may do good for the sake of the temporal benefit. He may not believe in religion, or in eternity, and yet may see that doing good will be for his advantage in this world. Suppose, then, that his eyes are opened, and he sees the reality of eternity. Then he may take up religion as a means of happiness in eternity. Now, everyone can see that there is no virtue in this.

The true and the false convert differ in this: the true convert chooses, as the end of his pursuit, the glory of God and the good of His kingdom. This end he chooses for its own sake, because he views this as the greatest good, as a greater good than his own individual happiness. Not that he is indifferent to his own happiness, but he prefers God's glory, because it is a greater good. He looks on the happiness of every individual according to its real importance, as far as he is capable of valuing it, and he chooses the greatest good as his supreme object.

Points on Which Saints and Sinners Agree and Disagree

They may agree in leading a strictly moral life. The difference is in their motives. The true saint leads a moral life from love of holiness, the deceived person from selfish considerations. He uses morality as a means to an end, to effect his own happiness. The true saint loves it as an end.

They may be equally prayerful, so far as the form of praying is concerned. The difference is in their motives. The true saint loves to pray. The other prays because he hopes to derive some benefit to himself from praying. The true saint expects a benefit from praying, but that is not his leading motive. The other prays for no other reason.

They may be equally zealous in religion. One may have great zeal, because his zeal is according to knowledge, and he sincerely desires and loves to promote Christianity for its own sake. The other may show equal zeal, for the sake of having his own salvation more assured, and because he is afraid of going to hell if he does not work for the Lord. And so he works to quiet his conscience, and not because he loves Christianity for its own sake.

They may be equally conscientious in the discharge of duty; the true convert because he loves to do duty, and the other because he dares not neglect it.

Both may pay equal regard to what is right; the true convert because he loves what is right, and the other because he knows he cannot be saved unless he does right. He is honest in his common business transactions, because it is the only way to secure his own interest. Verily, the false convert has his reward. He gets the reputation of being honest among men, but if he has no higher motive, he will have no reward from God.

They may agree in their desires in many respects. They may agree in their desires to serve God. The true convert because he loves the service of God, and the deceived person for the reward, as the hired servant serves his master.

They may agree in their desires to be useful. The true convert desires usefulness for its own sake, the deceived person because he knows that he may obtain the favor of God. And then, in proportion to his knowledge of the importance of having God's favor will be the intensity of his desires to be useful.

In desiring the conversion of souls, the true saint will seek to glorify God; the deceived person to gain the favor of God. He will be driven by this, just as he is in giving money. Just as it is possible that a person might give his money to the Bible Society, or the Missionary Society, from selfish motives alone—to procure happiness, or applause, or obtain the favor of God—he may just as easily desire the conversion of souls, and labor to promote it, from motives purely selfish.

The true saint will glorify God because he loves to see God glorified, and the deceived person because he knows that is the way to be saved. The true convert has his heart set on the glory of God, and His great end, and he desires to glorify God as an end, for its own sake. The other desires it as a means to *his* own ends, benefitting himself alone.

With regard to repentance, the true convert abhors sin on account of its hateful nature, because it dishonors God. Therefore he desires to repent of it. The other desires to repent, because he knows that unless he does repent he will be damned.

With respect to believing in Jesus Christ, the true saint wants his belief to glorify God, because he loves the truth for its own sake. The other desires to believe, that he may have a stronger hope of heaven.

With regard to obeying God, the true saint hopes to increase in holiness; the false professor because he desires the rewards of obedience. They may agree not only in their desires, but in their resolutions. They may both resolve to give up sin, to obey God, to lay themselves out in promoting Christianity and building up the kingdom of Christ. They may both resolve it with great strength of purpose, but with different motives.

They may also agree in their intentions. They may both really intend to glorify God, to convert men, to extend the kingdom of Christ, and to have the world converted. But the true saint does this from love to God and holiness, the other for the sake of securing his own happiness. One chooses it as an end, the other as a means to promote a selfish end.

They may both strive to be truly holy; the true saint because he loves holiness, and the deceived person because he knows that he can be happy no other way.

They may agree not only in their desires, resolutions and intentions, but also in their affection toward many objects. They may both love the Bible: the true saint delights in it, and feasts his soul on it because it is God's truth; the other loves it because he thinks it is to his best advantage to do so.

They may both love God; one because he sees God's character to be supremely excellent and lovely in itself and he loves it for its own sake; the other because he thinks God is his particular friend, who is going to make him happy forever: he connects the idea of God with his own interests.

They may both love Christ. The true convert loves His character; the deceived person because he thinks He will save *him* from hell, and give him eternal life. Why should he not love Him?

They may both love Christians; the true convert because he sees in them the image of Christ, and the deceived person because they belong to his own denomination, or because they are on his side and he feels the same interest and hopes with them.

They may also agree in hating the same things. They may both hate infidelity and oppose it strenuously—the true saint because it is opposed to God and holiness, and the deceived person because it injures an interest in which he is deeply concerned, and if true, destroys all his own hopes for eternity. So they may hate error; one because it is detestable in itself, and contrary to God; the other because it is contrary to his views and opinions.

I recollect seeing in writing an attack on a minister for publishing certain opinions, ". . . because," said the writer, "these sentiments would destroy all *my hopes* for eternity." A very good reason indeed!—or, at least, as good a reason as a selfish being needs for opposing an opinion.

They may both hate sin; the true convert because it is odious to God, and the deceived person because it is injurious to himself. Cases have occurred where an individual has hated his own sins and yet not forsaken them. How often the drunkard, as he looks back at what he once was and contrasts his present degradation with what he might have been, abhors his drink—not for its own sake, but because it has ruined him. And he still loves his cups, and continues to drink—although, when he looks at their effects, he feels indignation.

They may be both opposed to sinners. The opposition of true saints is a benevolent opposition, viewing and abhorring their character and conduct as calculated to subvert the kingdom of God. The other is opposed to sinners because they are opposed to the religion he has embraced, and because they are not on his side.

They may both rejoice in the same things. Both may rejoice in the prosperity of the Church and the conversion of souls; the true convert because he has his heart set on it and loves it for its own sake, and the greatest good. On the other hand, the deceived person is glad because that particular thing in which he thinks he has such a great interest is advancing.

Both may mourn and feel distressed at the weak condition of the church: the true convert because God is dishonored, and the deceived person because his own soul is not happy, or because religion is not in favor.

Both may love the society of the saints; the true convert because his soul enjoys their spiritual conversation, the other because he hopes to derive some advantage from their company. The first enjoys it because out of the abundance of the heart the mouth speaketh; the other because he loves to talk about the great interest he feels in religion, and the hope he has of going to heaven.

Both may love to attend Christian meetings. The true saint attends because his heart delights in acts of worship, in prayer and praise, in hearing the Word of God and in communion with God and His saints. However, the other attends because he thinks a church meeting is a good place to prop up his hope. He may have a hundred reasons for loving to attend these services, and yet none of them for their own sake, or because he loves in itself the worship and the service of God.

Both may find pleasure in the duty of the prayer closet. The true saint loves his closet, because he draws near to God and finds delight in communion with God, where there are no embarrassments to keep him from going right to God and conversing. The deceived person finds a kind of satisfaction in it, because it is his duty to pray in secret and he feels a self-righteous satisfaction in doing it. Not only that, he may feel a certain pleasure in it, from a kind of excitement of the mind which he mistakes for communion with God.

They may both love the doctrines of grace; the true saint because they are so glorious to God, the other because he thinks them a guarantee of his own salvation.

They may both love the precepts of God's law; the true saint because they are so excellent, holy, just and good; the other because he thinks they will make him happy if he loves them. Both may consent to the penalty of the law. The true saint consents to it in his own case, because he feels it to be just in itself for God to send him to hell. The deceived person because he thinks *he* is in no danger from it. He feels a respect for it, because he knows that it is right and his conscience approves it, but he has never consented to it in his own case.

They may be equally liberal in giving to benevolent societies. Two men may give equal sums to a benevolent object, from totally different motives. One gives to do good, and would be just as willing to give as not, if he knew that no other living person would give. The other gives for the credit of it, or to quiet his conscience, or because he hopes to purchase the favor of God.

They may be equally self-denying in many things. Self-denial is not confined to true saints. Look at the sacrifices and self-denials of the Muslims, going on their pilgrimage to Mecca. Look at the heathen, throwing themselves under the car of Juggernaut. Look at the poor ignorant papists, going up and down over the sharp stones on their bare knees till they stream with blood. A Protestant congregation will agree that there is no faith involved in these things. But there is self-denial. The true saint denies himself for the sake of doing more good to others. He is more set on this than on the indulgence of his own interest. The deceived person may go to equal lengths, but from purely selfish motives.

They may both be willing to suffer martyrdom. Read the lives of the martyrs, and you will have no doubt that some were willing to suffer from a wrong idea of the rewards of martyrdom, and would rush upon their own destruction because they were persuaded it was the sure road to eternal life.

In all these cases, the motives of one class are directly opposed to the other. The difference lies in the choice of different *ends*. One chooses his own interest, the other chooses God's interest, as his chief end. For a person to pretend that both these classes are aiming at the same end is to say that an unrepentant sinner is just as benevolent as a real Christian. Or, that a Christian is not benevolent like God, but is only seeking his own happiness, and seeking it in Christianity rather than in the world.

We Can Know Our True Character

Some ask, "If these two classes may be alike in so many particulars, how are we to know our own real character or to tell to which class we belong? We know that the heart is deceitful above all things, and desperately wicked. How are we to know whether we love God and holiness for their own sake, or if we are seeking the favor of God, and aiming at heaven for our own benefit?" Let me give several answers to that question.

First, if we are truly benevolent, it will be reflected in our daily transactions. This character, if real, will show itself in our business, if anywhere. If selfishness rules our conduct there, as sure as God reigns we are truly selfish. If in our dealings with people we are selfish, we are selfish in our dealings with God too. "For he that loveth not his brother whom he hath seen, how can he love God whom he hath not seen?" (1 John 4:20). Christianity is not merely love to God, but love to man also. And if our daily transactions show us to be selfish, we are unconverted. Disinterested benevolence is essential to Christian faith; a Christian loves his neighbor as himself.

Second, if your motives in Christianity are true, the duties of it will not be a task to you. You will not go about serving God as the laboring man goes to his toil for the sake of a living. If the laboring man takes pleasure in his labor, it is not for its own sake. He would not do it if he could help it. If he takes any pleasure in the task, it is for its anticipated results, the support and comfort of his family, or the increase of his property.

This is precisely the case of some people in regard to Christianity. They take it as a sick man takes his medicine, because they desire its effects, and they know they must have it or perish. It is a task that they never would do for its own sake. Suppose men love labor, as a child loves play. They would do it all day long, and never be tired of doing it, without any other inducement than the pleasure in doing it. So it is in Christianity, where it is loved for its own sake, there is no weariness in it.

Third, if selfishness is the prevailing character of your faith, it will sometimes take one form and sometimes another. For instance, if there is a time of general coldness in the church, real converts will still enjoy their own secret communion with God, although there may not be so much to attract public notice. But the deceived person will then invariably be found driving after the world. Now, let the true saints rise up, make a noise, and speak their joys aloud so that Christianity begins to be talked of again, and the deceived church member will soon begin to bustle about, appearing to be even more zealous than the true saint. He is compelled by his convictions and not affections. When there is no public interest, he feels no conviction; but when the church awakes, he is convicted and compelled to stir about to keep his conscience quiet. Yet, it may be only selfishness in another form.

Fourth, if you are selfish, your enjoyment of Christianity will depend mainly on the strength of your hopes of heaven, and not on the exercise of your affections in this world. Your enjoyments are not in the employments of Christianity themselves, but of a vastly different kind from those of the true saint. They are mostly from anticipating. When your evidences are renewed, and you feel very certain of going to heaven, then you enjoy Christianity a good deal. It depends on your hope, and not on your love for the things for which you hope. You hear persons tell of their having no enjoyment in Christianity when they lose their hopes. The reason is plain. If they loved Christianity for its own sake, their enjoyment would not depend on their hope.

A person who loves his employment is happy anywhere. And if you loved the employments of Christianity, you would be happy if God should put you in hell, provided He would only let you employ yourself in promoting the Christian faith. As long as you might pray and praise God, you think that you could be happy anywhere in the universe; for you would still be doing the things in which your happiness mainly consists. If the duties of religion are not the things in which you feel enjoyment, and if all your enjoyment depends on your hope, you have no true faith; it is all selfishness.

I do not say that true saints do not enjoy their hope. But that is not the great thing with them. They think very little about their own hopes. Their thoughts are employed about something else. The deceived person, on the contrary, is sensible that he does not enjoy the duties of Christian faith; but the more he does, the more confident he is of heaven. He takes only such kind of enjoyment in it, as a man does who thinks that by great labor he shall have great wealth.

Fifth, if you are selfish in religion, your enjoyments will be chiefly from anticipation. The true saint already enjoys the peace of God, and the joy of heaven has begun in his soul. He has not merely the prospect of it, but eternal life has actually begun in him. He has that faith which is the very substance of things hoped for. He has the very feelings of heaven in him; he anticipates joys higher in degree, but the same in kind. He knows that he has heaven begun in him, and is not obliged to wait till he dies to taste the joys of eternal life. His enjoyment is in proportion to his holiness, and not in proportion to his hope.

The sixth difference by which it may be known whether you are selfish in religion is this: the deceived person has only a purpose of obedience, and the other has a preference of obedience. This is an important distinction, and I fear few people make it. Multitudes have a purpose of obedience, who have not true preference of obedience. Preference is actual choice, or obedience of heart. You often hear some speak of their having had a purpose to do this or that act of obedience, but who fail to do it. And they will tell you how difficult it is to execute their purpose.

The true saint, on the other hand, really prefers and in his heart chooses obedience, and therefore he finds it easy to obey. The one has a purpose to obey, like that which Paul had before he was converted as he tells us in the seventh chapter of Romans. He had a strong purpose of obedience, but did not obey, because his heart was not in it. The true convert prefers obedience for its own sake; he actually chooses it and does it. The other purposes to be holy, because he knows that is the only way to be happy. The true saint chooses holiness for its own sake.

Seventh, the true convert and the deceived person also differ in their faith. The true saint has a confidence in the general character of God that leads him to unqualified submission to Him.

A great deal is said about the kinds of faith, but without much meaning. True confidence in the Lord's special promises depends on confidence in God's general character. There are only two principles on which any government, human or divine, is obeyed. These are fear and confidence. No matter whether it is the government of a family, or a ship, or a nation, or a universe, all obedience springs from one of these two motivations. In the first case, individuals obey from hope of reward and fear of the penalty. In the second, their choice to obey stems from that confidence in the character of the government that works by love. One child obeys his parent from confidence in his parent. The other yields an outward obedience from hope and fear.

The true convert has this faith or confidence in God that leads him to obey God because he loves Him. This is the obedience of faith. He has such confidence in God that he submits himself wholly into His hands. The other has only a partial faith, and only a reluctant submission. The devil has a partial faith. He believes and trembles.

A person may believe that Christ came to sinners, and on that ground may submit to Him to be saved. Yet, he does not submit wholly to Him, to be governed by Him. His submission is only on condition that he shall be saved. It is never with that unreserved confidence in God's whole character that leads him to say, "Thy will be done." He only submits to be saved.

This is the religion of law. The other is true gospel faith. One is selfish, the other benevolent. Here lies the true difference between the two classes. The religion of one is outward and hypocritical. The other is that of the heart and is holy and acceptable to God.

Eighth, and final, if your religion is selfish, you will rejoice particularly in the conversion of sinners when your own agency is concerned in it, but will have very little satisfaction in it where it is through the agency of others. The selfish person rejoices when he is active and successful in converting sinners, because he thinks he shall have a great reward. But instead of delighting in it when done by others, he will be envious.

The true saint sincerely delights to have others useful, and rejoices when others are instrumental in the conversion of sinners as much as if he had been the channel. There are some who will take interest in a revival, but only so far as they are connected with it. It would seem they'd rather sinners remain unconverted, than that they should be saved by the ministry of an evangelist or minister of another denomination. The true spirit of a child of God says, "Send, Lord, by whom thou wilt send, only let souls be saved, and thy name glorified!"

Some Objections to These Views

Some object to these views and complain, "Am I not to have any regard to my own happiness?" Yes, certainly, it is right to regard your own happiness according to its relative value. Put it in this scale, by the side of the glory of God and the good of the universe, and then give it the value which belongs to it. This is precisely what God does. And this is what He means when He commands you to love your neighbor as yourself.

You will in fact promote your own happiness, precisely to the extent that you leave it out of view. True happiness consists mainly in the gratification of virtuous desires. There may be pleasure in gratifying desires that are selfish, but it is not real happiness. But to be virtuous, your desires must be disinterested, that is, not self-centered. Your happiness will be in proportion to your disinterestedness.

Suppose a man sees a beggar sitting on a curbstone in the street, cold and hungry, without friends, and ready to perish. The man's feelings are touched, and he steps into a grocery close by, and buys him a loaf of bread. At once the countenance of the beggar lights up, and he looks up with unutterable gratitude. Now, plainly, the gratification the man receives from the act is proportionate to the selflessness of his motive. If he did it purely and solely out of disinterested benevolence, his gratification is complete in the act itself. But if he did it partly to make it known that he is a charitable and humane person, then his happiness is not complete until the deed is told to others.

Suppose you see a sinner in his sins; he is truly wicked and truly wretched. Your compassion is excited, and you convert and save him. If your motives were to obtain honor among men, and to secure the favor of God, you are not completely happy until the deed is told, and perhaps put in the church newspaper. But if you wished purely to save a soul from death, then as soon as you see that done, your gratification is complete and your joy unmingled. So it is in all Christian duties; your happiness is precisely in proportion as you are disinterested.

If you aim at doing good for its own sake, then you will be happy in proportion as you do good. But if you aim directly at your own happiness, and if you do good simply as a means of securing your own happiness, you will fail. You will be like the child pursuing his own shadow; he can never overtake it, because it always keeps just so far before him.

Suppose in the case I have mentioned, you had no desire to relieve the beggar's plight, but acted simply to obtain the applause of a certain individual. Then you will feel no pleasure at all in the relief of the beggar; but when that individual hears of it and commends it, then you are gratified. But you are not gratified in the thing itself.

Or suppose you aim at the conversion of sinners; but if it is not love of sinners that leads you to do it, how can the conversion of sinners make you happy? It will not gratify the desire that prompted the effort. The truth is, God has so constituted the mind of man that it must seek the happiness of others as its end or it cannot be happy. Here is the true reason why all the world, seeking their own happiness and not the happiness of others, fails to achieve their end. It is always just so far before them. If they would leave off seeking their own happiness, and lay themselves out to do good, they would be happy.

Some object, "But did not Christ regard the joy set before Him? And did not Moses also have respect unto the recompense of reward? And does not the Bible say we love God because He first loved us?"

Truly, Christ despised the shame and endured the cross, and had regard to the joy set before Him. But what was the joy set before Him? Not His own salvation, not His own happiness, but the great good He would do in the salvation of the world. He was perfectly happy in himself. The happiness of others was what He aimed at. This was the joy set before him. And that is what He obtained.

Also, Moses had respect to the recompense of reward. But was that his own comfort? Far from it. The recompense of reward was the salvation of the people of Israel. What did he say? When God proposed to destroy the nation, and make of him a great nation, if Moses had been selfish he would have said, "That is right, Lord; be it unto thy servant according to thy word." But what did he say? Why, his heart was so set on the salvation of his people, and the glory of God, that he would not think of it for a moment, but said, "If thou wilt, forgive their sin—; and if not, blot me, I pray thee, out of thy book, which thou hast written" (Ex. 32:32).

In another case, when God said He would destroy them, and make of Moses a greater and a mightier nation, Moses thought of God's glory, and said, "Then the Egyptians shall hear of it. . . . Then the nations which have heard the fame of thee will speak, saying, 'Because the Lord was not able to bring this people into the land' " (Num. 14:13, 15–16).

He could not bear to think of having his own interest exalted at the expense of God's glory. It was really a greater reward, to his benevolent mind, to have God glorified and the children of Israel saved, rather than have any personal advantage.

Where Scripture teaches, "We love Him, because He first loved us" (1 John 4:19), the language plainly bears two interpretations. Either

His love to us has provided the way for our return and the influence that brought us to love Him, or that we love Him for His favor shown to ourselves. That the latter is not the meaning is evident, because Jesus Christ has so expressly denounced that motivation in His Sermon on the Mount: "If ye love them which love you, what reward have ye? Do not even the publicans the same?" (Matt. 5:46). If we love God, not for His character but for His favors to us, Jesus Christ has declared us reprobate.

Others also object, asking, "Does not the Bible offer happiness as the reward of virtue?" Yes, the Bible speaks of happiness as the result of virtue, but nowhere declares virtue to be found in the pursuit of one's own happiness. The Bible repeatedly refutes this, and represents virtue as doing good to others.

In addition, we can see by the philosophy of the mind that it must be so. If a person desires the good of others, he will be happy to the extent that he gratifies that desire. Happiness is the result of virtue, but virtue does not consist in the direct pursuit of one's own happiness and is wholly inconsistent with it.

Another will complain, "God aims at our happiness, and shall we be more benevolent than God? Should we not be like God? May we not aim at the same thing that God aims at? Should we not be seeking the same end that God seeks?" This objection is misleading, futile and rotten. God is benevolent to others. He aims at the happiness of others and at our happiness. And to be like Him, we must aim at and delight in His happiness and glory, and the honor and glory of the universe, according to their real value.

Some ask, "Why does the Bible appeal continually to the hopes and fears of men, if a regard to our own happiness is not a proper motive to action?" The Bible appeals to the instincts God placed in men, not to their selfishness. Man dreads harm, and it is not wrong to avoid it. We may have a due regard to our own happiness, according to its value.

Consider also that mankind is so besotted with sin that God cannot get their attention to consider His true character, and their reasons for loving Him, unless He appeals to their hopes and fears. But when they are awakened, then He presents the gospel to them. When a minister has preached the terrors of the Lord until he has his hearers alarmed and aroused, so that they will give attention, then he has gone far enough in that line. Next, he ought to spread out all the character of God before them to engage their hearts to love Him for His own excellence.

Some also ask, "Did not Jesus say, 'Repent ye, and believe the gospel' " (Mark 1:15)? Yes, but he requires *true* repentance; that is, to forsake sin because it is hateful in itself. True repentance does not forsake sin on condition of pardon. True repentance does not bargain,

"I will be sorry for my sins, if you will forgive me." Jesus requires true faith and true submission; not conditional faith or partial submission. This is what the Bible insists on. It says we shall be saved, but on the condition of unconditional repentance and submission.

Finally, some object, "Does not the gospel hold out pardon as a motive to submission?" This depends on the sense in which you use the term *motive*. If you mean that God spreads His whole character out before people, as well as His reasons to engage the sinner's love and repentance, then, yes. His compassion and willingness to pardon are reasons for loving God, because they are a part of His glorious excellence that we are bound to love.

But if you mean by *motive* a condition, and that the sinner is to repent on condition he shall be pardoned; then, I say that the Bible nowhere holds out any such view of the matter. It never authorizes a sinner to say, "I will repent *if* You will forgive me," and nowhere offers pardon as a motive to repent in such a sense as this.

We see why so many church members have such differing views of the nature of the gospel. Some view it as a mere matter of accommodation to mankind, by which God is rendered less strict than He was under the law; they believe they may be fashionable or worldly, so that the gospel might come in and overlook their deficiencies and save them.

Other members view the gospel as a provision of divine benevolence, having for its main design to destroy sin and promote holiness. Therefore they declare that the gospel does not free them to be less holy than they ought to be under the law, but that its whole value consists in its power to make them, if possible, holier still.

We see why some people are so much more anxious to convert sinners than to see the church sanctified and God glorified by the good works of His people. Many feel a natural sympathy for sinners, and wish to have them saved from hell; and if that is gained, they have no further concern. But true saints are most affected by sin not because it produces death, but because it dishonors God. And they are most distressed to see Christians sin, because it dishonors God more.

Some people seem to care but little how the church lives, if they can only see the work of conversion go forward. They are not anxious to have God honored. It shows that they are not actuated by the love of holiness, but by a mere compassion for sinners.

6

TRUE SUBMISSION*

"Submit yourselves therefore to God" (James 4:7).

If you are deceived in regard to your hopes, and have built on a false foundation, the fundamental error in your case was you embraced, from selfish motives, what you thought was the gospel plan of salvation. Your selfish heart was unbroken. This is the source of your delusion, if you are deceived. If your selfishness was subdued, you are not deceived in your hope. If it was not, your faith is vain and so is your hope.

If you are deceived, and have a false hope, you are in the utmost danger if you continue to cling to your old hope, whenever you are awakened to consider your condition. Commonly, after a season of anxiety and self-examination, such church members and professing Christians settle down again on the old foundation. The reason is, their habits of mind have become fixed in that channel; therefore, by the laws of the mind it is difficult to break into a new course. If you ever mean to get right with God, you should see clearly that you have hitherto been wholly wrong, so that you need not multiply any more the kind of efforts that have deceived you up to now.

This kind of deception is quite common. How often will a great part of the church lie cold and dead until a revival commences? Then you will see them bustling about, and they get engaged, as they call it, in Christianity. They renew their efforts and multiply their prayers for a season; and this is what they call getting revived.

But it is only the same kind of faith that they had before. Such Christianity lasts no longer than the public excitement. As soon as the body of the church begins to diminish their efforts for the conversion of sinners, these individuals relapse into their former worldliness.

---

*Lectures to Professing Christians, 232–250.

71

They get as near to what they were before their supposed conversion as their pride and their fear of the censures of the church will let them. When a revival comes again, they renew the same round. So they live along by spasms, over and over again, revived and backslidden, revived and backslidden, alternately, as long as they live. The truth is, by a spurious conversion they are blinded to the fact that their selfishness never was broken down; and the more they multiply such kinds of efforts, the more sure they are to be lost.

What True Submission Is Not

True submission to God is not indifference. No two things can be more unlike than indifference and true submission. Nor does true submission consist in being willing to be sinful for the glory of God. Some have supposed that true submission would include even this. But this is a mistake. To be willing to be sinful is itself a sinful state of mind. And to be willing to do anything for the glory of God is to choose not to be sinful. The idea of being sinful for the glory of God is absurd.

True submission does not consist in a willingness to be punished. If we were now in hell, true submission would require that we should be willing to be punished. Because then it would be certain that it was God's will we should be punished. So, if we were in a world where no provision was made for the redemption of sinners, and where our punishment was therefore inevitable, it would be our duty to be willing to be punished.

If a man committed murder, and if there were no other way to secure the public safety but for him to be hanged, it would be his duty to be willing to be hanged for the public good. So if we were in a world solely under law, where there was no plan of salvation and no measure to secure the stability of government through the forgiveness of sinners, it would be the duty of everyone to be willing to be punished. In this world, genuine submission does not imply a willingness to be punished. It is not the will of God that all shall be punished; it is His will that all who truly repent and submit to God shall be saved (2 Pet. 3:9).

What True Submission Is

True submission consists in perfect acquiescence in all the providential dealings and orderings of God, whether relating to ourselves, or to others, or to the universe. Some people suppose they do acquiesce in the abstract in the providential government of God. Yet, if you converse with them you see them finding fault with God's arrangements in many things. They wonder why God allowed Adam to sin.

Or why He allowed sin to enter the universe at all. Or why He did this or that, or made this or that, or thus and so. In all these cases, supposing we could assign no reason at all that would be satisfactory, true submission implies a perfect acquiescence in whatever He has permitted or done. Feeling that, so far as His providence is concerned, it is all right.

True submission implies acquiescence in the precept of God's moral law. The general precept of God's moral law is, "Thou shalt love the Lord thy God with all thy heart, and with all thy soul, and with all thy strength, and with all thy mind; and thy neighbor as thyself" (Luke 10:27).

Perhaps some will say, "I do acquiesce in this precept, I feel that it is right, and I have no objection to this law." Here I want you to make the distinction carefully between a mental assent to God's law, and actual submission to it. Every mind naturally, and by its own common sense of what is right, approves of this law. Every devil in hell approves of it. God has so constituted the mind that every moral agent must mentally approve of His law. But this is not the acquiescence I am speaking of.

A person may approve to so great a degree that he is even delighted with it—without truly submitting to it. There are two ideas included in genuine submission.

First, true acquiescence to God's moral law includes actual obedience. It is vain for a child to pretend a real acquiescence in his father's commands, unless he actually obeys them. It is in vain for a citizen to pretend an acquiescence in the laws of the land, unless he obeys those laws.

Second, the main idea of submission is the yielding up of that which constitutes the great point in controversy. Simply this: people have taken their supreme affection away from God and His kingdom, and set up self-interest as the paramount object of regard. Instead of laying themselves out in doing good, as God requires, they have adopted the maxim that "charity begins at home."

This is the very point in debate between God and the sinner. The sinner aims at promoting his own interest as his supreme object. We must cease placing our own interests as supreme and let the interests of God and His kingdom rise in our affections just as much above our own interests as their real value is greater. The person who does not do this is a rebel against God.

Suppose a civil ruler decided to promote the general happiness of his nation, wisely enacting laws adapted to this end, and dedicating all his own resources in this object. Suppose he should then require every subject to do the same.

Then suppose an individual should go and set up his own private interest in opposition to the general interest. He is a rebel against the government, and against all that the government is set to promote. He must give up that point, and fall in line with the ruler and the obedient subjects in promoting the public good.

Now, the law of God absolutely requires that you should make your own happiness subordinate to the glory of God and the good of the universe. And until you do this, you are the enemy of God and the universe, and a child of hell.

The gospel requires the same as the law. I am astonished that many have maintained that it is right for a person to aim directly at his own salvation, and to make his own happiness the great object of pursuit. Plainly, God's law is different from this, and requires everyone to prize God's interest supremely. The gospel requires the same as the law, otherwise, Jesus Christ is the minister of sin, and came into the world to take up arms against God's government.

The gospel requires disinterested benevolence, or love to God and man—the same requirement as the law. The Bible says, "Seek ye first the kingdom of God, and His righteousness" (Matt. 6:33). What does that mean? Strange as it may seem, a writer has lately quoted this very text to prove that it is right to seek first our own salvation, or our own happiness, and to make that the leading object of pursuit.

But that is not the meaning. It requires everyone to make the promotion of the kingdom of God his great object. I suppose this enjoins the duty of aiming at being holy, and not at our own happiness. Happiness is connected with holiness, but it is not the same thing. To seek holiness or obedience to God, to honor and glorify Him, is a very different thing from seeking supremely our own happiness.

Scripture also says, "Whether therefore ye eat, or drink, or whatsoever ye do, do all to the glory of God" (1 Cor. 10:31). Some ask, "May we not eat and drink to please ourselves?" No. We may not even gratify our natural appetite for good, but as subordinate to the glory of God. This is what the gospel requires, for the apostle wrote this to the Christian church.

Another passage says, "Look not every man on his own things, but every man also on the things of others" (Phil. 2:4). It is a vain attempt to quote all of the passages that teach this. You may find, on almost every page of the Bible, some passage that means the same thing, requiring us not to seek our own good, but the benefit of others.

Our Savior says, "Whosoever will save his life shall lose it; and whosoever will lose his life for my sake shall save it" (Matt. 16:25). That is, if a person aims at his own interest, he shall lose his own interest. If he aims at saving his soul, as his supreme object, he will lose his own soul. He must make the good of others his supreme object, or he will be lost.

Again, He says, "There is no man that hath left house, or brethren, or sisters, or father, or mother, or wife, or children, or lands, for my sake and the gospel's, but he shall receive an hundred-fold now in this time, houses, and brethren, and sisters, and mothers, and children, and lands, with persecutions; and in the world to come, eternal life" (Mark 10:29–30).

Here some people may stumble, and say, "There is a reward held out as a motive." But, mark! What are you to do? Forsake self for the sake of a reward to self? No, but forsake self for the sake of Christ and His gospel; and the *consequence* will be as stated. That is the important distinction.

In 1 Cor. 13, Paul gives a full description of this selfless love, or charity, without which a person is nothing. Remarkably, he says a person may do, and yet be nothing. "Though I speak with the tongues of men and of angels, and have not charity, I am become as sounding brass, or a tinkling cymbal. And though I have the gift of prophecy, and understand all mysteries, and all knowledge; and though I have all faith, so that I could remove mountains, and have not charity, I am nothing. And though I bestow all my goods to feed the poor, and though I give my body to be burned, and have not charity, it profiteth me nothing" (1 Cor. 13:1–3).

But true gospel benevolence is of this character: "Charity suffereth long, and is kind; charity envieth not; charity vaunteth not itself, is not puffed up, doth not behave itself unseemly, seeketh not her own, is not easily provoked, thinketh no evil; rejoiceth not in iniquity, but rejoiceth in the truth; beareth all things, believeth all things, hopeth all things, endureth all things" (vv. 4–7).

". . . seeketh not her own." Notice that. Love has no selfish end, but seeks the happiness of others as its great end. Without this kind of benevolence, we know there is not a particle of Christian faith. The Bible is full of such passages showing that all pure Christianity consists in disinterested benevolence.

Objections

Some inquire, "Why does the Word of God contain threats of the wrath to come, if it is selfishness to be influenced by a fear of them?" People are so constituted that by the laws of their being they dread pain. The Scripture threatenings, therefore, answer many purposes. One is to arrest the attention of the selfish mind, and lead it to examine the reasons there are for loving and obeying God. When the Holy Spirit thus gets the attention, then He rouses the sinner's conscience, and engages him to consider and decide upon the reasonableness and duty of submitting to God.

Some ask, "Since God has given us these susceptibilities to pleasure and pain, is it wrong to be influenced by them?" It is neither right nor wrong. These susceptibilities have no moral character. In morals, there is a class of actions that come under the denomination of prudential considerations.

For instance, suppose you stand on a precipice, where, if you throw yourself down, you will undoubtedly break your neck. You are warned against it. Now, if you do not heed the warning, but throw yourself down, and destroy your life, that will be sin. But heeding the warning of itself is no virtue. It is simply prudent. There is no virtue in avoiding danger, although it may often be sinful not to avoid it. It is sinful for people to brave the wrath of God. But to be afraid of hell is not holy, no more than the fear of breaking your neck down a precipice is holy. It is simply a dictate of the human nature.

Others inquire, "Does not the Bible make it our immediate duty to seek our own happiness?" It is not sinful to seek our own happiness, according to its real value. On the contrary, it is a real duty to do so. And he who neglects to do this commits sin. But while it is right to seek our own happiness, and the constitutional laws of the mind require us to regard our own happiness, still our constitution does not indicate that it is right to pursue our own happiness as the chief good.

Suppose someone should argue, "Because our constitution requires food, therefore it is right to seek food as the supreme good." Would that be sound reasoning? Certainly not, for the Bible expressly forbids any such thing, and says, "Whether therefore ye eat, or drink, do all to the glory of God."

Some argue, "Each one's happiness is put particularly in his own power; and if everyone should seek his own happiness, the happiness of the whole will be secured, to the greatest amount that is possible."

I deny the conclusion altogether, for the laws of the mind are such that it is impossible for one to be happy while he makes his own happiness the supreme object. Happiness consists in the gratification of virtuous desires. But to be gratified, the thing must be obtained "that is desired." To be happy, therefore, the desires that are gratified must be right, and therefore they must be desires that are set outside of oneself.

If your desires revolve around yourself—for instance, if you desire the conversion of sinners for the sake of promoting your own happiness—you will never be happy. When sinners are converted you will not be happy, because it is not the thing on which your desire is centered. The law of the mind, therefore, renders it impossible: if any individual pursues his own happiness, he will never obtain it.

Two things are indispensable to true happiness. First, there must be virtuous desire. If the desire is not virtuous, conscience will remonstrate against it, and therefore a gratification would be attended with pain. Second, this desire must be gratified in the attainment of its object. The object must be desired for its own sake, or the gratification would not be complete, even should the object be obtained.

If the object is desired as a means to an end, the gratification would depend on obtaining the end by this means. But if something is desired as an end, for its own sake, obtaining it would produce unmingled gratification. The mind must, therefore, desire not its own happiness, for in this way it can never be attained, but the desire must center on some other object which is desired for its own sake, the attainment of which would be a gratification, and thus result in happiness.

If each one pursues his own happiness, as his supreme ambition, the interests of different individuals will clash and destroy the happiness of all. This is the very thing we see in the world. This is the reason for all the fraud, violence, oppression, and wickedness in earth and hell. It is because each is pursuing his own interest, resulting in a clash of interests.

The true way to secure our own happiness is not to pursue happiness as an end but to pursue another object, which, when obtained, will afford complete gratification: the glory of God and the good of the universe. The question is not whether it is right to desire and pursue our own happiness at all, but whether it is right to make our own happiness our supreme end.

Some say, "If happiness consists in gratifying virtuous desire, and I aim at gratifying virtuous desire, then this is aiming at my own happiness." The mind does not aim at gratifying the desire, but at accomplishing the thing desired.

Suppose you see a beggar, and you give him a loaf of bread. You aim at relieving the beggar. That is the object desired, and when that is done, your desire is gratified, and you are happy. But if, in relieving the beggar, the object you aimed at was your own happiness, then relieving the beggar will not gratify that desire. By making happiness your aim, you render it impossible to attain. Thus you see, both the law and the gospel require disinterested benevolence as the only condition in which you can be happy.

Submission in Regard to the Law and the Gospel

True submission implies acquiescence in the penalty of God's law. In this world, we are not simply under a government of arbitrary law. This world is a province of Jehovah's empire and stands in a peculiar relation to God's government. It has rebelled, and a new and special provision has been made by which God offers us mercy.

The conditions are that we obey the precepts of the law and submit to the justice of the penalty. It is a government of law, with the gospel appended to it. The gospel requires the same obedience as the law, and requires the sinner's acquiescence in the justice of the penalty. If the sinner were under undisputed justice, it would require that he should submit to the infliction of the penalty. But man is not, and never has been since the fall, under the government of mere justice, but has always known, more or less clearly, that mercy is offered. It has, therefore, never been required that people should be willing to be punished. In this respect gospel submission differs from legal submission.

Under absolute law, submission would consist in willingness to be punished. In this world, submission consists in acquiescence in the justice of the penalty, and regarding oneself as *deserving* the eternal wrath of God.

True submission implies acquiescence to the sovereignty of God. It is the duty of every sovereign to see that all his subjects submit to his government. And it is his duty to enact such laws that every individual, if he obeys perfectly, will promote the public good to the highest possible degree.

If anyone refuses to obey, it is his duty to take that individual by force and make him serve the public interest in the best way that is possible in his rebellion. If he will not promote the public good voluntarily, he must be made to do it involuntarily. The government must either hang him, or shut him up, or in some way make him an example by his suffering. Or, if the public good admits of mercy, it may show mercy in such a way that will best serve the general interest.

Now God is a sovereign ruler, and the submission He requires is no more than what He is bound to require. He would be neglecting His duty as a ruler, if He did not require it. And since you have refused to obey this requirement, you are now bound to throw yourself into His hands, for Him to dispose of you, for time and eternity, in the way that will most promote the interests of the universe. You have forfeited all claim to any portion in the happiness of the universe or the favor of God.

What's now required of you is, since you cannot render obedience for the past, you should acknowledge the justice of His law and leave your future destiny entirely and unconditionally at His disposal for time and eternity. You must submit all you have and all you are to Him. You have justly forfeited all, and are bound to give up all at His bidding, in any way that He calls, to promote the interests of His kingdom.

Finally, true submission requires submission to the terms of the gospel:

1. You must *repent* and have a hearty sorrow for sin, agreeing with

God and taking His part against yourself.

2. You must have *faith*, perfect trust and confidence toward God, such as leads you without hesitation to throw yourself, body and soul, and all you have and are, into His hand, to do with you as He thinks good.

3. You must have *holiness*, or disinterested benevolence. To receive salvation is a mere matter of pure grace, to which you have no claim on the score of justice.

4. You must *receive* Christ as your mediator and advocate, your atoning sacrifice, your ruler and teacher, and in all the offices in which He is presented to you in God's Word. In short, you are to be wholly acquiescent in God's appointed way of salvation.*

Do you see why there are so many false hopes in the church? The reason is, so many persons embrace what they consider the gospel without yielding obedience to the law. They look at the law with dread, and regard the gospel as a scheme to get away from the law. These tendencies have always been manifested among men.

There is a certain class that hold to the gospel and reject the law. And another class take the law and neglect the gospel. The Antinomians think to get rid of the law altogether. They suppose that the rule of life under the gospel is different than that under the law. The truth is that the rule of life is the same in both, and both require disinterested benevolence.

Now, if a person thinks that, under the gospel, he may give up the glory of God as his supreme object, and instead of loving God with all his heart, and soul, and strength, he may make his own salvation his supreme object, his hopes are false. He has embraced another gospel—which is no gospel at all.

But how are we to answer the common objection that faith in Christ implies making our own salvation our object or motive? First of all, what is faith? It is not believing that *you* shall be saved, but believing God's Word concerning His Son.

It is nowhere in Scripture revealed that you shall be saved. God has revealed the fact that Jesus Christ came into the world to save sinners. What you call *faith* is more properly called *hope*. The confident expectation that you shall be saved is inferred in an act of faith—an inference that you have a right to draw when you are conscious of obeying the law and believing the gospel; that is, when you exercise

---

*See Charles G. Finney, *Principles of Union with Christ*, Minneapolis: Bethany House Publishers, 1985, for his discussion of the relationship you can have with Christ in his various offices. This book is a brief daily devotional on the names of Christ and salvation in union with Him.

the feelings required in the law and gospel, you have a right to trust in Christ for your own salvation.

It is an error to suppose that despairing of mercy is essential to true submission. Plainly, under the gospel, everybody knows it is the will of God that every soul should be saved that submits wholeheartedly to its conditions. Suppose a man should come to me and ask, "What shall I do to be saved?" And I answer, "If you expect to be saved you must despair of being saved." What would he think? What inspired writer ever gave any such direction as this? No, the inspired answer is, "Love the Lord thy God, with all thy heart," "Repent, believe the gospel," and so on. Is there anything here that implies despair?

Truly, sinners sometimes *do* despair before they obtain true peace. But why? Not because despair is essential to true peace; but because of their ignorance, or because of wrong instructions given to them, or because of a misapprehension of the truth. Many anxious sinners despair because they get a false impression that they have sinned away their day of grace, or that they have committed the unpardonable sin, or that their sins are peculiarly aggravated so the gospel provision does not reach them.

Sometimes they despair for this reason: they know that there is mercy provided, and ready to be bestowed as soon as they will comply with the terms, but they find all their efforts at true submission vain. They find they are so proud and obstinate that they cannot get their own consent to the terms of salvation.

Perhaps most individuals who submit, do in fact come to a point where they give up all as lost. But is that necessary? That is the question. Now, you see, it is nothing but their own wickedness that drives them to despair. They are unwilling to take hold of the mercy that is offered. Their despair, then, instead of being essential to true submission under the gospel, is inconsistent with it, and no man ever embraced the gospel while in that state. It is sin to despair; it is horrid unbelief. To say it is essential to true submission is saying that sin is essential to true submission.

True submission is acquiescing in the whole government of God. It is acquiescing in His providential government, in His moral government, and in the penalty of His law. By submitting himself to this, a man acknowledges that he is himself deserving of an exceeding great and eternal weight of damnation, and of the necessity of the terms of salvation in the gospel. Under the gospel, it is no one's duty to be willing to be damned. The man who submits to the revealed law, and consents to be damned, is as much in rebellion as ever; for it is one of God's express requirements that he should obey the gospel.

To call on a sinner to be willing to be punished is a grand mistake for several reasons. It is to set aside the gospel, and place him under another government than that which exists. It sets before him a partial view of the character of God, to which he is required to submit. It keeps back the true motives of submission.

It presents not the real and true God, but a different being. It is practicing a deception on him, by holding out the idea that God desires his damnation, and he must submit to it; for God has taken His solemn oath that He desires not the death of the wicked, but that they turn from their wickedness and live. It is a slander upon God, and charging God with perjury. Every man under the gospel knows that God desires sinners to be saved, and it is impossible to hide the fact. The true ground on which salvation should be placed is that he is not to seek his own salvation, but to seek the glory of God—not to hold out the idea that God desires that he should go to hell.

What did the apostles tell sinners when they inquired what they must do to be saved? What did Peter tell them at Pentecost? What did Paul tell the jailer? To repent, forsake their selfishness, and believe the gospel. This is what men must do to be saved.

There is another difficulty in attempting to convert men in this way. It is attempting to convert them by the law, and setting aside the gospel. It is attempting to make them holy, without the appropriate influences to make them holy.

Prior to his conversion, Paul tried this way and found it never would answer. In the seventh chapter of Romans, he gives us the result in his own case. It drove him to confess that the law was holy and good, and he ought to obey it; and there it left him in distress, crying, "The good that I would I do not: but the evil which I would not, that I do" (v. 19). The law was not able to convert him, and he cried out, "O wretched man that I am! who shall deliver me from the body of this death?" (v. 24).

In response, the love of God in sending His Son Jesus Christ is presented to his mind, and that delivered him. In the next chapter he explained it: "What the law could not do, in that it was weak through the flesh, God sending His own Son in the likeness of sinful flesh, and for sin, condemned sin in the flesh: that the righteousness of the law might be fulfilled in us, who walk not after the flesh, but after the Spirit" (Rom. 8:3–4).

The whole Bible testifies that it is only the influence of the gospel that can bring sinners to obey the law. The law in itself will never do it. Shutting out the soul from the motives induced through the influence of the gospel, and compelling him to rely on the law alone will never convert a sinner.

I know there may be some who suppose they were converted in this way, and that they have submitted to the law absolutely, and without any influence from the gospel. But was it ever concealed from them for a moment that Christ had died for sinners, and that if they should repent and believe, they should be saved? These motives must have had their influence, for all the time that they think they were looking at the naked law, they expected that if they believed they should be saved.

I suppose the error of attempting to convert people by the law without the gospel lies in the old Hopkinsian notion that men, in order to be saved, must be willing to be damned.* It sets aside the fact that this world is, and always has been since the fall, under a dispensation of mercy. If we were under a government of mere law, true submission to God would require this. But we are not, in this sense, under the law, and never have been; immediately after the fall, God revealed to Adam the intimations of mercy.

An objection arises here in the mind of some, which I will remove. "Is not the offer of mercy, in the gospel, calculated to produce a selfish religion?" The offer of mercy may be accepted, and then perverted—as every other good thing may be—giving rise to a selfish religion. And God knew it would be so when He revealed the gospel. But observe: nothing is calculated to subdue the rebellious heart of man but this very exhibition of the benevolence of God revealed in the offer of mercy.

There was a father who had a stubborn and rebellious son, and he tried long to subdue him by chastisement. He loved his son, and longed to have him virtuous and obedient. But the child seemed to harden his heart against his repeated efforts. At length the poor father was quite discouraged, and burst out into a flood of convulsive weeping. "My son! My son! What shall I do? Can I save you? I have done all that I could to save you; O what more can I do?"

The son had looked at the rod with a brow of brass, but when he saw the tears rolling down his father's furrowed cheeks, and heard the convulsive sobs of anguish from his aged bosom, he too burst into tears, and cried out, "Whip me father! Do whip me, as much as you please, but don't cry!" Now the father had found the way to subdue that stubborn heart. Instead of holding over him nothing but the iron hand of law, he let out his soul before his son; and what was the effect? To crush him into hypocritical submission? No, the rod did that. The gushing tears of his father's love broke him down at once to true submission to his father's will.

So it is with sinners. The sinner braves the wrath of Almighty God, and hardens himself to receive the heaviest bolt of Jehovah's thunder; but when he sees the *love* of his Heavenly Father's heart, if there is anything that will make him abhor and curse himself, that will do it; when he sees God manifested in the flesh, stooping to take on human nature, hanging on the cross, and pouring out His soul in tears, and

---

*Samuel Hopkins (1721–1803) began writing in 1759, and published his *System of Doctrines* in 1793.

bloody sweat, and death. Is this calculated to make hypocrites? No, the sinner's heart melts, and he cries out, "O, do anything else, and I can bear it; but the love of the blessed Jesus overwhelms me."

This is the very nature of the mind, to be thus influenced. Therefore, exhibiting the love of God to sinners is the only way to make them truly submissive and truly benevolent. The law may make hypocrites; but nothing but the gospel can draw out the soul in true love to God.

7

SELFISHNESS IS NOT TRUE RELIGION*

"Seeketh not her own" (1 Corinthians 13:5).

In his letter to the Corinthians, Paul taught that charity, or Christian love, does not seek her own. A supreme regard for our own happiness is inconsistent with true Christianity. Unfortunately, a considerable number of people who profess to be Christians do not agree with this. Regardless, selfishness is not true Christianity; however since some maintain otherwise, it is necessary to examine the subject more carefully and give some arguments for what I regard to be the truth.

Loving Yourself—As Well As Your Neighbor

I am not disputing whether it is lawful to have any regard to our own happiness. On the contrary, I admit and maintain that regard for our own happiness, according to its value in the scale of other interests, is a part of our duty. God has commanded us to love our neighbors as ourselves. This plainly makes it a duty to love ourselves or regard our own happiness by the same rule that we regard that of others.

Plainly, it is right to regard the promises of God and threats of evil as they affect us according to the relative value of our own interests. But a threat against us individually is not as important as that which threatens a large number of people. A threat of evil against yourself is not as important as a threat against your family. Then suppose evil threatened a whole congregation, state, nation, or world. Although the happiness of one person is great, it is not to be regarded as supreme.

I am a minister. Suppose God were to say to me, "If you do not do your duty, then you shall be sent to hell." This is a great evil, and I

Lectures to Professing Christians, 251–269. See also the note at the end of this sermon.

ought to avoid it. But suppose He were to say, "If your congregation does not do her duty, they will all be sent to hell. But if you do your duty faithfully, then you will probably save the whole congregation." Is it right for me to be as much influenced by the fear of evil to myself as by the fear of having a whole congregation sent to hell? Plainly not.

The question is not whether our own eternal interests ought to be pursued in preference to our temporal interests. I expressly maintain—and so does the Bible—that we are bound to regard our eternal interests as altogether of more consequence than our temporal interests. Thus, the Bible says, "Labor not for the meat which perisheth, but for that meat which endureth unto everlasting life" (John 6:27).

In comparison with eternal life, we are not to regard or value our temporal interests at all. The same duty of preferring eternal to temporal interests is enjoined by our Savior when He said, "Lay not up for yourselves treasures upon earth, where moth and rust doth corrupt, and where thieves break through and steal; but lay up for yourselves treasures in heaven, where neither moth nor rust doth corrupt, and where thieves do not break through nor steal" (Matt. 6:19–20).

When Christ sent out His disciples two by two to preach and to work miracles, they came back full of joy and exultation because they found even the devils yielding to their power: "Lord, even the devils are subject unto us." Jesus said, "In this rejoice not, that the spirits are subject unto you; but rather rejoice, because your names are written in heaven" (Luke 10:20). The Bible teaches that eternal good is to be preferred in all our conduct to temporal good. But this is very different from maintaining that our own personal eternal interest is to be aimed at as the supreme object of regard.

When we are influenced by hope and fear, the things that are hoped or feared should be put into the scale according to their real value in comparison with other interests. More particularly, the eternal interests of others.

This can be clearly seen in the Bible, where there are many who were influenced at least to some degree by hope and fear, or by the prospect of reward, or by the joy that was set before them. Noah was moved with fear and built the ark. But, did fear for his personal safety motivate him? The Bible does not say this. He feared for the safety of his family. Moreover, he dreaded the destruction of the whole human race.

Hope or fear respecting their own personal interest was not the controlling motive for any good people mentioned in the Bible. It was right for them to be influenced by promises and threats; otherwise, they could not have loved their neighbors as themselves.

Our Own Happiness

Supreme regard for our own happiness cannot be true Christianity. You dishonor God if you fear your own damnation more than the damnation of all other people. Will a true Christian aim at securing his own happiness more than securing the happiness of all other people and the glory of God? If we consider our own interests supremely, are we acting consistently to the requirements of true Christianity or not? This is the proper point of inquiry, and you must bear this constantly in mind.

True Christianity is being like God. By this I mean that true Christians act on the same principles and grounds, and have the same feelings toward different objects as God does.

A supreme regard for your own happiness is not seen in God's example; it is totally unlike Him. The Bible says, "God is love" (1 John 4:8). Benevolence is the sum total of His character. All His other moral attributes, such as justice and mercy, are only facets of His benevolence.

His love is manifested in two forms: One is that of benevolence, goodwill, or desiring the happiness of others. The other is complacency, or approving the character of others who are holy. God's benevolence regards all beings who are capable of happiness. This is universal. Toward all holy beings, He exercises the love of complacency. In other words, God loves His neighbor as himself. He regards the interests of all beings according to their relative value, as much as His own.

He seeks His own happiness or glory as the supreme good, not because it His own, but because it truly is the supreme good. The sum total of His happiness as an infinite being is infinitely greater than the sum total of the happiness of all other beings, or of any possible number of finite creatures.

Take a very familiar illustration. Suppose a person who is kind to animals journeys on horseback, and along the way he and his horse fall into a river. Does benevolence require him to drown himself in order to save his horse? No. True benevolence would motivate him to save himself—and, if need be, allow his horse to perish. His happiness is of greater value than that of his horse, because a man is created in the image of God. But the difference between God and all created beings is infinitely greater than that between a man and his horse, or between the highest angel and the lowest insect.

Therefore, God regards the happiness of all beings according to their real value. Unless we do the same, we are unlike God. If we are like God, as His children should be like their Father, we must regard God's happiness and glory in the same light that He does. That is, His happiness must be regarded as the supreme good beyond everything else in the universe. If we desire our own happiness more than God's happiness, then we are infinitely unlike God.

To aim at our own happiness supremely is inconsistent with Christianity, because it is contrary to the spirit of Christ. Scripture says, "If any man have not the Spirit of Christ, he is none of His" (Rom. 8:9). The Bible repeatedly says that Christ did not seek His own way nor His own glory.

What did He seek? Was it His own personal salvation? No. Was it His own personal happiness? No. He sought the glory of His Father and the good of the universe through the salvation of people. He came on an errand of pure benevolence to benefit the kingdom of God, not to benefit himself. This was "the joy that was set before him" for which "He endured the cross, despising the shame" (Heb. 12:2). He came to do a great good by throwing himself out to labor and suffer for the salvation of people.

To regard our own happiness as the supreme object of pursuit is contrary to the law of God. The sum of God's law is this: "Thou shalt love the Lord thy God, with all thy heart, and with all thy soul, and with all thy strength, and with all thy mind; and thy neighbor as thyself" (Luke 10:27). This is the great thing required: benevolence toward God and man. The first thing is really to love the happiness and glory of God above all other things, because this is so infinitely lovely, desirable and properly the supreme good.

Some have objected that it is not our duty to seek the happiness of God, because His happiness is already secured. Suppose that the king of England is perfectly independent of me, and has his happiness secured without me. Does that make it any less my duty to wish him well, to desire his happiness and to rejoice in it? Because God is happy, in himself, independent of His creation, is that a reason why we should not love His happiness and rejoice in it?

We are bound by the terms of God's law to delight in God, because He is holy, infinitely holy. The law also binds us to exercise the same goodwill toward others that we do to ourselves; that is, to seek both their interests and our own according to their relative value. Are you doing this? We are bound to love and rejoice in the character of those who are good and holy.

Thus we see that the sum of the law of God is to exercise benevolence toward God and all beings according to their relative value, and rejoicing in everything good and holy. To regard our own happiness supremely, or to seek it as our supreme end, is contrary to the law of God, to both its letter and its spirit.

To seek your own happiness supremely is as contrary to the gospel of Jesus Christ as it is to the law of God. The Apostle Paul begins 1 Cor. 13 by writing, "Though I speak with the tongues of men and of angels, and have not charity, I am become as sounding brass, or a tinkling cymbal. And though I have the gift of prophecy, and understand all mysteries, and all knowledge; and though I have all faith, so that I could remove mountains, and have not charity, I am nothing" (vv. 1–2).

Charity means love. In the original it is the same word that is rendered love. "And though I bestow all my goods to feed the poor, and though I give my body to be burned, and have not charity, it profiteth me nothing" (v. 3).

Now mark! In no stronger language could he have expressed the idea that charity, or benevolence, is essential to true Christianity. See how he throws out his guards on every side so that it is impossible to mistake him. If a person has not true charity, he is nothing. He then proceeds to show the characteristics of this true charity: "Charity suffereth long, and is kind; charity envieth not; charity vaunteth not itself, is not puffed up, doth not behave itself unseemly, seeketh not her own, is not easily provoked, thinketh no evil; rejoiceth not in iniquity, but rejoiceth in the truth; beareth all things, believeth all things, hopeth all things, endureth all things" (vv. 4–7).

Here you see that one leading peculiarity of this love is that charity "seeketh not her own." Notice that. If charity is the mark of true Christianity—the only Christianity—then it "seeketh not her own." An established principle of God's government is that if a person aims supremely at his own interest he will lose his own interest.

The same is taught in the tenth chapter of this epistle, verse 24: "Let no man seek his own, but every man another's wealth." If you look at the passage, you will see that word "wealth" is in italic letters, meaning the word was added by the translators, and did not appear in the original Greek. They might just as well have used the word happiness, or welfare, as wealth. So in verse 33: "Even as I please all men in all things, *not seeking mine own profit*, but the profit of many, that they may be saved." Therefore I say, to make our own interest the supreme object of pursuit is as contrary to the gospel as it is to the law.

The Problem With Selfishness

Selfishness is contrary to conscience. The universal conscience of mankind has decided that a supreme regard to our own happiness is not virtue. People have always known that to serve God and benefit mankind is right, and that to seek supremely their own personal interest is not right. They have always regarded it mean and contemptible for individuals to seek their own happiness as the supreme object; consequently, we see the extent that people will go to in order to conceal their selfishness and to appear benevolent. It is impossible for anyone, unless his conscience is strangely blunted by sin, or perverted by false instruction, not to see that it is sinful to regard his own happiness above other and more important interests.

Selfishness is contrary to right reason. Right reason teaches us to regard all things according to their real value. God does this, and we should do the same. God has given us reason for this very purpose, that we should weigh and compare the relative value of things. People mock reason when they deny that it teaches us to regard things according to their real value. And so, it is contrary to reason to aim at and prefer our own interest as the supreme end.

Selfishness is contrary to common sense. What has the common sense of mankind decided on this point? Look at the common sense of mankind in regard to what is called patriotism. No man, in fighting for his country, was ever regarded a true patriot if his object was to achieve his own interest. Suppose it should appear that his object in fighting was to get himself crowned king; would anybody give him credit for patriotism? No. All men agree that it is patriotism when a man is disinterested—like Washington—and fights for his country, for his country's sake. The common sense of mankind has censured the spirit that seeks its own things, preferring its own interest to the greater interests of others. Evidently, all people so regard it. Otherwise, why is everyone so anxious to appear disinterested?

Selfishness is contrary to the constitution of the mind. I do not mean by this that it is impossible, by our very constitution, for us to seek our own happiness as the supreme object. But we are so constituted that if we do this, we never can attain it. Happiness is the gratification of desire. We must desire something, and gain the object we desire.

When a man desires his own happiness, the object of his desire will always keep just so far before him, like his shadow, so that the faster he pursues it, the faster it flies. Happiness is inseparably attached to the attainment of the object desired. Suppose I desire a thousand dollars. That is the thing on which my desire fastens, and when I get it that desire is gratified, and I am happy, so far as gratifying this desire goes to make me happy.

But if I desire the thousand dollars for the purpose of getting such things as a watch, or a dress, the desire is not gratified till I get those things; the money itself will not satisfy. But now suppose the thing I desired was my own happiness. Getting the thousand dollars then does not make me happy, because that is not the thing my desire was fixed on. And so getting the watch, or the dress, does not make me happy, for they do not gratify my desire.

God has so ordered things, and given such laws to the mind, that people can never gain happiness by pursuing it. This very fact plainly indicates the duty of disinterested benevolence. Indeed, God has made it impossible for people to be happy, except in proportion as they are disinterested.

Imagine two men walking along the street together. They come across a man that has just been run over by a cart, and lies injured in the street. They take him up, and carry him to the surgeon, and relieve him. Now it is plain that their gratification is in proportion to the intensity of their desire for his relief. If one of them felt but little and cared but little about the sufferings of the poor man, he will be but little gratified. But if his desire to have the man relieved amounted to agony, his gratification would be accordingly sweet.

Now suppose there were a third individual who had no desire to relieve the distressed man; certainly relieving him could be no gratification to that person. He could pass right by him, and see him die. When the man's sufferings are alleviated, the third man is not gratified at all. Therefore you see, happiness is attained to the same degree that one's desires are gratified.

In order to make the happiness of gratified desire complete, the desire itself must be virtuous. Otherwise, if the desire is selfish, the gratification will be mingled with pain from the conflict of the mind.

That all this is true is a matter of consciousness, and is proved to us by the very highest kind of testimony we can have. And for anyone to deny it is to charge God foolishly, as if He had given us a constitution that would not allow us to be happy in obeying Him.

Following from this is the fact that selfishness, to make our own interest the supreme object, is also inconsistent with our own happiness. People may enjoy a certain kind of pleasure, but not true happiness. The pleasure which does not spring from the gratification of virtuous desire is a deceptive delusion. The reason all people do not find happiness, when they are all so anxious for it, is that they are seeking *it*. If they would seek the glory of God, and the good of the universe as their supreme end, *it* would pursue them.

Selfishness is inconsistent with the public happiness. If each person aimed at his own happiness as his chief end, these interests would unavoidably clash and come into collision, and universal war and confusion would follow in the train of universal selfishness.

To maintain that a supreme regard to our own interest is true Christianity is to contradict the experience of all real saints. I believe every real saint knows that his supreme happiness consists in going out of himself, and regarding the glory of God and the good of others. If he does not know this he is no saint.

Selfishness is also inconsistent with the experience of all those who *have had* a selfish religion, and have found out their mistake and have gotten true religion. This is a common occurrence. I suppose I have known hundreds of cases. Some members in our church have recently discovered for themselves, through experience, that benevolence is true Christianity.

Selfishness is contrary to the experience of all the impenitent. Every impenitent sinner knows that he is aiming supremely at the promotion of his own interest, and knows that he has not true religion. The very thing that his conscience condemns him for is that he is regarding his own interest instead of the glory of God.

If Selfishness Were True Christianity

Now just turn the leaf over for a moment, and suppose that supreme regard for our own happiness were true Christianity; and then see what would follow.

Then it would follow that God is not holy. That is, if a supreme regard to our own interest, because it is our own, is true Christianity, then it would follow that God is not holy, for He does not follow this Christianity. God regards His own happiness, but it is because it is the greatest good, not because it is His own. But He is love, or benevolence; and if benevolence is not true Christianity, God's nature must be changed.

It would follow that the law of God must be altered. If a supreme regard to our own happiness is Christian, then the law should read, "Thou shalt love thyself with all thy heart and with all thy soul, and with all thy mind, and with all thy strength, and God and thy neighbor infinitely less than thyself."

It would follow that the gospel must be reversed. Instead of saying, "Whether therefore ye eat, or drink, or whatsoever ye do, do all to the glory of God," it should read, "Do all for your own happiness." Instead of, "He that will save his life shall lose it," we should find it saying, "He that is supremely anxious to save his own life shall save it; but he that is benevolent, and willing to lose his life for the good of others, shall lose it."

It would follow that the people's consciences should be changed so as to testify in favor of selfishness, and condemn and reprobate everything like disinterested benevolence.

It would follow that it is only right that things be weighed *not* according to their relative value, but to our own set of values. By such reasoning, our own little interest is of more value than the greatest interests of God and the universe.

It would be common sense, then, that true patriotism would consist in everyone seeking his own interest instead of the public good, and each one seeking to build himself up as high as he can.

It would follow that the human constitution must be reversed. If supreme selfishness is virtue, the human constitution was made wrong. It is so made that people can be happy only by being benevolent. And if this doctrine is true, that Christianity consists in seeking our own happiness as a supreme good, then the more Christianity a man has the more miserable he is.

It would follow that the whole framework of society would have to be changed. As it is now, the good of the community depends on the extent to which everyone regards the public interest. And if selfishness is the supreme value, then the community good must be redefined so that it would be best promoted when everyone is scrambling for his own interest, regardless of the interests of others.

It would follow that the experience of the saints would have to be reversed. Instead of finding, as they now do, that the more benevolence they have the more happiness they enjoy; they should testify that the more they aim at their own good, the more they enjoy of Christianity and the favor of God.

It would follow that the impenitent sinner should be found to testify that he is supremely happy in supreme selfishness, and finds true happiness in it.

The fact is plain. Most people do not know what true happiness *is*, and they are seeking it in that which can never produce it. They do not find it because they are pursuing it. If they would turn around and pursue holiness, happiness would pursue them. If they would become disinterested, and lay themselves out to do good, they could not help but be happy. If they choose happiness as an end, it flies before them. True happiness consists in the gratification of virtuous desires; if they would set themselves to glorify God, and do good, they would find happiness. The only class of people who never do find it, in this world, or the world to come, are those who seek it as an end.

The constitution of the human mind and of the universe affords a beautiful illustration of the economy of God. Suppose man could find happiness only by pursuing his own happiness. Then each individual would have only the happiness that he himself had gained, and all the happiness in the universe would be only the sum total of what individuals had gained, with the offset of all the pain and misery produced by conflicting interests.

Now notice! God has so constituted things that while each lays himself out to promote the happiness of others, his own happiness is secured and made complete. How vastly greater, then, is the amount of happiness in the universe, than it would have been, had selfishness been the law of God's kingdom. Each one who obeys the law of God fully secures his own happiness by his benevolence, and the happiness of the whole is increased by how much each receives from all others.

Many say, "Who will take care of my happiness if I do not? If I am to care only for my neighbor's interest, and neglect my own, none of us will be happy." That would be true, if your care for your neighbor's happiness were a detraction from your own. But if your happiness consists in doing good and promoting the happiness of others, the more you do for others, the more you promote your own happiness.

Supreme regard to our own interest is selfishness, and nothing else. It would be selfishness in God, if He regarded His own interest supremely because it is His own. And it is selfishness in people. Whoever maintains that a supreme regard to our own interest is true Christianity maintains that selfishness is true Christianity.

If selfishness is virtue, then benevolence is sin. They are direct opposites and cannot both be virtue. Only a selfish man sets up his own interest over God's, giving it a preference, and placing it in opposition to God's interest. And if this is virtue, then Jesus Christ departed from the principles of virtue by seeking the good of mankind as He did. But who will pretend this?

Those who regard their own interest as supreme, and yet think they have true Christianity, are deceived. I say it solemnly, without reservation, because I believe it is true, and I would say it if it was the last thing I was to say before going to the judgment. Dear reader, whoever you are, if you are doing this, you are not a Christian. Don't call this being narrow-minded. I am not narrow-minded. I would not denounce anyone. But as God is true, and your soul is going to the judgment, you have not the Christianity of the Bible.

Some will ask here, "What! are we to have no regard to our happiness, and if so, how are we to decide whether it is supreme of not?" I do not say that you are to have *no* regard for it. I say, you may regard it according to its relative value.

Is there any real practical difficulty here? I appeal to your conscience. You know, if you are honest, what it is that you regard supremely. Are these interests, your own interests on one side, and God's glory and the good of the universe on the other, so nearly balanced in your mind that you cannot tell which you prefer? It is impossible! If you are not as sure that you prefer the glory of God to your own interest, as you are sure that you exist, you may take it for granted that you are all wrong.

You see why the enjoyment of so many professors of religion depends on their evidences. These persons are all the time hunting after evidence; and just in proportion as that varies, their enjoyments wax and wane. If they really regarded the glory of God and the good of mankind, their enjoyment would not depend on their evidences. Those who are purely selfish may enjoy much in religion, but it is by anticipation. The idea of going to heaven is pleasing to them. But those who go out of themselves, and are purely benevolent, have a present heaven in their breasts.

You see that all of you who had no peace and joy in religion before you had a hope are deceived. Perhaps I can give an outline of your experience. You were awakened and were distressed—you had reason to be, by the fear of going to hell. By and by, perhaps while you were engaged in prayer, or while some person was conversing with you, your distress left you. You thought your sins were pardoned. A gleam of joy shot through your mind, and warmed up your heart into a glow that you took for an assurance of salvation, and this again increased your joy.

How very different is the experience of a true Christian! His peace does not depend on his hope; but true submission and benevolence produce peace and joy, independent of his hope.

Suppose the case of a man in prison, condemned to be hanged the next day. He is in great distress, pacing his cell, and waiting for the day. Not long after, a messenger comes with a pardon. He seizes the paper, turns it up to the dim light that comes through his grate, reads the word *pardon*, and almost faints with emotion, and leaps for joy. He supposes the paper to be genuine.

Now suppose it turns out that the paper is counterfeit. Suddenly his joy is all gone. So in the case of a deceived person. He was afraid of going to hell, and of course he rejoices if he believes he is pardoned. If the devil should tell him so, and he believed it, his joy would be just as great while the belief lasts, as if it were a reality.

True Christian joy does not depend on evidence. He submits himself into the hands of God with such confidence, and that very act gives him peace. He had a terrible conflict with God, but all at once he yields the controversy, and says, "God will do right, let God's will be done." Then he begins to pray, he is subdued, he melts down before God, and that very act affords sweet, calm, and heavenly joy.

Perhaps he may go for hours, or even for a day or two, full of joy in God, without thinking of his own salvation. You ask him if he has a hope, and he replies that he never thought of it. His joy does not depend on the belief that he is pardoned, but consists in a state of mind acquiescing to the government of God. In such a state of mind, he could not but be happy.

Now let me ask which religion have you? If you exercise true Christianity, even if God should put you into hell, and there let you exercise supreme love to Him, and the same love to your neighbor as to yourself; that itself is a state of mind inconsistent with being miserable.

I wish this to be fully understood. These hope-seekers will be always disappointed. If you run after hope, you will never have a hope good for anything. But if you pursue holiness, then hope, peace and joy will come. Is our religion the love of holiness, the love of God and of souls? Or is it only a hope?

Do you see why anxious sinners do not find peace? They are looking at their own guilt and danger. They regard God as an avenger, shrinking from His terrors; they will make it impossible for themselves to ever come at peace. While looking at the wrath of God, making them wither and tremble, they cannot love Him. They hide from Him.

Anxious sinners, let me tell you a secret. If you keep looking at that feature of God's character, it will drive you to despair, which is inconsistent with true submission. You should look at His whole character, and see the reasons why you should love Him, and throw yourself upon Him without reserve, and without distrust. Instead of shrinking from Him, come right to Him, and say, "O, Father in heaven, Thou art not inexorable, and Thou art sovereign, but Thou art good. I submit to Thy government, and give myself to Thee, with all I have and all I am, body and soul, for time and for eternity."*

---

*Finney appended the following note to the above sermon concerning his sermon "Religion of the Law and the Gospel." Since this sermon is based upon Romans 9:30–33, it can be found in *Principles of Victory*, pages 137–145. *Principles of Victory* and *Principles of Liberty* contain Finney's sermons on Romans.

Finney's own note follows: "The subject for the next lecture, *Religion of the Law and the Gospel*, will be the distinction between legal submission and gospel submission, or between the religion of the law and the religion of faith.

Let me observe that when I began to preach on the subject of selfishness in Christianity, I did not dream that it would be regarded by anyone as a controversial subject. I have no fondness for controversy, and I should as soon think of calling the doctrine of the existence of God a controversial subject, as this. The question is one of greatest importance, and we ought to weigh the arguments, and decide according to the Word of God. Soon we shall go together to the bar of God, and you must determine whether you will go there with selfishness in your hearts, or with that disinterested benevolence that seeks not her own. Will you be now honest? For as God is true, if you are seeking your own, you will soon be in hell, unless you repent. Oh, be honest! Lay aside prejudice and act for eternity.

8

LOVE OF THE WORLD*

"Love not the world, neither the things that are in the world. If any man love the world, the love of the Father is not in him" (John 2:15).

The text above gives a clear directive regarding how Christians are to view the world. It remains for us to understand three things: what "love of the world" means, who loves the world in this sense, and the fact that those who love the world do not love God.

Love of the World

The love of the world John speaks of in the text above does not refer to every desire for worldly objects. God has made us so that a certain amount and certain kinds of worldly objects are indispensable to our existence. We need food and clothing, implements for farming and trade, and various worldly things. The proper desire for these things is not sinful nor inconsistent with the love of God.

Love of the world is to make worldly things the principal objects of desire and pursuit. To love *them* and desire *them* more than to love God and others, to be more anxious to obtain *them* and spend more time in their acquisition than in efforts to glorify God and save souls is to love the world in the sense of the text. Where the love of God and others is supreme in the heart, there may be a suitable desire for worldly objects. But where a person manifests a disposition to prefer the acquisition of wealth or of worldly objects, and aims rather at obtaining worldly things than at glorifying God and doing good to others, certainly love of the world is supreme in his heart.

Sermons on Important Subjects, 257–277.

The Love of the World in Practice

All who cheat and defraud to obtain the things of the world love the world supremely. A person who will cheat and defraud his neighbor obviously does not love him as he does himself. A person who disobeys God in order to obtain worldly goods does not love God supremely: this is self-evident. It is a simple matter of fact that he loves the things of the world supremely.

Those who have anxieties and care mostly about worldly things love the world. If they are more anxious for these things, and pursue them more earnestly than they pursue God's glory and the good of others, then they love the world supremely.

Now some may ask, "If a person's purpose for obtaining money is to do good with the money, can he not be anxious to obtain worldly things?" I answer that a person may desire to obtain money for the purpose of glorifying God with it, but in that case the *principal* anxiety, care and desire would not *terminate* upon the acquisition of the money, but upon what he hopes to accomplish through the money.

To suppose that a person whose supreme object is to glorify God and do good to others should concern himself *principally* about worldly things is the same absurdity as to suppose that he was more anxious about the means than about the end which he hoped to accomplish by those means. The end gives value to the means. The end is the main object of thought and desire. To suppose that a person's anxieties and cares would cluster about the means of effecting the end rather than about the end itself is plainly absurd and impossible.

Suppose a gentleman is engaged to be married and has commenced a journey for that purpose. His heart is greatly set upon the end he has in view. Do you think that either the delights or cares of his journey will occupy more of his thoughts and absorb more of his affections than the purpose for which he has undertaken the journey? Who does not know that in such a case, if his heart were greatly set upon obtaining his bride, he would pass from place to place, hardly conscious of the incidents along the way? His bride and his marriage would fill up his thoughts by day and be the subject of his dreams by night. All his cares and desires regarding the speed of his transportation would be for the more speedy accomplishment of his heart's desire.

Now, suppose a person loves God supremely and desires money and worldly goods only so that he may glorify God and benefit society thereby. Can such a person be so anxious and so busy about the means as to lose sight of the end? Can his purpose be swallowed up in his efforts to obtain the means to accomplish it? This cannot be. And now I appeal to the two classes of people already mentioned: you who practice fraud and take advantage of the ignorance of others, overreaching and cheating them in little or great things—do you pretend to love God? If so, you are a hypocrite.

You who are filled with worries and concerns about worldly things—whose time, thoughts and affections are swallowed up in efforts to obtain them—know assuredly that you love the world, and the love of God is not in you.

Everyone who consults only his own interest and advantage in the transaction of his business loves the world. God requires you to love your neighbor as yourself. He says, "Look not every man on his own things, but every man also on the things of others" (Phil. 2:4). And, "Let no man seek his own, but every man another's wealth" (1 Cor. 10:24). These are express commandments from God. They are the very spirit and substance of the gospel.

Benevolence is a desire to do good to others. A willingness to deny yourself for the purpose of promoting the interest of your neighbor is the very spirit of Christ: the heart and soul of His gospel.

Now, suppose a person in his bargains with others aimed only at promoting his *own* interest, seeking his own wealth before another's. Suppose he did not look to the welfare of others, but his eye and heart were fixed upon his own side of the bargain. Suppose he did not aim at benefitting the person with whom he transacted business, but concerned himself primarily with taking care of himself. This would be the very opposite of the spirit of the gospel. Could this man love his neighbor as himself? Could he love God supremely, since God has prohibited all selfishness on pain of eternal death?

No! If he loved God, he would not disobey Him for the sake of making money. If he loved his neighbor as himself, if he felt that it was more blessed to give than to receive, if he had the Spirit of Christ, he would naturally feel and manifest as great a desire for the interests of those with whom he dealt as for his own interest. He would be more anxious to give a good bargain than to get it. Self-denial, to promote the happiness and the interest of others, would be his joy, would constitute his happiness, would be that to which he would be most inclined.

Now, let me ask you, *Can you deny this principle?* What is your spiritual state? Have you the love of God in you? How do you transact business? Do you consult the interests of those with whom you deal as much as you do your own? Or, in all your bargains, do you aim simply at securing a profit for yourself? If you do, the love of God is not in you. You have not the beginning of piety in your heart.

Anyone who feels chagrined and grieved, upon discovering that the person with whom he has dealt has the best of the bargain, and has made a greater profit than himself, does not have the mind of Christ. If he did, he would rejoice in his neighbor's good fortune, and he would aim to benefit the person with whom he deals as much as possible. And if afterward he learned that his neighbor had made a good bargain, and had been greatly benefitted by it, it would gratify him all the more.

Now, how is it with you? Do you find yourself gratified and delighted when you find that you have greatly contributed to the interests of those with whom you deal, in having given them the best side of the bargain? Be honest, try yourself by this rule. See whether you love your neighbor as yourself. See whether you love God supremely. He requires you to seek not your own, but your neighbor's wealth. To look not upon your own interest, but the interest of others. Do you live by the spirit of these principles? Have you the same spirit and temper as God, who lays down the rule of action? If not, you have not the love of God in you.

All those who make bargains only when they can make a profit by it do not love their neighbors as themselves. There are many who will never trade unless they can promote their own interests. How much their bargain might mean to someone else does not matter to them, for the interest of the other person is not taken into account at all. They do not think of making a bargain to benefit others, and will turn away from the proposal instantly, unless they can promote their own selfish ends. They will stand and bow, and be very accommodating, kind and attentive, while there is any prospect of their making a good percentage on their product. But the negotiation is broken off instantly, without courtesy or good manners, whenever it is settled that they can make nothing by the bargain. They do not consult the interests of those with whom they deal, and by this they show that the world is their god.

All those who will take advantage of the ignorance of those with whom they deal, to get a good bargain out of them, love the world supremely. Cases of this kind occur often. A customer comes in, and he is instantly measured from head to foot by every eye. They survey him all around to see whether he understands the value of the articles he wishes to purchase; whether it will be difficult to get a good bargain out of him or not; whether it will do to set the price of goods high, and how high; and whether it is likely that he will buy much or little. And if he wishes to make a heavy bill, some of the first articles he asks for are put low; thus baits are laid to lead him on, from step to step, until he imagines that all the articles are reasonably priced.

Those who sell useless articles to people for the sake of profit do not have the love of God in them. A person who does this cannot be consulting the interest of his neighbor at all. He must be acting on principles of pure selfishness. He takes the money without an equivalent exchange, and consents that they should spend it for that which is not bread, and their labor for that which does not satisfy. This is the direct opposite of the Spirit of Christ.

All those who sell harmful articles for the sake of the profit do not have the love of God in them. The person who sells articles, which he knows to be pernicious, to his fellow men for the sake of gain has the very spirit of hell. Shall a person, who will sell rum or make whiskey—dealing out death and damnation to others, and making them pay for it as well—shall he pretend to love God? For shame! You hypocrite! You wretch! You enemy of God and man! You wolf in sheep's clothing! Take off your mask, and write your name "Satan" on your sign-board.

There are those who will sell articles that are not only useless, but harmful; designed to promote the pride and vanity of people and take their hearts from God, fastening them upon the baubles of this vain world. Some tempt the deceitful hearts of people, and enlist them in the chase of fashion, gaiety and worldliness. Now, instead of being pious, those who do this take the devil's place and tempt mankind to sin.

All those who transact business upon principles of commercial justice rather than on principles of benevolence love the world supremely. Business principles, or the principles of commercial justice, are the principles of supreme selfishness. They have been established by selfish people for selfish purposes, without even the pretense of conformity to the law of love.

Upon these so-called principles, it is neither demanded nor expected that anyone should seek another's wealth, but that everyone should take care of himself, purchase as low and sell as high as he can; take advantage of the state of the market, the scarcity of the articles in which he deals, and in short, to go the whole circle of selfish projects to promote the interest of self.

Can a person love God supremely (and his neighbor as himself), who daily and habitually transacts business upon the principles of commercial justice, founded, as they are, in that which is the direct opposite of the requirement of God? Can a person love God if every day he is engaged in business transactions; the sum, substance, and the detail of which are designed to promote self-interest; that do not even pretend to aim at the promotion of the interest of others, but self is the beginning, the middle, and the end of the whole matter?

All those who engage in business to the neglect of spiritual exercises love the world supremely. Many professing Christians seem as reluctant to do good with their money as unrepentant sinners are to repent. They profess to engage in business for the glory of God, but instead of using their money for this purpose, they enlarge their capital and their business, and transact business upon the principles of worldly people, and practice upon themselves a constant delusion. Instead of using their money as they go along to build up of the kingdom of Jesus Christ, they add their yearly profit to their capital. Soon, their whole time, thoughts, and affections are engrossed with money-making. Now, why do you not see that you who practice this are deceiving yourselves?

The only way in which money can be used for the glory of God and the good of others is to promote their spirituality and holiness. If you pursue business in a manner that is inconsistent with your own spirituality, you might as well talk of getting drunk or swearing for the glory of God, as of making money for His glory.

For you to neglect communion with God, under the pretense of making money for Him, is sheer hypocrisy. If you prefer business to prayer, or busy yourself in your office, shop or business and neglect your prayer closet, the love of God is not in you. To pretend that you love God is just as absurd as to suppose that your eagerness to make money for the glory of God leads you to neglect communion with Him, or that your great zeal to serve Him and great love for Him leads you to neglect communion with Him.

Those who use their business as an excuse to not attend meetings do not have the love of God in them, though they claim to use the profits for the conversion of sinners. Obviously, such people are not transacting business for God. It is true that the only possible use of making money for the glory of God is to use it for the conversion and sanctification of sinners; this is the great end of doing business for God. But to be so busy in making money as to neglect to make a direct and personal effort for the conversion of sinners is absurd. Such behavior demonstrates that the object of making money is not to convert, save and sanctify sinners. Plainly, in such a case the money is sought from the love of it, and not for the purpose of building up the kingdom of Jesus Christ.

All those whose business diverts their thoughts and affections from God love the world. If they were transacting business for God, the more busy and engaged they were in His service, in doing His will, and in making money for Him, the more would He be present to all their thoughts, and the deeper and more mellow would be their piety.

All rich people love the world supremely. Jesus Christ has said that it is easier for a camel to go through the eye of a needle than for a rich man to enter the kingdom of heaven. Yes, you say, that is true, if he sets his heart upon his riches. Now, what I affirm is every rich man *under the gospel* does set his heart upon his riches. If he did not, he would not be rich. If he loved the kingdom of God *supremely*, he would give his riches to promote that kingdom.

We always do that which is most important to us. If you see an article of furniture, or dress, or anything else that you prefer to a greater degree than the money you possess, you are certain to make the exchange, and give your money for the article, if it is in your power. This is certain, for your volition governs your conduct.

Now, if a person loves the Lord Jesus Christ and the souls of others more than he does his money; if, upon the whole, he prefers the glory of God and the salvation of others to his own selfish interests, then it is as certain that he will cease to be rich, and give his money to promote those objects. In the same way, a rich person who hoards his wealth—even after he is faced with the gospel, and is made aware that his money can be used for the glory of God and the conversion of souls—demonstrates beyond the shadow of a doubt that he loves the world supremely. To say that he is rich, but does not set his heart upon riches—that he continues to retain his wealth, and yet does not set his heart upon it—is manifestly absurd and false. For, certainly, nothing but a supreme attachment to his wealth could cause him to hold on to the possession of it, when every wind is loaded down with the cries of those who are ready to perish, beseeching him to send to them the bread of life.

But perhaps someone will argue that much depends upon the instructions that a particular rich person has received from the Lord concerning his riches: he may be fully convinced that he may *lawfully* retain and enjoy his wealth. But this does not change the situation, for the question is not what he may *lawfully* do, but what he *desires* to do with his money.

Suppose a certain woman's husband is in slavery, whom that woman tenderly loves. The price of his ransom is fixed, and she is determined to pay the price by her earnings and savings. How will she behave herself? Of what use is it to tell her that she may *lawfully* purchase articles of dress and convenience, and that it is *lawful* for her to have the comforts of life. Will she so spend her money? No. She will scarcely allow herself a pair of shoes. She will practice the most rigid economy, and take satisfaction in denying herself everything but that which is absolutely essential, until she has set aside the sum demanded for her husband's ransom.

It is of no use to preach to her of the *lawfulness* of appropriating her money to other purposes. She has one all-absorbing object in view. She values money only as it will contribute to the promotion of this object. Neither false instruction nor seemingly prudent instruction with regard to the *lawfulness* of spending her money for other things will induce her to change her practice. Every penny that she can spare is set aside for the promotion of this object of her heart's desire.

So, if a person loves God supremely, and longs for the prosperity of His kingdom more than for anything else, he will not even consider whether he may lawfully enjoy an estate. He prefers to build up the kingdom of Christ with his resources, and accounts his money as of no value, except as it can contribute to this object. Therefore, if a person is rich, and continues to be rich even under the influence of the gospel, there can be no other reason for it than that he prefers wealth to the promotion of the kingdom of Jesus Christ.

Still others find reason to evade the point, observing that Abraham and Job and David and Solomon were all rich men. That is true, and yet the command had never been given in their day to preach the gospel to every creature. There is no reason to think that any of them dreamed that the world would be converted in the way we now know it will—and must—be converted. They could not, therefore, have had the same motives that we have for using their wealth for the conversion of the world. We have no reason to believe that their property could have been used for the conversion of the world, in the sense that we can use ours. Because of this, it was no certain sign, if they kept their wealth, that they preferred it to the kingdom and glory of God.

All of those who lay up their surplus income—that which is not necessary for the support of themselves and their families—do not have the love of God in them. If they lay it up, it must be because they love it. If they preferred the kingdom of God, they would immediately use what they could spare, after providing for the necessities of their families, to the building up of His kingdom.

Suppose a person were on the coast of Africa and earnestly longed to return to his home, but had no means of paying his passage. If someone presented him with a purse of gold, would he save it, or would he immediately spend it, in order to gratify the all-absorbing desire of his heart and pay his passage to his native country? This would be the very reason why he would prize the gift. In his eyes, it would be valuable for the simple reason that he might accomplish the object of his heart's desire with it. Can a person love supremely the kingdom of Christ and yearn for its coming and extension, and yet hoard his money instead of spending it freely for this supremely desirable purpose?

Although a person may give his surplus income, if it requires no self-denial, he gives to God that which costs him nothing, and he gives no substantial evidence that he loves God. If he gratifies all his desires and the desires of his family, if he provides all the comforts and conveniences of life for them, and simply gives whatever remains of his income over and above his expenditures, then he really practices no self-denial. He enjoys all that can be enjoyed of wealth, and is really ridding himself of the trouble of taking care of it by giving the balance of his yearly income to the cause of Christ. This is like a safety-valve to let off the surplus steam that would otherwise burst the boiler.

Should everyone give up *all* of his capital and means in order to promote the cause of Christ? This is neither necessary nor prudent; retaining capital, of itself, is not sinful. Indeed, it is expedient to lay aside a certain amount of it in order to promote the wisest transaction of business, and to care for the needs of one's family. After these expenses are cared for, however, a person's capital is to be used as a tool with which he serves God and his generation.

I cannot see that using one's money in this manner is inconsistent with the love of God. But for a person to live and die rich, to hoard his income, to enjoy his wealth, and leave his substance to his children fits the Psalmist's description of a wicked man who has his portion of this world.

All those who are more interested in secular news that relates to money transactions than in the accounts of revivals of Christianity and in those things that pertain to the kingdom of Christ love the world supremely. Show me a person who looks over the secular news after the price of stocks, and who gets excited about bank questions and speculations, but who does not read or take an interest in reports of revivals and the outward movements of the Church; if he professes to love God, his profession is base hypocrisy.

All those who are more depressed and feel more keenly about commercial embarrassments than they do the low state of Christianity and the state of dying sinners, love the world supremely. This is too plain to need either proof or illustration.

All those who would sooner engage in moneyed speculations than they would in revivals of Christianity love the world supremely. Some who profess to be Christians are easily excited when great speculations are to be made, when stocks are high or real estate is on the rise; but if an effort is to be made to promote a revival of Christianity, they are too much engrossed in their speculations to give their time and hearts to it.

They may pretend that they are making money for God, but their true motives are easily uncovered, for the promotion of revivals of Christianity is the only object of appropriating money to the cause of Christ. If the great object of embarking in these speculations is to promote revival and to build up Christ's kingdom, it is strange that in the course of pursuing the means to do it, they lose their desire to promote directly the end at which they aim. The naked matter of fact is that if they prefer business speculations to revivals, then they love money and the world supremely.

All those who disobey the commandments of God for the purpose of making or saving money love the world supremely. A person who travels on Sunday to secure a debt or to avoid the expense of spending a Sunday in a hotel when on a journey, certainly loves money supremely. If he considered the property in his possession as belonging to God, could he think that God would rather he violate the holy Sabbath than to lose a debt or spend a few dollars by stopping on the Sabbath?

All those who do not feel more gratified with the appropriation of money to the cause of Christ than with any other use of it love the world supremely. Take again the case of the woman who is earning money to relieve her husband from slavery. What other appropriation could she make of money that would so much gratify her heart? It is this object that gives value to money in her estimation.

Should a person give her a purse of gold, would she say, "Now I can buy myself a nice new dress. Now I can furnish my home and live in fashion"? No. Bursting into tears of joy and gratitude, she would exclaim, "Now I can redeem my husband!" In the same way, a person who loves God and longs for the coming of His kingdom will feel most gratified by spending money for the promotion of that precious purpose.

Jesus Christ said that "it is more blessed to give than to receive" (Acts 20:35). The truly benevolent person receives the highest and holiest pleasure in disposing of his possessions in the manner that best promotes the glory of God and the good of his fellow man. Instead of giving to those causes grudgingly and sparingly, he will pour out his treasures with the fullest, readiest heart. For this is what his heart most longs for. His spirit is longing with unutterable desires, which can only be fulfilled in this manner. Therefore, he accounts nothing a privation or a sacrifice which is appropriated to furthering the cause of Christ.

Does the miser account the hoarding of money a privation, a sacrifice, or a grievance? No, he deems hoarding as the best possible use for his money. To every other object he gives sparingly, and takes but little satisfaction in any expenditures that he is obliged to make; his heart is set upon accumulating treasures. Every penny that is saved and put into his iron chest is disposed of according to his heart's desire.

The Christian's heart is just as truly set upon building up the kingdom of Jesus Christ as the miser's heart is upon hoarding his wealth. In other expenditures, therefore, he will naturally be sparing; but in the promotion of the great object of his heart's desire, he will be liberal and bountiful and enjoy most of all the appropriation of money to that object.

All those who prefer financial investments over contributing to the promotion of the interests of Christ's kingdom love the world supremely. If they loved God supremely, they would desire to invest only to the extent that it enables them to make the contribution. If they made a hundred or a thousand dollars, they would say, "O for an opportunity now to use this money in the cause of Christ." But if they love their own gain, and are not ready to contribute joyfully in the work of Christ, then they love the world, and have not the love of God in them.

All those who prefer seeing a customer come in and *spend* money rather than seeing an agent of some benevolent society come in who wants to *receive* money for the promotion of Christ's kingdom love the world supremely. The person who smiles and appears delighted when a customer comes in, but is sour and formal—perhaps even uncivil—when an agent calls to collect funds for the building up of Christ's kingdom, this demonstrates, beyond all doubt, where that business-man's heart is. It shows that he loves his money more than he loves his God.

All those who do not really enjoy giving more than receiving love the world supremely. If they loved God supremely, their supreme object and joy in receiving would be that they might immediately turn around and give to the promotion of His kingdom. But if their incessant cry is "give, give," and they wish always to receive, and do not enjoy the giving of the money as they do the receiving of it, it must be because they love the world.

All those who are more frugal in their expenditures for the kingdom of Christ than in what they spend upon themselves and their families love the world supremely. There are multitudes of professedly pious people who imagine that everything connected with the worship and service of God should be of the cheapest kind, while they practice a very different principle in their own homes and for their families and for themselves.

If a church is to be fixed up, they make sure that everything is done with as little expense as possible. If there are carpets, they must be of the cheapest kind. If there are cushions in the pews, or lights or other conveniences, almost anything will do, provided it is cheap. Things are allowed to be out of order, filth is allowed to accumulate, and the house of God lies in waste, all under the pious pretense of Christian economy.

Many churches have no light, and some have no stoves, and still others have their panes of glass broken out. The doors of others are so dilapidated that they will scarcely shut. Other churches are either unpainted, or so faded that if it were someone's house you would suppose it to be the abode of a drunkard. Most of the churches in the country have no carpets; and carpets are more needed in churches than in any other house—in order to prevent the disturbance that always occurs where people are going out and in upon an uncarpeted floor.

And in the city there are many who are entirely unwilling to bear the expense of fitting up a church as lavishly as they fit up their own dwellings. All such conduct has its foundation in the love of the world, and in supreme selfishness, regardless of the fact that their actions are condoned and excused under the pretense of Christian economy.

People are always most free in giving their money to the promotion of the objects dearest to their hearts. This is simply a matter of fact. If, therefore, the heart is set supremely upon honoring God with our substance, it is certain that we will be bountiful and liberal in our expenditures in order to fit up places for God's worship, investing in all those things that are essential to decency, to comfort, and enjoyment in His service.

You Can't Love God and Mammon

The text is a form of expression that is to be understood as expressing a very strong negative: "If any man love the world, the love of the Father is not in him." That is, the love of God is certainly *not* in him. This is the language and the doctrine of the whole Bible; so that, so far as Scripture testimony goes, the proof is conclusive.

It is impossible for a person to have two supreme objects of affection; if he has any acceptable love to God, it must be supreme. To affirm that a person loves the world in the sense of this text and that he loves God with any acceptable love is a contradiction. It is the same as to say that he loves both God and the world supremely.

A person cannot love supremely two objects that are entirely in opposition to each other. The apostle explains the reason for it in the verses immediately following the text: ". . . for all that is in the world, the lust of the flesh, the lust of the eyes, and the pride of life, is not of the Father, but is of the world" (v. 16). The love of the world and the love of God are directly opposite states of mind; to exercise them both at the same time is impossible.

If a person transacts worldly business upon the principles of the gospel, it is infinitely better for the world in every respect. If everyone sought to promote the happiness and interest of others, the amount of property and of every other good would be greatly increased. Some people behave as though society would cease to exist unless they consulted solely their own interest.

"What!" he says, "You want me to seek not my own interest, but the interest of others? What would become of my own interest?" He doesn't understand that his interest would be secured, if, while being concerned about the benefit of others, others were also being concerned about his.

In this way, the secular interests of people would be at least as highly advanced as they are under the present arrangement of society, if not more so. In addition, the spirit that would be cherished and cultivated by this course of conduct would shed a refreshingly sweet and healing balm of influence over all the discords of selfishness. Peace, love, and heaven would reign in the hearts of people.

But does anyone object and say, "Because worldly people will not practice these principles, Christians should not either lest they intend to give up all the business of the world into worldly hands." This is a radical and ruinous mistake. Suppose it were known that Christians universally discarded all selfishness in their business, and acted entirely upon principles of benevolence; that in all their dealings Christian businessmen sought the interest of those with whom they deal as fervently as they seek their own. No sooner would this fact be known than worldly people would be forced to transact business upon these same principles, or give up all the business of the world into the hands of the Christians.

For who would choose to deal with a person who acted upon selfish principles, when he might just as well transact business with those who would not only treat him justly, but with entire benevolence. It is perfectly within the power of the church to compel worldly people to transact business upon gospel principles or not transact business at all. And woe to the church if she does not reverse and annihilate the whole system of doing business on principles of selfishness.

Perhaps some will say that if these things are true, then who can be saved? Certainly not those who govern their affairs upon principles of commercial justice, which is actually founded on selfishness. Such men are satisfied to be honest in this sense of honesty instead of being governed by the law of love; they mind earthly things, and consider it more blessed to receive than to give, seeking their own wealth, and not that of their neighbors. If there is any truth in the Word of God, all such people are on the way to hell.

Some call this uncharitable; if so, they are hypocrites, for the doctrine is true, whatever the inference may be. I do not pretend to be more charitable than God is, and to hope that those people are pious of whom God has said that His love is not in them. I will not be charitable enough to throw away my Bible, or suppose that the lovers of the world are the friends of God, instead of His enemies. That multitudes of people who profess to be Christians are deceived, and that they love the world supremely is as evident as if they had sworn an oath to do this very thing. But just because the great mass of professing Christians give evidence of this state of mind, is no reason to dispute our Bibles and charitably hope that they may be saved in the end.

This love of the world also accounts for why so few professing Christians have a spirit of prayer. The truth is, the love of God is not in them. Look around any great commercial city. Nearly the whole population is there for the purposes of worldly gain. The principles upon which almost the entire business of the city is transacted is supremely selfish. How then can a spirit of prayer prevail in such a place as this? This same principle prevails almost universally through the country. Without hesitation, farmers, mechanics, merchants, and people of every occupation transact their business upon selfish principles and seek supremely their own and not their neighbor's wealth. It is impossible that the love of God should prevail in the church, or in any heart, while actuated by such principles.

You see from this subject why young converts so uniformly wax cold in Christianity. Let any person pass through one business season, acting upon business principles, and it is impossible that the love of God should be alive in his heart, for he is assiduously cultivating and cherishing a spirit of selfishness. In all of his daily pursuits, he does not intend to seek the good of others, but his own. So, can we be at a loss for the reasons of such universal backsliding?

For these reasons, you may observe that the religion of the great mass of the church is not the religion of love, but of fear. They fear the Lord, but serve their own gods. They are dragged along by their consciences to perform what they suppose to be their duty. They have a dry, legal, earthly spirit, and their pretended service is hypocrisy and utter wickedness.

And that is why lives are so little effected by all the means that are used for the building up of the kingdom of Jesus Christ. People would much rather give their money than to live holy lives and walk with God. An effort seems to be in the making to convert the world with money. Endless investments are entered into by professedly pious people. While their heart and soul and lives are absorbed in the spirit of this world, they try to persuade themselves that their money will be a substitute for a holy life, and compensate for the lack of their own personal effort to save the souls of people. But, rely upon it, God will teach them their mistake.

The spontaneous conduct of the primitive church shows what true piety will do in leading people to renounce the world. While the love of God pervaded the church, people were motivated by very different principles than those of commercial justice. They sought not their own, but the things of Jesus Christ.

Still others, finding safety in numbers, ask, "But how can it be as you say? Are nearly all the church wrong?" They are, upon this subject. In most things the church of the present day is orthodox in theory, but vastly heretical in practice. It is not anything new for the church to be nearly all wrong. More than once or twice nearly the entire body of the church has departed from God, and satisfied itself with the religion of selfishness.

Lastly, I beg of you, if you are convicted of worldliness, do not go away and say that you *hope* that you love God, in spite of some, or nearly all, of these evidences against you. I declare to you before God and the Lord Jesus Christ, if these marks of worldliness are upon you, the love of God is not in you. And "be ye not deceived; God is not mocked: for whatsoever a man soweth, that shall he also reap. For he that soweth to his flesh shall of the flesh reap corruption; but he that soweth to the Spirit, shall of the spirit reap life everlasting" (Gal. 5:6–7).

9

THE WAY OF SALVATION*

"Sirs, what must I do to be saved? And they said, Believe on the Lord Jesus Christ, and thou shalt be saved" (Acts 16:30–31).

" . . . who of God is made unto us wisdom, and righteousness, and sanctification, and redemption" (1 Corinthians 1:30).

Salvation includes several things: sanctification, justification, eternal life, and glory. The primary focus is placed on the areas of sanctification and justification. Sanctification is purifying the mind, making it holy. Justification relates to the manner in which we are accepted and treated by God.

The Way of Salvation

Salvation is accomplished by faith as opposed to works. Let me give a brief view of the gospel plan of salvation, and contrast it to the original plan which was proposed to save mankind.

Soon after their creation, the human race was given the standard of the law of God; people were to be saved on the basis of perfect and eternal obedience to that law. Adam, as the first man, was the natural head of the race.

Some have supposed God made a covenant with Adam such as this: If he continued to obey the law for a limited period, then all his posterity would be confirmed in holiness and happiness forever. I am unable to ascertain the reason for this belief; I am not aware that the doctrine is taught in the Bible. If it were true, the condition of mankind now would not differ materially from what it was at first; in fact, it has declined markedly ever since the time of Adam.

If the salvation of the race originally relied solely on the obedience

---

Lectures to Professing Christians, 383–398.

of one man, I do not see how it could be called a covenant of works as far as the race is concerned. For if their weal or woe were suspended on the conduct of one head, it was a covenant of grace to them in the same manner that the present system is a covenant of grace. For according to that view, all that related to works depended on one man, just as it does under the gospel. According to that view, the rest of the race had no more to do with works than we have now, but all that relates to works was done by the representative.

Now, I believe that even if Adam had continued in obedience forever, securing his own salvation, his posterity would have needed to do the same in order to be saved. Perhaps if he had always obeyed God, the natural influence of his example would have brought about such a state of things that as a matter of fact all his posterity would have continued in holiness. But the salvation of each individual would still have depended on that individual's own works. If the works of the first father were to determine the fate of the race, if on account of his obedience they were to be secured in holiness and happiness forever; then, I do not see how this differs from the covenant of grace, or the gospel.

As a matter of fact, Adam was the natural head of the human race. The consequences of his sin have touched us, *but his sin is not literally counted our sin.* The truth is simply this: Because of his position as our natural head, it follows that Adam's sin has resulted in the sin and ruin of his posterity. I believe that mankind was originally under a covenant of works; although Adam was their head or representative, his obedience or disobedience could not have drawn them irresistibly into sin and condemnation, irrespective of their own acts.

The Bible teaches that "by one man's disobedience many were made sinners" (Rom. 5:29). Once Adam had fallen, there was not the least hope—by the law—of saving any of mankind. Then *the plan* was revealed for saving mankind by a proceeding of mere grace, a provision that had been formed in the counsels of eternity, on foresight of this event. Salvation was now placed on an entirely new foundation: by a covenant of redemption. You will find this covenant in Psalm 89, and other places in the Old Testament. This is a covenant between the Father and the Son regarding the salvation of mankind. It is the foundation of another covenant, the covenant of grace.

In the covenant of redemption, man is merely the subject of the covenant between God the Father and the Son. In this covenant, the Son is made the head or representative of His people. Adam was the natural head of the human family, and Christ is the covenant head of His church.

On this covenant of redemption was founded the covenant of grace. In the covenant of redemption, the Son stipulated with the Father to work out an atonement. The Father stipulated that He should have a seed, or people, gathered from out of the human race. The covenant of grace was made with human beings and was revealed to Adam after the Fall and more fully revealed later, to Abraham.

Of this covenant, Jesus Christ was to be the Mediator, the One who would administer it. It was a covenant of grace, in opposition to the original covenant of works, under which Adam and his posterity were first placed. Salvation was now to be obtained by faith, instead of works, because the obedience and death of Jesus Christ were to be regarded as the reason why any individual was to be saved, not that individual's personal obedience.

Not that His obedience was, strictly speaking, performed for us. As a man, Christ was under the necessity of obeying the law for himself. If He did not obey it, He became a transgressor as well. And yet there is a sense in which it may be said that His obedience is reckoned to our account. His obedience so highly honored the law, and His death so fully satisfied the demands of public justice, that grace (not justice) has reckoned His righteousness to us.

If He had obeyed the law strictly for us, and had owed no obedience for himself, then I cannot see why justice should not account His obedience to us. In this way we could have obtained salvation on the score of right instead of asking it on the score of grace or favor. But it is only in this sense accounted ours: He, being God and man, voluntarily assumed our nature, and then voluntarily laid down His life to make atonement. His act casts such a glory on the law of God that grace is willing to consider His obedience as ours in this sense, and, on His account, to treat us as if we were righteous.

Christ is also the covenant head of those who believe. He is not the natural head, as Adam was, but our covenant relation to Him is such that whatever is given to Him is given to us. Whatever He is, both in His divine and human nature; whatever He has done, either as God or man, is given to us by covenant, or promise, and is absolutely ours. Please understand this: The church, as a body, has never yet understood the fullness and richness of this covenant; namely, that all there is in Christ is given to us in the covenant of grace.

We receive this grace by faith. We do not become interested in this righteousness by works, or by anything we do previous to the exercise of faith. But as soon as we exercise faith, all that Christ has done, all there is of Christ, all that is contained in the covenant of grace becomes ours by faith. Hence, the inspired writers make so much of faith.

Faith is the voluntary compliance on our part with the condition of the covenant. Faith is the eye that discerns, the hand that takes hold, the medium by which we possess the blessings of the covenant. By the act of faith, the soul becomes actually possessed of all that is

embraced in the covenant. If the bonds of sin are not broken immediately, and the soul set at liberty at once, it is because the particular
act of faith has not embraced enough of who Christ is, and of what He
has done.

When Christ is received and believed on, He is made to us our
wisdom, and righteousness, and sanctification, and redemption. But
what is meant by these things? How, and in what sense?

This is a very peculiar verse, and my mind has long dwelt on it
with great anxiety to know its exact and full meaning. I have prayed
over it, as much as over any passage in the Bible, that I might be
enlightened to understand its real significance. I have long been in the
habit, when my mind fastened on any passage that I did not understand, to pray over it till I felt satisfied. I have never dared to preach
on this verse, because I never felt fully satisfied that I understood it.
But I think I understand it now; at any rate, I am willing to give my
opinion on it. And if I have any right knowledge respecting its meaning, I am sure I have received it from the Spirit of God.*

Christ Our Wisdom

Jesus Christ is often called "the Wisdom of God." And in the book
of Proverbs He is called Wisdom. But how is He made to us Wisdom?
We have absolutely all the benefits of His wisdom. If we exercise the
faith we ought, we are just as certain to be directed by His wisdom.

In all respects, this is the same as if we had the same wisdom,
originally, of our own or else it cannot be true that He is made unto
us wisdom. Since He is the infinite source of wisdom, He is made unto
us wisdom. We are partakers of His wisdom, and it is guaranteed to
us. At any time, if we trust in Him, we may have it as certainly, and
in any degree we need, to guide us infallibly, as if we had it originally
ourselves. That is what we need from the gospel, and what the gospel
must furnish, to be suited to our needs.

The person who has not learned this, has not known anything as
he ought. If he thinks his own theories and speculations are going to
bring him to any right knowledge regarding Christianity, he knows
nothing at all, as yet. His carnal, earthly heart can no more study the
realities of Christianity so as to get any available knowledge of them
than the heart of a beast. "What man knoweth the things of a man,
save the spirit of man which is in him? Even so the things of God
knoweth no man, but the Spirit of God" (1 Cor. 2:11).

---

*After much prayer, Finney later published a series of devotions on the meaning of
the names of Jesus Christ using the teaching in this sermon as his foundation.
These devotions can be found in *Principles of Union With Christ*.

What can we know, without experience, of the character or Spirit of God? Do you say, "We can reason about God." But of what good is reason? Suppose a soul contained only intellect, and had no other powers, and I should undertake to teach that pure intellect what it was to love. I could lecture, and reason, and philosophize about love, and yet it would be impossible to make that pure intellect understand what love is, unless it not only has power to exercise love, but has actually exercised it! It is just as if I should talk about colors to a man born blind. He hears the word, but what idea can he attach to it, unless he has seen? It is impossible to get him to comprehend the difference of colors. The term *color* has no meaning to him; it is a mere word.

Just so in Christianity. One who has not experienced it, may reason upon it. He may demonstrate the perfection of God, as he would demonstrate a proposition in Euclid. But that which is the spirit and life of the gospel can no more be carried to the mind by mere words, without experience, than love can be carried to a pure intellect, or colors to a man born blind. You may speak the truth to him so as to crush him down to hell with conviction; but to give the spiritual meaning of things, without the Spirit of God, is as absurd as to lecture a blind man about colors.

There are two things, then, contained in the idea of wisdom. Since Christ is our representative, we are interested in all His wisdom, and all the wisdom He has is exercised for us. His infinite wisdom is actually employed for our benefit. Second, His wisdom, just as much as we need, is guaranteed always ready to be imparted to us, whenever we exercise faith in Him for wisdom. From His infinite fullness, in this respect, we may receive all we need. And if we do not receive from Him the wisdom we need, in every case it is because we do not exercise faith.

Christ Our Righteousness

He is made unto us Righteousness. Here my mind has long labored to understand the distinction the apostle intended to make between righteousness and sanctification. Righteousness means holiness, or obedience to law; and sanctification seems to mean the same thing.*

The difference is this: when the apostle wrote that Jesus was made unto us righteousness, he meant that Christ is our *outward* righteousness; His obedience is, under the covenant of grace, accounted to us. Not in the sense that on the ground of justice He obeyed "for us." God

---

*For Finney's developing views on sanctification see *Principles of Sanctification*, *Principles of Discipleship*, *Principles of Holiness*, and the forthcoming *Principles of Christian Obedience*.

does not account us just because our substitute has obeyed; but that we are so identified with His obedience, that as a matter of grace, we are treated as if we had ourselves obeyed.

There is a view of this subject which differs slightly: that the righteousness of Christ is imputed to us, so that we are considered to have been always holy. At one time it was taught, and extensively maintained, that righteousness was so imputed to us that we had a right to demand salvation on the score of justice.

My view of the matter is entirely different. It is this: Christ's righteousness becomes ours as a gift. God has so united us to Christ, as on His Son's account that the Father treats us with favor. It is just like a case where a father had done some outstanding service for his country, and the government thinks it proper to reward such exemplary service. Not only will that individual be rewarded, but all his family will receive favors on his account, because they are the children of a man who had greatly benefitted his country.

Human governments do this, and the reason for it is very plain. It is just so in the divine government. Christ's disciples are in such a sense considered one with Him, and God is so highly delighted with the unsurpassed service Christ has done the kingdom, from the circumstances under which He became a Savior, that God accounts His Son's righteousness to men as though it were their own. In other words, the Father treats them just as He would treat Christ himself. Bear in mind that I am referring to what I call the "outward righteousness"; the reason why God accepts and saves them is that they believe in Christ. And this reason includes both the obedience of Christ to the law, and His obedience unto death, as demonstrated by his suffering upon the cross to make atonement.

Christ Our Sanctification

Sanctification is inward purity. Christ is our inward purity. The control that Christ exercises over us is done by His Spirit working in us, to will and to do. He sheds His love abroad in our hearts, so controlling us that we are actually made holy through the faith that is of the operation of God.

That Christ is our sanctification, or our holiness, means that He is the author of our holiness. He is not only the procuring cause of that holiness, by His atonement and intercession, but by His direct communion with the soul He himself produces holiness. He is the immediate cause of our being sanctified. He works in us, not by suspending our own agency; but He controls our minds to sanctify us by the influences of His Spirit in us, in a way perfectly consistent with our freedom. And this, also, is received by faith.

By faith, Christ is received and enthroned as *king* in our hearts. The mind, confident in Christ, yields itself up to Him, to be led by His Spirit, and guided and controlled by His hand. The act of the mind, throwing the soul into the hand of Christ for sanctification, is faith. Nothing is needed but for the mind to break off from any confidence in itself, and to give itself up to Him, to be led and absolutely controlled by Him, just as a small boy puts out his little hand to that of his father, so that the father might lead the child anywhere he pleases. If the child is distrustful, or not willing to be led, or if he has confidence in his own wisdom and strength, he will break away and try to run away. But if all that self-confidence fails, he will cease from his own efforts, and run back to his father again, to be led entirely at his father's will.

I suppose this is similar to the act of faith by which an individual gives his mind up to be led and controlled by Christ. He ceases from his own efforts to guide, control and sanctify himself. He just gives himself up, as yielding as air, and leaves himself in the hands of Christ as his sanctification.

Christ Our Redemption

Here the apostle plainly refers to the Jewish practice of redeeming estates, or redeeming relatives who had been sold for debt. When an estate had been sold out of the family, or an individual had been deprived of liberty because of debt, both could be redeemed by paying the price of redemption. There are very frequent allusions in the Bible to this practice.

Where Christ is spoken of as our redemption, I suppose it means just what it says. While we are in our sins, under the law we are sold as slaves. In the hand of public justice, we are bound over to death, with no possible way to redeem ourselves from the curse of the law. Now, Christ makes himself the price of our redemption. In other words, He is our redemption money; He buys us out from under the law by paying himself as a ransom. "Christ hath redeemed us from the curse of the law, being made a curse for us . . ." (Gal. 3:13). Thus, also, He redeems us from the power of sin.

Under this covenant of grace, our own works—or anything that we have done, or can do, as works of law—have nothing to do with our salvation. In your mind separate entirely salvation by works from salvation by grace. Our salvation by grace is founded on a reason entirely outside of ourselves. Before, it depended on ourselves. Now we receive salvation as a free gift, solely on account of Jesus Christ.

He is the author, ground, and reason for our salvation. Whether we love God or not is of no account, so far as it is a ground of our salvation. The whole is entirely a matter of grace, through Jesus

Christ. Do not understand me to say that there is no necessity for love to God or good works. I know that without holiness "no man shall see the Lord" (Heb. 12:14). But the necessity of holiness and the ground of salvation are two separate things. Our own holiness does not enter at all into the ground or reason for our acceptance and salvation.

We are not going to be indebted to Christ only until we are sanctified, and all the rest of the time stand in our own righteousness. However perfect and holy we may become, in this life, or to all eternity, Jesus Christ will forever be the sole reason in the universe why we are not in hell. However holy we may become, it will be forever true that we have sinned, and in the eyes of justice, nothing short of our eternal damnation can satisfy the law. But now Jesus Christ has undertaken to help, and He forever remains the sole ground of our salvation.

According to this plan, we have the benefit of His obedience to the law, just as if He had obeyed for us. Not that He did obey for us, but we have the benefits of His obedience, by the gift of grace, the same as if He had done so.

The Work of Faith

Faith in Christ puts us in possession of Christ as the sum and substance of the blessings of the gospel. Christ was the very blessing promised in the Abrahamic covenant. Throughout the Scriptures He is held forth as the sum and substance of all God's favors to man. He is "the Bread of Life," "the Water of Life," "our Strength," "our All." The gospel has taxed all the powers of language to describe the extent and variety of His relationships to us, and to show that faith is used to put believers in possession of Jesus Christ in all these areas.

The manner in which faith puts the mind in possession of all these blessings is this: It annihilates all those things that stand in the way of our communion with Christ. He says, "Behold, I stand at the door and knock: if any man hear my voice, and open the door, I will come in to him, and will sup with him, and he with me" (Rev. 3:20). The door He speaks of is an obstacle to our fellowship with Christ, something that stands in the way.

Consider wisdom, for example. Why do we not receive Christ as our wisdom? Because we depend on our own wisdom, and think we have in ourselves some available knowledge of the things of God. As long as we depend on our own wisdom we keep the door shut to receiving the perfect wisdom—that of Christ. Now, let us just throw away all wisdom of our own, and acknowledge how infinitely empty we are of any available knowledge as to the way of salvation, until Christ shall teach us. Until we do this, there is a door between us and Christ. We hold back something of our own; instead of coming and throwing ourselves perfectly into the hands of Christ, we come to Him expecting that He will strengthen our own wisdom.

How does faith put us in possession of the righteousness of Christ? This is the way. Until our mind takes hold of the righteousness of Christ, we are alive to our own righteousness. We are naturally engaged in working out a righteousness of our own. Until we cease entirely from our own works, by absolutely throwing ourselves on Christ for righteousness, we do not come to Christ.

Christ will not patch up our own righteousness to make it answer the purpose. If we depend on our prayers, our tears, our charities, or anything we have done, or expect to do, He will not receive us. But the moment an individual takes hold of Christ, he receives and appropriates all Christ's righteousness as his own; as a perfect and unchangeable reason for his acceptance with God, by grace.

It is the same with regard to sanctification and redemption. Until an individual receives Christ, he does not cease from his own works. But the moment he does that, by this very act he throws the entire responsibility upon Christ. The moment the mind yields itself up to Christ, the responsibility comes upon Him, just as the person who undertakes to conduct a blind man is responsible for his safe conduct. The believer, by the act of faith, trusts Christ for his obedience and sanctification. By giving himself up to Christ, all the veracity of the Godhead is put at stake, that he shall be led right and made holy.

With regard to redemption, as long as the sinner supposes that his own sufferings, his prayers, tears, or mental agony, are of any avail, he will never receive Christ.

There is no such thing as spiritual life in us, or anything acceptable to God, until we actually believe in Christ. The very act of believing receives Christ as just that influence which alone can wake up the mind to spiritual life. We are no more, as Christians, than what we believe Christ to be for us.

Many seem to wait to do something before they receive Christ. Some wait to become more dead to the world. Some desire a broken heart. Some want their doubts cleared up before they come to Christ. *This is a grand mistake.* It is expecting to accomplish *without faith* that which is only the result of faith.

Your heart will not be broken, your doubts will not be cleared up, you will never die to the world until you believe. The moment you grasp the things of Christ, your mind will see, as in the light of eternity, the emptiness of the world, of reputation, riches, honor, and pleasure. To expect this first, prior to the exercise of faith, is beginning at the wrong end. It is seeking that as a preparation for faith which is always the result of faith.

Perfect faith will produce perfect love. When the mind duly recognizes Christ, and receives Him in His various relations; when the faith is unwavering and the views clear, there will be nothing left in the mind contrary to the law of God. Abiding faith will produce abiding love. Increasing faith will produce increasing love.

Love may be perfect at all times, and yet be in different degrees at different times. An individual may love God perfectly and eternally, and yet his love must increase in vigor to all eternity. As the saints in glory see more and more of God's excellences, they will love Him more and more, and yet will have perfect love all the time. That is, there will be nothing inconsistent with love in the mind, while the degrees of love will be different as their views of the character of God unfold. As God opens to their view the wonders of His glorious benevolence, their souls will thrill with new love for God. In this life, the exercises of love vary greatly in degree.

Sometimes God unfolds to His saints the wonders of His government, and gives them such views as astonish and enthrall them, and then love is greatly raised in degree. And yet the love may have been perfect before; that is, the love of God was supreme and single, unmingled with inconsistent affections.

And it is not unreasonable to suppose that it will be so to all eternity; occasions will occur in which the love of the saints will be brought into more lively exercise by new unfoldings of God's glory. As God reveals to them wonder after wonder, their love will increase indefinitely, and they will have continually enlarged understandings of its strength and fervor to all eternity.

You see, beloved, the way in which you can be made holy, and the manner by which you can be sanctified. Whenever you come to Christ, and receive Him for all that He is, and accept a whole salvation by grace, you will have all that Christ is to you: wisdom, and righteousness, and sanctification, and redemption. There is nothing but unbelief to hinder you from enjoying it all now. You need not wait for any preparation. There is no preparation that is of any avail. You must *receive* a whole salvation, as a *free gift*.

When will you thus lay hold of Christ? When will you believe? Faith, true faith, always works by love, purifies the heart, and overcomes the world. Whenever you find any difficulty in your way, you may know the problem. It is a lack of faith. No matter what may befall you outwardly, if you find yourself thrown backward in Christianity, or your mind thrown into confusion, unbelief is the cause, and faith the remedy.

If you lay hold of Christ, and keep hold, all the devils in hell can never drive you from God, or put out your light. But if you let unbelief prevail, you may go on in this miserable, halting way, talking about sanctification, using words without knowledge, and dishonoring God, till you die.

10

CONDITIONS OF BEING SAVED*

"What must I do to be saved?" (Acts 16:30).

Paul and Silas had gone to Philippi to preach the gospel. Their preaching excited great opposition and tumult. They were arrested and thrown into prison, and the jailer was to make sure they didn't escape. At midnight, they were praying and singing praises when God came down. The earth quaked, the prison rocked, its doors burst open, and their chains fell off. The jailer sprang up, frightened, and supposing his prisoners had fled was about to take his own life, when Paul called out: "Do thyself no harm: for we are all here." The jailer then called for a light and came trembling, falling down before Paul and Silas. Bringing them out, he asked them, "Sirs, what must I do to be saved?"

What Sinners Must Not Do

It has now come to be necessary to tell people what they must *not* do in order to be saved. When the gospel was first preached, Satan had not introduced as many delusions to mislead people as he has now. Then, it was enough to give the simple and direct answer, telling people only what they must do at once. But this seems to be not enough now. So many delusions and perversions have bewildered and darkened the minds of people that they often need a great deal of instruction to lead them back to those simple views of the subject that prevailed at first. Hence, the importance of showing what sinners must *not* do, if they intend to be saved.

They must not imagine that there is nothing to be done. In Paul's time, nobody seems to have thought of this, for back then the doctrine

---

Sermons on Gospel Themes, 161–191.

of universalism was not as much developed. People then would not dream that they could be saved without doing anything. If this idea had been rife at Philippi, the question of our text would not have been asked. No trembling sinner would have cried out, *What must I do to be saved?*

If people imagine they have nothing to do, it is not likely they will be saved. It is not in the nature of falsehood and lies to save people's souls, and surely nothing is more false than this notion. People know they have something to do to be saved. Why, then, do they pretend that all people will be saved whether they do their duty or constantly refuse to do it? The very idea is preposterous, and is entertained only by the most blatant outrage upon common sense and an enlightened conscience.

You should not mistake what you have to do. The duty required of sinners is very simple, and would be easily understood were it not for the false ideas that prevail today, as to the nature of Christianity, and to the things that God requires as conditions of salvation. On these points, erroneous opinions prevail to a most alarming extent. Hence, the danger of mistake. Beware lest you be deceived in a matter of so vital importance.

Do not say or imagine that you cannot do what God requires. On the contrary, always assume that you can. If you assume that you cannot, this very assumption will be fatal to your salvation.

Do not procrastinate. If you ever hope to be saved, you must set your face like a flint against this most pernicious delusion. Probably no other mode of evading present duty has ever prevailed so extensively as this, or has destroyed so many souls. Almost all people in gospel lands intend to prepare for death—intend to repent and become Christians before they die. Even universalists expect to become religious at some time—perhaps after death, perhaps after being purified from their sins by purgatorial fires—but *somehow* they expect to become holy, for they know they *must* before they can see God and enjoy His presence.

But observe, they put this matter of becoming holy off to the most distant time possible. Feeling a strong aversion to becoming holy now, they flatter themselves that God will make them holy in the next world, no matter how much they may frustrate His efforts to do it in this one. As long as it remains in their power to choose whether to become holy or not, they prolong the time to enjoy sin. They leave it to God to make them holy in the next world—if they can't prevent it there! Consistency is a jewel! All who put off being Christians now, cherishing the delusion of becoming so in some future time, whether in this world or the next, are acting out this same inconsistency. They fondly hope that they are now doing their utmost to prevent what will eventually occur.

Many sinners press their way to hell under this delusion. Often, when pressed with the claims of God, they will even name the time when they will repent. That time may be very near—perhaps as soon as they get home from the church meeting, or as soon as the sermon is over. Or, it may be more remote: when they have finished their education, for example, or become settled in life, or have made a little more money, or when they are ready to abandon some business of questionable morality. But, no matter whether the time set is near or remote, the delusion is fatal—procrastination is murder to the soul.

Such sinners are little aware that Satan himself has poured out his spirit upon them and is leading them whithersoever he will. He little cares whether they put off for a longer time or a shorter. If he can persuade people to a long delay, he likes it well. If only to a short one, he feels quite sure he can renew the delay and get another extension—so it answers his purpose fully in the end.

Now mark, sinner, if you ever mean to be saved you must resist and grieve away this spirit of Satan. You must cease to procrastinate. You can never be converted as long as you delay, promising yourself that you will become a Christian at some future time. Did you ever bring anything to pass in your temporal business by procrastination? Did procrastination ever begin, prosecute, and accomplish any important business?

Suppose you are made aware of some business of vast consequence—involving your character, or your whole estate, or perhaps even your life—to be transacted in Cleveland. You do not know precisely how soon it *must* be done. It may be done with safety now, and with greater facility now than later. However, it might possibly be done if you decide to delay a little, although every moment's delay involves an absolute uncertainty of your being able to do it at all. You do not know but that a single hour's delay will make you too late.

Under those circumstances, what would a man of sense and discretion do? Would he not rise up from his bed and prepare to leave immediately? Or would he sleep on, well knowing the matter involved such risks and uncertainties? No. You know that the risk of a hundred dollars pending on such conditions would stir the warm blood of any man of business, and you could not tempt him to delay an hour. "Oh," he would say, "I must attend to this great business at once; everything else must give way."

But suppose the man should act as a procrastinating sinner does, and promise himself that "tomorrow will be as this day and much more abundant"—and do nothing that day, nor the next, nor the next month, nor the next year. Would you not think it strange? Would you not expect his business to be done, his money to be secured, his interests to be promoted?

So the sinner accomplishes nothing but his own ruin as long as he procrastinates. Until he says, "Now is my time, *today* I will do my duty," he is only playing the fool and laying up his wages accordingly. Oh, it is infinite madness to defer a matter of such vast interest and of such perilous uncertainty.

If you would be saved you must not wait for God to do what He commands *you* to do. God will surely do all that He can for your salvation. All that He can do, He either has already done it, or stands ready to do as soon as you demonstrate a willingness to allow Him to accomplish these things.

Long before you were born, He anticipated your needs as a sinner, and began on the most generous scale to make provision for them. He gave His Son to die for you, thus doing all that needed to be done by way of an atonement. For a long time He has been shaping His providence to give you a keen sense of awareness as to your duty. He has sent you His Word and Spirit. Indeed, He has given you the highest possible evidences that He will be energetic and prompt on His part—as one in earnest for your salvation. *You know this.*

What sinner reading this fears lest God should be negligent on His part in the matter of his salvation? None. Many are annoyed that God should press them so earnestly and be so diligent in the work of securing their salvation. And now, can you quiet your conscience with the excuse of waiting for God to do *your duty*?

The fact is there are things for you to do that God cannot do for you. Those things that He has enjoined and revealed as the conditions of your salvation He cannot and will not do himself. If He could have done them himself, He would not have asked you to do them. Every sinner ought to consider this.

God requires of you repentance and faith because it is naturally impossible that anyone else but you should do them. They are your own personal responsibilities: the voluntary exercises of your own mind; no other being in heaven, earth or hell can do these things for you. As far as substitution was naturally possible, God has introduced it, as in the case of the atonement. He has never hesitated to bear all the self-denials that the work of salvation has required.

Do not flee to any refuge of lies. Lies cannot save you. Truth, not lies, alone can save. People must be sanctified by the truth. There is no plainer teaching in the Bible than this, and no Bible doctrine is better sustained by reason than the principles of sanctification.

I have often wondered how people could suppose that universalism could save anyone. Does universalism sanctify anyone? At this time the universalists say that you must be punished for your sins, and that through punishment these sins will be put away—as if the fires of purgatory would thoroughly consume all sin and bring out the sinner pure. Is this being sanctified *by the truth*? You might as well hope to be saved by eating liquid fire! You might as well expect fire to purify your soul from sin in this world as in the next!

It is amazing that people should hope to be sanctified and saved by this great error, or, indeed, by any error whatever. God says you must be sanctified *by the truth*. Suppose you could believe the delusions of the universalists. Would that make you holy? Do you think it would make you humble, heavenly minded, sin hating, or benevolent? Can you believe any such thing? Be assured that Satan is only the Father of lies, and he cannot save you. In fact, he would not if he could. He intends his lies not to save you, but to destroy your very soul. Nothing but lies could be more suited to his purpose. Lies are the natural poison of the soul. Take them at your peril!

Don't seek for any self-indulgent method of salvation. The great effort among sinners has always been to be saved in some way through self-indulgence. They are slow to admit that self-denial is indispensable; that *total, unqualified self-denial is the condition of being saved*. I warn you; do not suppose that you can be saved in some easy, self-pleasing way. People ought to know that it is naturally indispensable to salvation that selfishness be utterly put away, and its demands resisted and put down.

Does the system of salvation I am preaching so chime with the intuitions of your reason that you know within yourself that this gospel is the thing you most need? Ask yourself: Does the gospel in all its parts and relations meet the demands of my intellect? Are its requisitions obviously just and right? Do the conditions of salvation it prescribes obviously befit man's moral position before God, and his moral relations to the government of God? Putting these and similar questions to myself, I am constrained to answer in the affirmative.

The longer I live the more fully I see that the gospel system is the only one that can both meet the demands of the human intelligence, and supply the needs of man's sinning, depraved heart. The duties enjoined upon the sinner are just those things that I know are naturally the conditions of salvation. Why, then, should any sinner think of being saved on any other condition? Why desire it, even if it were ever so practical?

Don't imagine you will ever have a more favorable time. Unrepentant sinners are prone to imagine that now is not the right time. So they put it off, in hope of a better time. They think perhaps that they shall have more conviction and fewer obstacles and less hindrances.

So thought Felix. He did not intend to forego salvation any more than you do, but he was very busy just then. He had certain ends to be secured that seemed peculiarly pressing, and so he begged to be excused on the promise of very faithful attention to the subject at the expected convenient season. But did the convenient season ever come? Never.

Nor does it ever come to those who in like manner resist God's solemn call and grieve away His Spirit. Thousands are now waiting in the pains of hell who said just as he did: "Go thy way for this time; when I have a convenient season I will call for thee" (Acts 24:25).

Oh, sinner, *when will your convenient season come?* Are you aware that no season will ever be "convenient" for you, unless God calls up your attention earnestly and solemnly to the subject? And can you expect Him to do this at the time of *your* choice, when you scorn His call at the time of *His* choice? Have you not heard Him say:

> Because I have called, and ye refused; I have stretched out my hand, and no man regarded; but ye have set at naught all my counsel, and would none of my reproof: I also will laugh at your calamity; I will mock when your fear cometh. When your fear cometh as desolation, and your destruction cometh as a whirlwind; when distress and anguish cometh upon you. Then shall they call upon me, but I will not answer; they shall seek me early, but they shall not find me. (Prov. 1:24–28)

Oh, sinner, that will be a fearful and a final doom! Do you suppose that you will find another time as good, and one in which you can just as easily repent, as now? Many are ready to suppose that though there may be no better time for themselves, there will at least be one *as good*. Vain delusion!

Sinner, you already owe ten thousand talents; do you suppose that you will find it just as easy to be forgiven this debt later, having shown that you don't care how much and how long you prolong payment? In a case like this, where everything turns upon your securing the good-will of your creditor, do you hope to gain it by positively insulting Him to His face?

Or take another view of the case. In your heart you know that one day you must repent of your sin, or be forever damned. You know also that each successive sin increases the hardness of your heart, making it more difficult to repent. How, then, can you reasonably hope that a future time will be equally favorable for your repentance, when you have hardened your neck like an iron sinew, and made your heart like an adamant stone? Can you hope that repentance will yet be as easy to you as ever?

You know, sinner, that God requires you to break off from your sins *now*. But you look up into His face and say to Him, "Lord, is it just as well to stop abusing you at some future convenient time? If I can only be saved at last, I shall think it all my gain to go on insulting and abusing You, as long as You will possibly tolerate it. And since you are so very compassionate and patient, I may venture on in sin and rebellion against you for many months and years longer. Lord, don't hurry me. Let me have my way. Let me abuse You, and spit in your face—all will be well if I only repent in season so as finally to be saved. Indeed, I know that You are entreating me to repent now, but I much prefer to wait a season."

And now, do you suppose that God will set His seal to this, that He will say, "You are right, sinner; I set my seal of approval upon your course. It is well that you take these views of your duty to your Maker and your Father. Go on. Your course will ensure your salvation." Do you expect such a response from God?

If you ever expect to be saved, don't wait to see what others will do or say. Recently, I was astonished to find that a young lady under conviction of sin was in great trouble about what a beloved brother would think of her if she should give her heart to God. She knew her duty, but he was an unrepentant sinner, and how could she know what he would think if she repented now.

It amounts to this. She would come before God and say, "O great God, I know I ought to repent, but I can't, for I don't know whether or not my brother will like it. I know that he too is a sinner, and must repent or lose his soul, but I am much more afraid of his frown than I am of Yours, and I care more for his approval than I do for Yours. Consequently, I dare not repent until he does!"

How shocking this is! Strange that on such a subject people will ask, "What will others say of me?" Do you not answer to God alone? What, then, have others to say about your duty to Him? God requires you to repent, and them also. *Now, why don't you do it at once?*

Not long ago, as I was preaching abroad, one of the principal men of the city came to the meeting for inquiry, apparently much convicted and in great distress for his soul. But being a man of high political standing, and supposing himself to be very dependent upon his friends, he insisted that he must consult them, and have a regard for their feelings in this matter. I could not possibly convince him of his error, although I spent three hours in the effort. He seemed almost ready to repent—I thought he certainly would. But he slipped away, and I expect he will be found at last among the lost in perdition. Would you not expect such a result if he tore himself away under such an excuse as that?

Oh, sinner, you must not care what others say of you. Let them say what they please. Remember, the question is between your own soul and God, and "if thou be wise, thou shalt be wise for thyself: but if thou scornest, thou alone shalt bear it" (Prov. 9:12). You must die alone, and must appear for yourself before God in judgment!

Go, young woman, ask your brother, "Can you answer for me when

I come to the judgment? Can you pledge yourself that you can stand in my place and answer for me there?" Now, until you have reason to believe that he can, it is wise for you to disregard his opinion if it stands at all in your way. Whoever interposes any objection to your immediate repentance, fail not to ask him, "Can you shield my soul in the judgment? If I can be assured that you can and will, then I will make you my savior. But if not, then I must attend to my own salvation, and leave you to attend to yours."

I never shall forget the time my own mind was turned upon this point. Seeking a quiet place for prayer, I went into a deep grove, found a perfectly secluded spot behind some large logs, and knelt down. Suddenly, a leaf rustled and I sprang up, thinking, *somebody must be coming and I shall be seen here at prayer.* I had not been aware that I cared what others said of me, but looking back upon my exercises of mind there, I could see that I did care infinitely too much what others thought of me.

Closing my eyes again to pray, I heard a rustling leaf again, and the thought came over me like a wave of the sea, "I am ashamed of confessing my sin!" thought I, "Ashamed of being found speaking with God!"

Oh, how ashamed I felt of this shame! I can never describe the strong and overpowering impression that this thought made on my mind. I cried aloud at the very top of my voice; though everyone on earth and all the devils in hell were present to hear me and see me, I would not shrink and would not cease to cry out to God. For what is it to me if others see me seeking the face of my God and Savior? I am hastening to the judgment. *There* I shall not be ashamed to have the Judge my friend. *There* I shall not be ashamed to have sought His face and His pardon here. *There* will be no shrinking away from the gaze of the universe.

Oh, if sinners at the judgment could shrink away, how gladly would they; but they cannot! Nor can they stand in each other's places, to answer for each other's sins. That young woman, can she say then, "Oh, my brother, you must answer for me. For to please you, I rejected Christ and lost my soul"? That brother is himself a guilty rebel, confounded and agonized, and quailing before the awful Judge. How can he take your part in such an awful hour! Fear not his displeasure now, but rather warn him while you can to escape for his life before the wrath of the Lord waxes hot against him and there be no escape.

If you would be saved, you must not indulge prejudices against God, or His ministers, or against Christians, or against anything associated with Christianity. There are some people of peculiar temperament who are greatly in danger of losing their souls because they are tempted to strong prejudices.

Once committed either in favor of or against any persons or things, they are exceedingly apt to become so fixed as never more to look at the thing honestly. And when the objects of their prejudice—whether people or things—are so connected with Christianity that their prejudices prevent their fulfilling the great conditions of salvation, the effect can be nothing else than ruinous. For it is naturally indispensable to salvation that you should be entirely without guile. Your soul must act before God in the open sincerity of truth, or you cannot be converted.

I have known people in revivals to remain a long time under great conviction, without submitting themselves to God, and by careful inquiry I have found them wholly hedged in by their prejudices, and yet so blind to this fact that they would not admit that they had any prejudice at all. In my observation of convicted sinners, I have found this among the most common obstacles in the way of the salvation of souls. People become committed against Christianity; remaining in this state, it is naturally impossible that they should repent. God will not honor your prejudices or lower His prescribed conditions of salvation to accommodate your feelings.

You must give up all hostile feelings in cases where you have been really injured. Sometimes I have seen people evidently shut out from the kingdom of heaven simply because, having once been injured, they would not forgive and forget. Maintaining such a spirit of resistance and revenge, they could not, in the nature of the case, repent of their sin toward God, nor could God forgive them. Naturally, they lost heaven. I have heard some say, "I cannot forgive. I will not forgive. I have been injured, and I never will forgive that wrong." Now mark: you must not hold on to such feelings. If you do, you cannot be saved.

You must not allow yourself to stumble over the prejudices of others. I have often been struck by certain families, where the parents or older persons had prejudices against the minister, and I have wondered why those parents were not more wise than to lay stumbling blocks before their children to ruin their souls. This is often the true reason why children are not converted. Their minds are turned against the gospel when they are turned against those from whom they hear it preached. I would rather have people come into my family and curse and swear before my children than to have them speak against those who preach the gospel to them. Therefore I say to all parents: *Take care what you say, if you would not shut the gate of heaven against your own children!*

Do not allow yourself to take some fixed position and then allow the stand you have taken to deter you from any obvious duty. People sometimes commit themselves against taking what is called "the anxious seat"; consequently, they refuse to go forward under circumstances when it is obviously proper that they should—and where their refusal to do so places them in an attitude unfavorable (and perhaps fatal) to their conversion. Let every sinner beware of this!

Do not hold on to anything about which you have any doubt of its lawfulness or propriety. Cases often occur in which people are not fully satisfied that a thing is wrong, and yet are not satisfied that it is right. Now, in cases of this sort, it should not be enough to say, "Such and such Christians do so." You ought to have better reasons than this for your course of conduct.

If you ever expect to be saved, you must abandon all practices that you even suspect to be wrong. This principle seems to be involved in the passage, "He that doubteth is damned if he eat, because he eateth not of faith: for whatsoever is not of faith is sin" (Rom. 14:23). To do that which is of doubtful propriety is to allow yourself to tamper with the divine authority, and cannot fail to break down in your mind that solemn dread of sinning which, if you would ever be saved, you must carefully cherish.

If you would be saved, do not look at professing Christians and wait for them to become as engaged as they should be in the great work of God. If they are not what they ought to be, let them alone. Let them bear their own awful responsibility. It often happens that convicted sinners compare themselves with professed Christians, and excuse themselves for delaying their duty because professed Christians are delaying theirs. Sinners must not do this if they would ever be saved. It is very probable that you will always find enough guilty professing Christians to stumble over into hell if you allow yourself to do so.

But on the other hand, many who profess to be Christians may not be nearly as bad as you suppose; you must not be censorious, putting the worst constructions upon their conduct. You have other work to do than this. Let them stand or fall to their own master. Unless you abandon the practice of picking flaws in the conduct of professed Christians, it is utterly impossible that you should be saved.

Do not depend upon professing Christians—on their prayers or influence in any way. I have known children to hang a long time upon the prayers of their parents, putting those prayers in the place of Jesus Christ, or at least in the place of their own present efforts to do their duty. Now, this course pleases Satan entirely; he needs to do nothing more to ensure your destruction. Therefore, depend on no prayers—not even those of the holiest Christians on earth. The matter of your conversion lies between yourself and God alone, as much as if you were the only sinner in all the world, or as if there were no other beings in the universe but yourself and God.

Do not seek for any apology or excuse whatever. I dwell upon this and urge it the more because I so often find persons resting on some excuse without being themselves aware of it. In conversation with them upon their spiritual state, I see this and say, "There you are resting on that excuse." "Am I?" they exclaim, "I did not know it."

Do not seek for stumbling blocks. Sinners, a little disturbed in their stupidity, begin to cast about for stumbling blocks for self-vindication. All at once they become wide awake to the faults of professing Christians, as if they had to bear the care of all the churches. The real fact is, they are all engaged to find something to which they can take exception, so that they can thereby blunt the keen edge of truth upon their own consciences. This never facilitates their own salvation.

Do not tempt the forbearance of God. If you do, you are in the utmost danger of being given over forever. Do not presume that you may continue on yet longer in your sins, and still find the gate of mercy. This presumption has paved the way for the ruin of many souls.

Do not despair of salvation and settle down in unbelief, saying, "There is no mercy for me." You must not despair in any such sense as to shut yourself out from the kingdom. You may well despair of being saved without Christ and without repentance; but you are bound to believe the gospel and to do this is to believe the glad tidings that Jesus Christ has come to save sinners, even such a one as yourself, and that the one who comes to Him He "will in no wise cast out" (John 6:37). You have no right to disbelieve this, and act as if there were no truth in it.

You must not wait for more conviction of sin. Why do you need any more? You know your guilt and your present duty. Nothing can be more preposterous therefore, than to wait for more conviction. If you did not know that you are a sinner, or that you are guilty of sin, there might be some fitness in seeking for conviction of the truth on these points.

Do not wait for more or for different feelings. Sinners often say, "I must feel differently before I can come to Christ," or "I must have *more* feeling." As if this were the great thing that God requires of them. They are altogether mistaken.

Do not wait to be better prepared. While you wait, you are growing worse and worse, and are fast rendering your salvation impossible.

Don't wait for God to change your heart. Why should you wait for Him to do what He has commanded *you* to do, and waits for you to do in obedience to His command?

Don't try to recommend yourself to God by prayers or tears or by anything else whatsoever. Do you suppose your prayers put God under any obligation to forgive you? Suppose you owed someone five hundred dollars, and should go a hundred times a week and beg him to cancel your debt. Now, would you enter your many requests in account against your creditor, as so much claim against him? Suppose you intended to pursue this course till you had canceled the debt; could you hope to prove anything by this course—except that you were insane? And yet, sinners seem to suppose that their many prayers and tears lay the Lord Jesus Christ under real obligation to forgive them.

Never rely on anything else whatever than Jesus Christ and Him crucified. It is preposterous for you to hope, as many do, to make some propitiation by your own sufferings. In my early experience I thought I could not expect to be converted at once. I thought that I had to be bowed down for a long time. I said to myself, "God will not pity me until I feel worse than I do now. I can't expect Him to forgive me till I feel a greater agony of my soul than I do now." Even if I could have gone on augmenting my sufferings till they equalled the miseries of hell, it could not have changed God. The fact is: God does not ask you to suffer. Your sufferings cannot avail for atonement. Why, therefore, should you attempt to thrust aside the system of God's providing and thrust in one of your own?

There is another view of the case. The thing God demands of you is that you should bow your stubborn will to Him. Just as a disobedient child, when required to submit, might fall to weeping and groaning and to every expression of agony, and might even torture himself in hopes of moving the pity of his father, rather than submit to parental authority. He would be very glad to put his own sufferings in the place of the submission demanded. This is what the sinner is doing. He would substitute his own sufferings in the place of submission to God, and move the pity of the Lord so much that He would recede from the hard condition of repentance and submission.

If you would be saved you must not listen at all to those who pity you and who impliedly take your part against God, trying to make you think you are not as bad as you are. I once knew a woman who, after a long season of distressing conviction, fell into great despair. Her health sank, and she seemed about to die. All this time, she found no relief but seemed only to wax worse and worse, sinking down in stern and awful despair. Her friends, instead of dealing plainly and faithfully with her by probing her guilty heart to the bottom, had taken the course of pitying her and almost complained of the Lord that He would not have compassion on the poor agonized, dying woman. At length, as she seemed in the last stages of life, so weak as to be scarcely able to speak in a low voice, there happened in a minister who better understood how to deal with convicted sinners. The woman's friends cautioned him to deal very carefully with her, as she was in a dreadful state and greatly to be pitied. But he judged it best to deal with her very faithfully.

As he approached her bedside, she raised her faint voice and begged for a little water. He said, "Unless you repent, you will soon be where there is not a drop of water to cool your tongue."

"Oh," she cried, "*must I go to hell?*"

"Yes, you must, and you will soon, unless you repent and submit to God. Why don't you repent and submit immediately?"

"Oh," she replied, "it is an awful thing to go to hell!"

"Yes, and for that very reason God has provided an atonement through Jesus Christ, but *you won't accept it.* He brings the cup of salvation to your lips, and you thrust it away. Why will you do this? Why will you persist in being an enemy of God and scorn His offered salvation, when you might become His friend and have salvation if you would?"

This was the strain of their conversation, and in the end the woman saw her guilt and her duty and turning to the Lord found pardon and peace.

Therefore, I say, if your conscience convicts you of sin, don't let anyone take your part against God. Your wound needs not a bandage, but a *probe.* Don't fear the probe. It is the only thing that can save you. Don't seek to hide your guilt or veil your eyes from seeing it, nor be afraid to know the worst, for you must know the very worst, and the sooner you know it the better.

I warn you, don't look after some physician to give you an opiate, for you don't need it. Shun, as you would death itself, all those who would speak to you smooth things and prophesy deceits. They would surely ruin your soul.

Do not suppose that if you become a Christian, it will interfere with any of the necessary or appropriate duties of life, or with anything whatever to which you ought to attend. No, Christianity never interferes with any real duty. This is far from the case, in fact. A proper attention to your various duties is indispensable to your being a Christian. You cannot serve God without doing your real duties.

Moreover, if you would be saved, you must not give heed to anything that would hinder you. It is infinitely important that your soul should be saved. No consideration thrown in your way should be allowed to have the weight of a straw or a feather.

Jesus Christ has illustrated and enforced this by several parables, especially in the one which compares the kingdom of heaven to "a merchant man, seeking goodly pearls: who when he had found one pearl of great price, went and sold all that he had, and bought it" (Matt. 13:45–46). In another parable, the kingdom of heaven is said to be like "treasure hid in a field; the which when a man hath found, he hideth, and for joy thereof goeth and selleth all that he hath and buyeth that field" (Matt. 13:44). Thus forcibly are people taught that they must be ready to sacrifice whatever is required in order to gain the kingdom of heaven.

You must not seek Christian faith selfishly. You must not make your own salvation or happiness the supreme end. Beware, for if you make this your supreme end you will get a false hope, and will probably glide down the pathway of the hypocrite into the deepest hell.

What Sinners Must Do

It is of the utmost importance that you should understand what you must do clearly. You need to know that you must return to God and to understand what this means. The difficulty between you and God is that you have stolen yourself and run away from His service. You rightly belong to God. He created you for himself, and hence has a perfectly righteous claim to the homage of your heart, and the service of your life. But you, instead of living to meet His claims, have run away—have deserted from God's service and have lived to please yourself. Now, your duty is to return and restore yourself to God.

You must return and confess your sins to God. You must confess that you have been all wrong, and that God has been all right. Go before the Lord and lay open the depth of your guilt. Tell Him you deserve just as much damnation as He has threatened.

These confessions are naturally indispensable to your being forgiven. In accordance with this the Lord says, "If then their uncircumcised hearts be humbled, and they then *accept of the punishment* of their iniquity, then will I remember my covenant" (Lev. 26:41–42). Then God can forgive. But as long as you remain stubborn on this point, and will not concede that God is right, or admit that you are wrong, He can never forgive you.

You must moreover confess to anyone you have injured. And is it not a fact that you have injured some, and perhaps many of your fellow men? Have you not slandered your neighbor and said things which you have no right to say? Have you not in some instances, which you could call to mind if you would, lied to them, or about them, or covered up or perverted the truth? And have you not been willing that others should have false impressions of you or of your conduct? If so, you must renounce all such iniquity, for "He that covereth his sins shall not prosper: but whoso confesseth and forsaketh them shall have mercy" (Prov. 28:13).

Furthermore, you must not only confess your sins to God and to those you have injured, but you must also make restitution. You have not taken the position of a penitent before God and man until you have done this also. God cannot treat you as a penitent until you have done it. I do not mean by this that God cannot forgive you until you have carried into effect your purpose of restitution by finishing the outward act, for sometimes it may demand time, and may in some cases be itself impossible to you. But the purpose must be sincere and thorough before you can be forgiven by God.

You must renounce yourself.

(1) You must renounce your own righteousness forever, discarding the very idea of having any righteousness in yourself.

(2) You must renounce your own will, and be ever ready to say not in word only, but in heart, "Thy will be done, on earth as it is in heaven." You must consent most heartily that God's will shall be your supreme law.

(3) You must renounce your own way and let God have His own way in everything. Never allow yourself to fret about any of His designs. Since God's agency extends to all events, you ought to recognize His hand in all things. And of course, to fret at anything whatever is to fret against God who has at least *permitted* that thing to occur as it does. So long as you allow yourself to fret you are not right with God. You must come before God as a little child, subdued and trustful at His feet. Let the weather be fair or foul, consent that God should have His way. Let all things go well with you, or ill; yet let God do His pleasure, and let it be your part to submit in perfect resignation. Until you take this ground, you cannot be saved.

You must come to Christ.

You must accept Christ truly and fully as your Savior. Renouncing all thought of depending on anything you have done or can do, you must accept Christ as your atoning sacrifice and as your ever-living Mediator before God. Without the least qualification or reserve, you must place yourself under His wing as your Savior.

You must seek supremely to please Christ and not yourself.

It is naturally impossible for you to be saved until you come into this attitude of mind—until you are so well pleased with Christ in all respects as to find your pleasure in doing His pleasure. It is in the nature of things impossible that you should be happy in any other state of mind, or unhappy in this one, for His pleasure is infinitely good and right.

When, therefore, His good pleasure becomes your good pleasure, and your will harmonizes entirely with His, then you will be happy for the same reason that He is happy, and you cannot fail to be happy any more than Jesus Christ can. And this becoming supremely happy in God's will is essentially the idea of salvation. In this state of mind, you are saved. Out of it you cannot be.

It has often been impressed upon me that many people who profess to be Christians are deplorably and utterly mistaken. Their real feeling is that Christ's service is an iron collar—an insufferably hard yoke. Hence, they labor exceedingly to throw off some of this burden. They try to make it out that Christ does not require much, if any, self-denial, and little, if any, deviation from the course of worldliness and sin. They struggle to get the standard of Christian duty down to a level with the fashions and customs of the world, hoping to make it easier to live a Christian life and wear Christ's yoke!

But taking Christ's yoke as it really is, it becomes in their view an iron collar. Doing the will of Christ, instead of their own, is a hard business, not a joyful one. Now, since doing Christ's will *is* Christianity (and who can doubt it?), then *in their state of mind* they will be supremely wretched.

Let me ask those who groan under the idea that they *must* be religious, who deem it awfully hard, how much religion of this kind would it take to make hell? Surely not much! It gives you no joy to do God's pleasure, and yet you are forced to the doing of His pleasure as the only way to be saved. You are thereby perpetually dragooned into the doing of what you hate as the only means of escaping hell. Would not this be itself a hell? Can you not see that in this state of mind you are not saved and cannot be?

To be saved you must come into a state of mind in which you will ask no higher joy than to do God's pleasure. This alone will be forever enough to fill your cup to overflowing.

You must have all confidence in Christ.

You must absolutely believe in Him, believe all His words of promise. They were given to you to be believed, and unless you believe them they can do you no good at all. So, far from helping you without your exercise of faith in them, they will only aggravate your guilt of unbelief.

God would be believed when He speaks in love to lost sinners. He gave them these "exceeding great and precious promises: that by these ye might be partakers of the divine nature, having escaped the corruption that is in the world through lust" (2 Pet. 1:4). But thousands of those who profess to be Christians do not know how to use these promises; they might just as well have been written on the sands of the sea.

Sinners, too, will go to hell in unbroken masses, unless they believe and take hold of God by faith in His promise. Oh, His awful wrath is out against them! And He says, "I would go through them, I would burn them together. Or let him take hold of my strength, that he may make peace with me; and he shall make peace with Me" (Isa. 25:4–5). Do you ask how to take hold? By faith. Yes, *by faith*. Believe His words and *take hold*! Take hold of His strong arm and swing right out over hell, and don't be afraid any more than if there were no hell.

But you say, "I do believe, and yet I am not saved." No, you don't believe. A woman said to me, "I believe, I know I do, and yet here I am in my sins." "No," I said, "you don't. Have you as much confidence in God as you would have in me if I had promised you a dollar? Do you ever pray to God? And, if so, do you come with any such confidence as you would have if you came to me to ask for a promised dollar? Oh, until you have as much faith in God as this, aye and more, until you have more confidence in God than you would have in ten thousand men, your faith does not honor God and you cannot hope to please Him. You must say, 'Let God be true, though every man be a liar' " (Rom. 3:4).

But, you say, "Oh, I am a sinner, and how can I believe?" I know you are a sinner, and so are all people to whom God has given these promises. "Oh, but I am a *great sinner*," you say. Well, "This is a faithful saying, and worthy of all acceptation, that Christ Jesus came into the world to save sinners; of whom," Paul writes, "I am chief" (1 Tim. 1:15). So you need not despair.

You must forsake all that you have to be Christ's disciple.

There must be absolute and total *self-denial*. By this I do not mean that you are never to eat again, or never again to clothe yourself, or never more enjoy the society of your friends—no, not this. But I mean that you should cease entirely from using any of these enjoyments selfishly. You must no longer think to own yourself—your time, your possessions, or anything you have ever called your own. All these things must be God's, not yours.

In this sense you are to forsake all that you have, namely, in the sense of laying all upon God's altar to be devoted supremely and only to His service. When you come back to God for pardon and salvation, come with all you have to lay all at His feet. Come with your body, to offer it as a living sacrifice upon His altar. Come with your soul and all its powers, and yield them in willing consecration to your God and Savior. Come, bring them all along— body, soul, intellect, imagination, acquirements—all, without reserve.

Do you say, "Must I bring them *all*"? Yes, all— absolutely ALL. Do not keep back anything. Don't sin against your own soul, like Ananias and Sapphira, by keeping back a part. Renounce your own claim to everything, and recognize God's right to all. Say, "Lord, these things are not mine. I had stolen them, but they were never mine. They were always yours. I'll have them no longer. Lord, these things are all yours; henceforth and forever. Now, what will you have me to do? I have no business of my own to do. I am wholly at your disposal. Lord, what work have you for me to do?"

In this spirit you must renounce the world, the flesh, and Satan. Your fellowship is henceforth to be with Christ, and not with those objects. You are to live for Christ, and not for the world, the flesh, or the devil.

You must believe the record God has given of His Son.

The unbelieving person does not receive the record, does not set to his seal that God is true. "This is the record, that God hath given us eternal life, and this life is in His Son" (1 John 5:11). The condition of your having it is that you believe the record, and of course that you act accordingly.

Suppose there is a poor man living at your next door, and the mail brings him a letter stating that a rich man has died in England, leaving him 100,000 pounds sterling, and the cashier of a neighboring bank writes him that he has received the amount on deposit for him, and holds it subject to his order. "Well," the poor man says, "I can't believe the record. I can't believe there ever was any such rich man. I can't believe there is 100,000 pounds sterling for me." So he must live and die as poor as Lazarus, because he won't believe the record.

Now, mark. This is just the case with the unbelieving sinner. God has given you eternal life, and it waits your order. But you don't get it because you will not believe, and therefore will not make out the order, and present in due form the application.

"Ah," you say, "But I must have some feeling before I can believe. How can I believe till I have the feeling?" In the same way, the poor man might say, "How can I believe that the 100,000 pounds is mine? I have not got a farthing of it now. I am as poor as ever." Yes, you are poor because you *will not believe*. If you would believe, you might go and buy out every store in this country. Still you cry, "I am as poor as ever. I can't believe it. See my poor worn clothes. I was never more ragged in my life. I have not a particle of the feeling and the comforts of a rich man."

It's the same with the sinner who won't believe until he gets the inward experience! He must wait to have some of the feeling of a saved sinner before he can believe the record and take hold of the salvation! Preposterous! So the poor man must wait to get his new clothes and fine house before he can believe his documents and draw for his money. Of course he dooms himself to everlasting poverty, although mountains of gold were all his own.

Now sinner, you must understand. Why should you be lost when eternal life is bought and offered you by the last will and testament of the Lord Jesus Christ? Will you not believe the record and draw for the amount at once? Do for mercy's sake understand this, and not lose heaven by your own folly!

If you would be saved you must accept a *prepared salvation*, one already prepared and full and present. You must be willing to give up all your sins, and be saved from them, *all, now and henceforth*! Until you consent to this, you cannot be saved at all. Many would be willing to be saved in heaven, if they might hold on to some sins while on earth—or rather they *think* they would like heaven on such terms. But the fact is, they would as much dislike a pure heart and a holy life in heaven as they do on earth, and they deceive themselves utterly in supposing that they are ready or even willing to go to such a heaven as God has prepared for His people.

No, there can be no heaven except for those who accept a salvation *from all sin* in this world. They must take the gospel as a system that holds no compromise with sin—and contemplates full deliverance from sin even now, and makes provision accordingly. Any other gospel is not the true one, and to accept of Christ's gospel in any other sense is to not accept it all. Its first and its last condition is *sworn and eternal renunciation of all sin.*

11

THE WHOLE COUNSEL OF GOD*

"Wherefore I take you to record this day, that I am pure from the blood of all men. For I have not shunned to declare unto you all the counsel of God" (Acts 20:26–27).

The meaning of the words "pure from the blood of all men" can best be explained by a reference to the prophet Ezekiel. In the third chapter of his prophecy we read:

> Son of man, I have made thee a watchman unto the house of Israel: therefore hear the word at my mouth, and give them warning from me. When I say unto the wicked, Thou shalt surely die; and thou givest him not warning, nor speakest to warn the wicked from his wicked way, to save his life; the same wicked man shall die in his iniquity; but his blood will I require at thine hand. Yet if thou warn the wicked, and he turn not from his wickedness, nor from his wicked way, he shall die in his iniquity; but thou hast delivered thy soul. Again, when a righteous man doth turn from his righteousness, and commit iniquity, and I lay a stumblingblock before him, he shall die: because thou hast not given him warning, he shall die in his sin, and his righteousness which he hath done shall not be remembered: but his blood will I require at thine hand. Nevertheless if thou warn the righteous man, that the righteous sin not, and he doth not sin, he shall surely live, because he is warned; [or because he takes warning], also thou hast delivered thy soul. (Ezek. 3:17–21)

This passage explains what the apostle meant. You know also that,

---

*The Penny Pulpit, A farewell sermon preached on Wednesday evening, April 2, 1851, at the Tabernacle, Moorfields. Finney preached from the text at the particular request of the pastor, Dr. Campbell. He noted to the congregation that he had hesitated to do so, because he did not want it inferred that he was comparing himself with the apostle, which was far from his design or purpose.

according to Scripture, a man's life is in his blood. Of course this language is figurative: the life of the soul is called its blood. To be clear from the blood of men, then, is to be clear of the charge of unfaithfulness to their souls. To be clear from the blood of all men in the sense that the apostle claims himself to be means that he is not to blame if they should lose their souls. He had discharged his duty to them. If their souls were lost *they* were answerable for it, not himself.

Notice that the soul is of infinite value and that it cannot be lost without infinite guilt laid somewhere, because infinite responsibility must be incurred somewhere. I would also point out the conditions upon which all who have this responsibility may be clear of the blood of the soul.

The Soul Has Infinite Value

This is a theme so vast that when an individual gives up his mind to consider and dwell upon it he is completely confounded. It is like eternity: the mind seems to topple in the attempt to grasp and understand it.

In the Bible, great value is always placed on the soul. You all know that everything that is really valuable must promote the welfare and well-being of the mind. Nothing can be valuable in itself but that which constitutes the well-being of mind. Take all the mind out of the universe, and what is left of any real value? Joy and sorrow, pain and pleasure, all belong to the mind. Especially is this true of all intelligent minds, the minds of moral agents. It is, of course, the souls of moral agents of which I now speak. Of mere brute beasts we can know but little; and therefore, we cannot say much about them. When we speak of the souls of men, we refer to something that is immortal.

The first thought in reference to the value of the soul is this: its eternity of existence. It lives forever! Once souls have begun to be, they will never cease to be. They will grow older and older, and live onward and onward and onward, as long as God shall live! Now think of that!

Another consideration is this: from the very nature of mind, it must be either happy or miserable. Further, since the mind is so enduring, its enjoyments or sufferings will continually and everlastingly increase. This must be the result of a natural and necessary law. The means of greater happiness or misery will be forever enlarging. The soul, once it begins to exist, will go on enjoying or suffering for ever and ever, and its capacity for enjoyment or suffering also increases with its duration. Its capacity at any time in a future state will be full of either the one set of feelings or the other.

Consequently, the period must arrive when each individual shall be either enjoying or suffering more than would fill the conceptions of all finite creatures. If you could unite in one mind all the intellect of the universe at this moment (excepting only that of God himself) it still would not be capable of comprehending either the joy or the suffering that may be comprehended by any single mind at some period in eternity.

The soul of every individual, whether that of the youngest child or the weakest mind, will have to live forever. After the elements have been melted by the fire, and the universe has rolled together as a scroll and passed away with a great noise, whatever your mind is able to grasp now, you will be able to look back upon the lengthened ages that you have lived. You will remember all your sorrows and your joys, and be able to say, "Ah! I have enjoyed (or suffered, as the case may be) in my personal experience to a greater degree than all the creatures of God are capable of feeling—both before I was born, and before I came to this place."

And when you have said that, you will be infinitely short of the truth, for there will be others after you, who will feel these things deeper still, whose intelligence in eternity will surpass even yours. They will exclaim, "I have received more favors, mercy, and grace from God now, than those before me had received when I first started into existence. And all those after me have been progressing and receiving additional favors just as I have. They are as far ahead of me now as they were then, for God has not confined His favors to me."

The time will arrive when the last admitted inhabitant of heaven will be able to say, "I know more of God now than they all knew when I came here. I am older now than they all were then. My single cup of knowledge will now hold more than at that time all theirs would hold combined. Indeed that which runs over the side of mine would have filled theirs." But what have you said even when you have said this? Behind there lies an eternity still. You may roll on the waves of the ocean in that direction for ever, for there is neither shore nor bound; neither height, nor depth, nor bottom; infinity is on every side!

How many hundreds of years has Paul been in heaven, and with him his spiritual children, those who were converted under his ministry! At some period in eternity the youngest child now alive, or ever will live, who gets to heaven will be able to say, "I now know a thousand times more about God and heaven than Paul did when he was upon earth, or than all the Church of God combined knew at that time." But after all, this is only a very faint conception of eternity and the progress of the mind in a future state. Draw out your imagination to the greatest possible or conceivable extent. Let any computation be made. Let your mind stretch itself to its utmost tension, and what then?

Why, you have only set your foot on the threshold of eternity. You are no nearer to the end than when you made the first step. The joy of heaven is always and absolutely perfect. The soul will be continually and forever rising nearer to God, but there will never be any approaching to a close in anything there, since everything is absolutely infinite!

Now look at the other side. Think of an individual who goes on and on sinning, just as if there was no such place as hell! There was a first time when you consented to sin, and there was a first pang of conscience in your little mind, and a tear gathered in your little eye. Could anybody have looked into your little heart, and beheld that twinge of your little mind, and seen that heavy sigh, and have supposed that you would ever sin again?

Ah! But you have repeated it again and again, and on you have gone until now! Just think then for a moment of that individual going into eternity! Then all restraint is taken away. The pleasures of sin too are all cut off. All good influences have died away for ever. He has received all his good gifts and good things.

He abused God's mercy, rejected God's gospel, grieved God's Spirit. In spite of the Spirit of grace, he went on in sin. Now, therefore, he is sinning with increasing vigor—rushing on in sin! Ah! think of the many sorrows, the many agonizings, the many hours of remorse that the sinner has to endure even here. But then, in a future world, when conscience will do its duty perfectly, when there is no diverting the attention from his true condition; when he cannot shut his eyes to the truth; what will be his agony and remorse then, when he feels that his soul is lost, and lost for ever? He cannot repent of his sins then. No! rather, he goes on sinning still.

Sinner, if you are numbered with the lost, that awful period in eternity will arrive when you will have sinned more than all the devils in hell have sinned up to the present hour! All the devils in that world have not yet created such a source of misery, as at some period you will have done if you are lost! Nay! All the devils, and all the wicked men who have left our world to be their companions in woe, combining their efforts have not committed so many sins as you will be able to claim as your own.

The period must arrive when to attempt to number your sins would be an inexpressible source of the deepest agony. Who can count them? Who can conceive of them? Who can compute them? What but an infinite mind could look at them without being so overcome as to wail out in the agonies of despair—if the mind were not infinitely holy.

There is no real believing in immortality, taking it as a truth into the mind, and contemplating the extent of it, without an individual feeling as if his nerves were on fire with such convictions as these.

Infinite Responsibility for an Infinite Soul

God is, in a threefold sense, the owner of everyone of these souls. First, He created them all. Second, He preserved them all. Third, He redeemed them all by the precious blood of Christ. They cost Him an infinite price, and He will not see them lost without making inquisition for blood, without imparting the responsibility. By a word He gave existence to the material universe. He speaks, and by the energy of His own word, world rises upon world, and system upon system. By the same means He can people them all. But He cannot redeem sinners in this way.

Because they have sinned, they are spiritually dead, and have incurred the penalty of the divine law. To save them from the resulting destruction required a different work to that of creation. Salvation could not be performed with a word. To redeem these souls cost Him an infinite price. To ordain those laws by which people came into existence was comparatively a trifling performance; although that required the power of God. But to redeem you, sinner, to purchase you back, to relieve you from the penalty of the divine law, to make an atonement that God might be just and yet save you, cost an infinite and terrible price!

God's beloved and only Son endured intense suffering, labor, persecution, and misrepresentation for more than thirty years for you. Finally, your redemption cost Him His life. Ah! under the charge of blasphemy the Son of God must die for you and for me! God, for man, gave His only Son, His well-beloved Son, in whom He was well pleased. The Son of God must die! What a sacrifice! It was infinite!

Think brethren, of the immense self-denial to which heaven was subjected! Think of that work which the family of the Divine Trinity; the glory of the Godhead, Father, Son, and Holy Spirit, combined to carry on with the greatest self-denial; and all this to save the soul! What a testimony is this to its value!

We learn here God's opinion of the value of the soul. Think on the self-denial on the part of the Father, that He could consent to send off His only and well-beloved Son as a missionary to this world. What must the inhabitants of heaven have thought of it? What a scene must there have been in heaven when the Son of the Eternal Father was prepared and sent off as a missionary to save this dying world!

We talk about missionaries to the heathen, and the self-denial they have to practice. We organize meetings when they are going to sail for distant climes that we may manifest our sympathy and mingle our tears with theirs, sing hymns to God, and pray together and give them our blessings and our prayers. All this is highly proper.

But what must have been the state of things when God announced in heaven that His Son was going on a missionary journey to this world to save us rebels by His blood! There must have been tears of grief, tears of inexpressible joy, sympathy for the inhabitants of this world, astonishment at the love of God, and wonder at the undertaking of the Son of God. The whole scheme, when it was first published in heaven, must have filled every part of that world with unutterable joy and sympathy. Oh, how many millions of hearts were united in sympathy with this wonderful mission that the Son of God had undertaken.

Notice! God has committed to each person one of these immortal souls. He has made provision for its eternal life, although it was doomed to die, and He has enjoined it upon each one to take care of his soul. He asks you, "What shall a man give in exchange for his soul? . . . For what is a man profited, if he shall gain the whole world, and lose his own soul?" (Matt. 16:26).

In every way God expresses His own idea of the infinite value of the soul. He has charged everyone to look to it, and to make it his first business to save it from eternal death. "Seek ye first the kingdom of God, and His righteousness" (Matt. 6:33); and those who do this are promised that they shall lose nothing by it for, "all other things shall be added unto you." Everything else that you need shall be thrown in, if you will only be careful not to lose your soul!

"Seek ye first the kingdom of God, and His righteousness." This is the charge that is given to everyone! God says, "I commit to you an immortal soul: take care you do not lose it! I prize it infinitely. I have given my Son to die for it. I love it with an everlasting love! But I cannot save it without your concurrence: I must have your consent. I must have your heart. I must have your sympathy. Take care that you do not lose it; but it is impossible to save it without your consent. Take care that you set about its salvation! Let this be your first, your great, your perpetual concern—the saving of your soul. Oh take care of it!"

But the infinite gift of salvation brings with it an added responsibility: an individual who receives this gift is held accountable not only for his own soul, but is charged with caring for those souls around him. Ministers, especially, have received this charge. "Son of man," says God, to every one of them, "I have set thee a watchman to the house of Israel: therefore hear the word at my mouth, and give them warning from me. When I say unto the wicked Thou shalt surely die; and thou givest him not warning, nor speakest to warn the wicked from his wicked way, to save his life; the same wicked man shall die in his iniquity, but his blood will I require at thine hand. Yet if thou warn the wicked, and he turn not from his wickedness, nor from his wicked way, he shall die in his iniquity, but thou hast delivered thy soul."

God has given a solemn charge to the church at large on this subject, and to each individual member of the church, not only to regard his own soul, but to watch, take care, remember, pray for, warn, and exhort, laboring for the souls of those around him. Christian parents, teachers, brothers, sisters, and all classes of Christians are to care for their own souls, and for the souls of those around them. "What I say unto one I say unto all, Watch."

God has also laid a charge upon all men to love their neighbors as themselves, to care for the souls of their neighbors as they would for their own. Every wicked man is bound to love God, to love the soul of his neighbor, and to love his own soul; and to neglect neither his own soul nor the souls of those under his influence.

The Blood of Sinners Is Never Silent

Plainly, we cannot be clear of the blood of souls unless we have done what we wisely and properly could to prevent their being lost. Of course, if we live in sin ourselves, we are guilty of our own blood. If we are in such a state, we cannot do our duty to others, and we are not clear of their blood. It may be useful to examine the different classes of duty which arise out of, and attach to, the various relations in which people stand.

Ministers, for instance, are public teachers, and as such they must be "instant in season, and out of season" (2 Tim. 4:2). Ministers must preach the truth, the whole truth, and nothing but the truth. They must lay themselves on the altar and not shun to declare the whole counsel of God. They must not keep back anything that is profitable to their hearers. They must select such truths as they think most needful to be known, and faithfully declare them. They must seek zealously to apply them to the hearts and consciences of those to whom they minister.

Further, they must live in such a manner as to show that they believe in their own hearts what they preach. They must not think that they will be clear from the blood of souls, merely because they publish the truth with their lips. They must preach also in their temper and life. They must be true and serious teachers in everything.

Church officers, deacons and others, also ought to consider their responsibility. Let them remember that it is great. They can be clear from the blood of souls only by living in such a manner as to be what they ought to be in every relation in which they sustain.

Parents have a great responsibility as well, for they exert a greater influence over their children than all the world beside. As a result, they will do more for or against the souls of their children than all other beings in the world. They begin the work of life or death, so far as influence is concerned, and also carry it on and ripen it. If their children are lost, because they have neglected to do their duty, their hands are red to the elbows with their children's blood!

Think of that! See that mother's hand? Has she been murdering her children? What is she about? She lives not, prays not, labors not for the salvation of her children! Oh, Mother! What are you about?

It is difficult, of course, to descend into all the relations of life to show how responsibility attaches itself to them all. But let what I have said be suggestive. You may apply it to Sunday school teachers, missionaries, brothers and sisters, young converts, and older Christians— each one sustains unique responsibilities.

No one can be guiltless of the blood of souls who does not do his duty, whatever it may be, who does not labor faithfully, as God shall give him an opportunity, and in the spirit and with the power with which God offers to clothe him for the salvation of souls.

To have a clear conscience in respect of this great matter is of inestimable value. For example, what an infinite consolation it must be to God the Father, Son, and Holy Spirit to know that nothing that could have been wisely and benevolently done for the salvation of people was omitted. Everything that could be done for this great end by an infinite and enlightened benevolence was done; nothing was omitted. So, when God sees the sufferings of the wicked of the whole universe, when He looks at them and pours His eye over them, and listens to their terrible wailings, just think of the consolation He will have in being able to say, "I am clear of their blood! I am clear! I call the universe to record that I am clear!"

I suppose this to be one of the great objects of the general judgment, that God, (if I may use such an expression) may clear His character, and vindicate His conduct in the presence of the entire universe; and bring all created intelligence to pronounce sentence of deserved damnation upon the wicked.

At the present, we cannot pronounce upon God's conduct any further than the law of our own intelligent consciousness affirms that He must be right, and so far as He has condescended to explain himself to us. But the time is coming when He will reveal everything to us. Every transaction of the divine government shall be disclosed at a period when suns and moons have ceased to rise and set; and days and years as we number them have ceased to cycle away; when people shall have ceased to grow, and their eyes are not dim with age, for they have ceased to die, and are immortal.

Then the time shall come to consider the whole matter. And God possesses the means, for His infinite mind has recorded all the facts; and thus He will bring into perfect remembrance the transactions of the entire universe from first to last. Doubtless, He will explain the reasons for His own conduct, and show the design He had in the creation, and in all the providential arrangements of His government.

Then every mouth shall be stopped, not one will be able to say a single word more of the impropriety of anything that God has done. The whole world will become guilty before God. Everything that He has done will receive the unanimous consent of the entire universe. They will declare that He is infinitely far from the least fault in all this matter, when He has placed everything in such a light that there can be no doubt of His perfect wisdom and benevolence. Then He will know that they know, as He now knows and will eternally know, that He has done all that infinite love, power and wisdom could do to save those immortal souls that He regarded as of such infinite value.

Suppose God's conscience condemns Him, that He knows He has done that which His own infinite mind must pronounce wrong and unbecoming in himself to do. Such a thought would fill His infinite mind with sorrow and remorse all through eternity, rolling onward and onward through a life of accumulating misery. Suppose He could accuse himself of any error, or wrong, or oversight, or anything that He should have attended to, or could have done wisely, but did not do, for the salvation of souls. It would fill His own mind with a pang that would really make it an infinite hell!

But there will be no such thing in the mind of God. The awfulness of that final moment of judgment will be weighed against His eternal clearness of consciousness, filling His infinite mind with satisfaction. When the universes look upon the ten thousand million of murdered souls, more than can ever be computed, who shall stand revealed at the day of judgment, the question will be asked, "Who has committed these murders?" God says, I am clear! The Father says, I am clear! The Son says, I am clear! The Holy Ghost says, I am clear! Now then, inquisition must be made for blood. Who has been guilty of this deed? What deeds of death are here? What dreadful things have been done? Who are the guilty parties?

Paul said to those to whom he had preached that they knew very well, from their own observation, that he was clear of their blood. He called upon them again to make a record of the fact that he might take it with him and use it at the solemn judgment, and confront them with it before the throne of God. He would prove by their own testimony that he was clear from the blood of them all. What consolation this is for a faithful minister!

It must be a dreadful thing on the other hand for an unfaithful minister to meet his people in the day of judgment! Indeed it is a dreadful thing for such a minister to leave a people amongst whom he has been laboring. Suppose he leaves them with conscious misgivings, or direct accusations, such as "You have been an unfaithful minister, you have been seeking your own popularity" (for his conscience may perhaps accuse him of that). Or "You have labored for filthy lucre, you have been indolent, you have truckled to the most false and pernicious sentiments; in short, you have not rightly represented God and His gospel, and have concealed the truth lest it should give offense to men." Suppose conscience speaks thus, "You have sought to create a reputation for yourself. You have not labored for the conversion of souls! Ah! you will soon have to die, and they to whom you have ministered also will depart into eternity."

How do you expect to meet these souls in the solemn judgment? You will have to meet them face to face. What a meeting that will be. Yes, we shall meet again. We shall meet at the bar of God, and see Him face to face. What will be the object of our meeting at that awful tribunal? Why, for God to tell the universe that He has done everything that He wisely could for the salvation of your souls; and you to give an account of the manner in which you have received or rejected His offers of mercy!

Now we are all going on, and will shortly appear before the great white throne, on which shall sit the Judge in terrible majesty, with the heavens and the earth all fleeing from His presence. Then the books shall be opened; yes, and all the dead shall be judged out of those books; and the sea shall give up its dead.

Never was I at sea but these words have come with solemn emphasis to my mind, and I expect that in a few days, when I am on the mighty waters, they will recur to me again. "The sea gave up the dead which were in it; and death and hell delivered up the dead which were in them" (Rev. 20:13). Ah! that will be a solemn time for ministers, for hearers, for parents, for children, for old and young. Yes, it will be a solemn time for all, for saints and sinners both. Ah! we must each give an account of himself to God. What a responsibility this is!

I was a pastor for eighteen years, and I have labored a great deal as an evangelist. Hundreds, maybe thousands, therefore, who have sat under my ministry, have gone before me into the eternal world. I shall follow them, and a great mass of others will follow me. By and by we shall all be congregated. And what then? I know that it is one thing to talk, and another thing to walk right up with open face before God, and take His judgment in the matter.

All secrets will then be laid open, the deepest intentions of the mind will be revealed; every motive of my heart, and every sermon that I have preached will be closely scanned and scrutinized. The truth upon every point will be brought up, and the whole universe will hear it. Ah, that will be a solemn time for me, for scores of thousands in America and in Great Britain will either have to face me down or I them. Think of that! I am not going to say all that Paul said.

It must be an awful thing for congregations to meet their ministers, those who have had pastors, or heard only occasional preaching. Brethren, think of it. I have often thought that of all the relations existing in this world, that of pastor and people is the most solemn; for God will surely make inquisition for blood. He must require this at someone's hand; and it will be a solemn time for the pastor if he is to blame.

No soul will be lost without the inquiry being made, "Who has done this deed? Who has shed this blood? Who has filled the world of hell with mourning, lamentation, and woe?" The cry will resound, loud and withering, *Who has done it?*

As I have said, the Father, Son, and Holy Ghost will say, *We have not done it.* Prophets and apostles will say, *We have not done it.* The faithful in all ages will say, *We have not done it.* Who then has been guilty of this dreadful and accursed deed? I will tell you who. First, the sinner has done it himself. Second, unfaithful ministers have done it; unfaithful deacons, elders, and leading members in the church have done it; unfaithful parents have done it; unfaithful children have done it; unfaithful brothers and sisters have done it; unfaithful Sunday school teachers have done it; in short, all unfaithful men have done it; they are red with the blood of souls.

You may know that they have been guilty of murder, for the blood of their victims is upon their garments. Cast your eyes upon them and behold. They are red from head to foot with the blood of men! All can see that they have done it. Everyone is covered with his neighbor's blood. The hands of countless men are imbued in the blood of their own soul, the souls of their children, or of their flocks, and all those to whom they have been unfaithful. Oh, brethren, I say again, just think of it! See that murderer standing over his victim, his weapons dripping blood; caught in the very act of murder; he cannot deny it, for blood is upon him.

But see the unfaithful minister in the day of judgment. He comes on to his trial, but he cannot look up. Those who sat under his ministry have caught sight of him, and they say to each other: "That is our minister. You remember his pretty tastes, his dazzling oratory, his graceful amblings, and his captivating blandishments. You remember about his pretty sermons, and you recollect how afraid he was to say *hell*, or let us know there was such a place. You recollect how he trimmed and truckled, how he opposed this thing and that thing, because it was not genteel. He was against all reform or progress in Christianity. Do you remember all that? Well, that was our minister." See him looking down. He is speaking, what does he say? What does he say? See the eye of the Judge looking through and through that unfaithful minister, that man who pretended to preach the gospel, and dealt deceitfully with souls. How much guilt there is upon him! What an awful thing that must be! How dreadful his position.

I have sometimes in my own experience had great searchings of heart on this matter, lest I should have preached myself instead of the gospel. Thousands of times when I have pressed myself close up, I have had fear lest the blood of souls was upon me. When I have heard that this man and that man was gone, who had sat under my ministry, I have often asked myself, "Have I done my duty by that man? Was I faithful? Or was I indolent? Did I shun to declare the whole counsel of God?"

I have often thought of this also (and I say it, not boastfully as you know), that I could say so far as I know myself I had never kept back what I thought the people needed most to know. I never kept back what I believed the people most needed to be told, because I was either afraid of them on the one hand or any other motive on the other. *I never had courage to keep back the truth.*

When people have said sometimes, "How dare you preach this thing and the other," I have told them that I had not courage to disobey God, and rush to the solemn judgment with the blood of souls on my hands. Indeed I have no such courage! *Whom should I fear, God or man?* How much faith must a man have if he cannot walk right up and tell the sinner the truth of God to his face. And if he cannot do this, how can he walk right up to the face of God and then give an account of himself to the great Searcher of hearts! He who is more afraid of men than of God must be an infidel.

I have already intimated that in the judgment sinners will find themselves without excuse. As in the case of Ezekiel, their blood will be upon their own head; but that is not all: it is also true that there may be moral guilt in not doing our duty, in our warning, praying, and laboring for our neighbors as we ought. I have also spoken of faithless ministers meeting their people at the day of judgment, and the disposition they will have to curse him.

I have sometimes wondered if their strong feelings of hate will find vent; whether there will be an audible expression of them. For example, whether at the judgment the multitude whom the unfaithful minister has misled will be permitted to give audible vent to the natural feelings of indignation that burn within their breasts; whether they will be allowed to curse him. They will be wicked enough and have reason enough, but will they be allowed to curse him? They have more reason to curse him, perhaps, than all the world beside. More reason to say, "O thou most accursed and wicked man, did you not trifle with my soul? Did I not look up to you as my religious teacher? Did I not yield myself up to your guidance; and did you not deceive me with lies, and by keeping from me the truth, by which I might have been saved?"

Such feelings will exist; but will the Judge permit them to find audible expression? If so, is it too much to suppose that they will hiss, and groan, and curse, while they weep and gnash their teeth! The same thing will doubtless also be true of parents.

But let me turn over this picture, and look upon another. What a meeting it will be when all the patriarchs, Abraham, Isaac, and Jacob; and the prophets, Elijah, and Elisha, and Isaiah, and Jeremiah, and Ezekiel, and all the minor prophets, and all the apostles, and faithful ministers of a later time shall assemble in heaven!

I have often thought of that wonderful convention that took place when the Savior was upon earth—the most wonderful, perhaps, that ever occurred in this world. You remember the history of the event we know as the Transfiguration. Christ took Peter, James, and John with Him up into a mountain and was transfigured before them, and there appeared Moses and Elijah—the two great representatives of the old dispensation. By Moses came the law, and Elijah represented the whole race of prophets; together they stood in conference with the Head of the Church Triumphant, about the death that He should accomplish at Jerusalem.

What a scene of wonder was that! We are told that the glory was so intense that the apostles were quite overcome, and Peter said, "It is good for us to be here: if thou wilt, let us make here three tabernacles; one for thee, and one for Moses, and one for Elias" (Matt. 17:4). They were so near heaven, so filled with awe and delight, that they knew not what they said.

Now just think for a moment how it will be by and by. Moses, for example, has been dead for thousands of years, and has long since become surrounded by a multitude who have found their way to heaven through his direct instruction, or by means of his writings that have been handed down from generation to generation.

All the saints will doubtless know Moses when they get there, of whom they have heard so much, as well as the patriarch Abraham, and the apostles and prophets. And when the newly arrived saint shall have a little time, after gazing at the wonders and glories of the place, he will look around for these ancient worthies, and perhaps shake them by the hand, and weep tears of gratitude and joy upon their necks.

Whitefield, and the multitudes who heard his voice, will meet in heaven. Think of that! How many thousands are gone that once saw and heard him. And they now find themselves again united in that blessed world as perfectly rational and intelligent beings, still able to mingle their hearts and their joys. The time will come when the whole Church of God, pastors and people, will be gathered home to glory.

Oh, how fast they are going. I have heard of the departure of some well-known ministers, together with this man and that man, names with which I am familiar. And so we are all following on, fathers, mothers, ministers, brothers, sisters, all are going. What a glorious thought that when we meet in that world of light and joy, the heavenly Jerusalem, it will be to part no more at all. Those of us who shall have washed our robes, and made them white in the blood of the Lamb, we shall meet to say farewell no more.

Notice now what happened shortly after Paul declared that he was pure from the blood of all men. "And when he had thus spoken, he kneeled down and prayed with them all. And they all wept sore, and fell on Paul's neck and kissed him, sorrowing most of all for the words which he spake, that they should see his face no more. And they accompanied him unto the ship."

What a beautiful parting. How deeply affecting. But I must not detain you. I have only to ask this of you, with all humility: may I not ask you who have been my hearers since I have been in London, as a matter of justice to record tonight this fact, that according to my ability I have dealt faithfully with your souls. I challenge you now to record this fact, for I am sure that you bear this testimony in your own consciences, will you bear it in mind at the solemn judgment, that so far as I have had ability, I have kept nothing back that you needed to know. I do not say this boastfully: God will judge between us.

But some I fear I shall leave in their sins after all. Remember, I shall meet *even you* again. Have you yet begun the great work of preparing for the judgment? If not, you have heard most solemn appeals and warnings. Let me ask you once more, will you think? Will you act? Will you rid me of all responsibility by saying, "Yes, yes, if I perish, it is not your fault, you have done your work faithfully, you have not daubed with untempered mortar, and I consent that the fact should be recorded in the solemn judgment that you are clear."

But I want not only to be able to feel the conviction of this in my own conscience, but that my record should be on high. I know it is vain for me to seek to justify myself, unless it is recorded in heaven that I have dealt faithfully with you. I trust I have. I shall see most of you probably no more, till we meet in the judgment; and oh, what a meeting that will be!

It is not my custom to preach farewell sermons, but when I have done my work, I must tear myself away, and leave the great Judge to seal up the record that shall be opened at the last day. Now all I have to say is this: the last leaf connected with my ministry, in this place, is now to be folded and put away amongst the files of eternity, to be exhibited when you and I shall stand before God in perfect light, with no self-excusing, no false pleas. We shall all be transparent, honest and open there.

And, now sinner, may I beg of God to search my own heart and prepare me for that scene, and to prepare you for it too. May I be allowed this once to call heaven and earth to record upon your souls, that in my weakness, and so far as I have had ability, I have set before you life and death, blessing and cursing, the gospel and the law, the rule of life? I have opened, so far as I have been able, the gate of mercy, and shown you the heart of Jesus. Will you accept it?

12

REGENERATION*

"Marvel not that I said unto thee, Ye must be born again" (John 3:7).

The context of the passage is probably familiar to you:

There was a man of the Pharisees, named Nicodemus, a ruler of the Jews: the same came to Jesus by night, and said unto him, "Rabbi, we know that thou art a teacher come from God: for no man can do these miracles that thou doest, except God be with him." Jesus answered and said unto him, "Verily, verily, I say unto thee, except a man be born again, he cannot see the kingdom of God." Nicodemus saith unto him, "How can a man be born when he is old? Can he enter the second time into his mother's womb, and be born?" Jesus answered, "Verily, verily, I say unto thee, except a man be born of water and of the Spirit, he cannot enter into the kingdom of God. That which is born of the flesh is flesh; and that which is born of the Spirit is spirit. Marvel not that I said unto thee, Ye must be born again. The wind bloweth were it listeth, and thou hearest the sound thereof, but canst not tell whence it cometh and whither it goeth: so is every one that is born of the Spirit." Nicodemus answered and said unto him, "How can these things be?" Jesus answered and said unto him, "Art thou a master of Israel, and knowest not these things?" In other words, "Are you a Jewish doctor and do not understand the doctrine of the new birth? Have you never experienced it? A teacher in Israel, and yet ignorant of this great truth?" (John 3:1–10)

What the New Birth Is Not

I am well aware that many are apt to form very false ideas concerning the new birth. Therefore, we must consider what regeneration is not.

---

*From *The Penny Pulpit*, preached on Wednesday evening, November 21, 1849, at Borough Road Chapel, Southwark.

First, the new birth does not consist in the creation of any new faculty, either of mind or of body. Both Christians and sinners have the same powers and faculties both of mind and body. Sinners do not need any new faculties. Sinners only need to use those faculties that they already possess, in the manner in which God requires them to be used. They need no other powers of mind or body than those they have. And God requires them to have no other powers than those created in them. Consequently, the new birth cannot include or imply the creation of any new powers of either body or mind.

Second, the new birth does not change the capacity or structure of any of the powers of the body or the mind. In regeneration there is no change in the structure of the human faculties, nor does God require any such change. What change is needed in any power either of mind or body? None! Then, no such change occurs in regeneration or the new birth.

Third, the new birth does not imply any change in the feelings of the mind that produce a change in a man's actions. By this I mean that regeneration is not a change that is introduced into the sensibilities or feelings. To be sure, new feelings arise in the mind. However, these new feelings do not *constitute* regeneration, nor do they *produce* regeneration.

Fourth, regeneration does not consist in any change in which man is purely passive. Regeneration or the new birth does not consist in any change in which man has no voluntary agency himself.

What the New Birth Is

The Scriptures represent the new birth, or regeneration, to be *a change of character*—a change from sinfulness to holiness. Now, there must be some voluntary action on the part of the sinner, or there will not be a change of his moral character. If he is passive, there will be no change of character. What do we mean by moral character, and how is a man's character changed? The character depends upon the will, and when a man's will is changed his character is changed. Regeneration, then, is not involuntary, but a change of *will*, and thereby a change of *character*—a departing from a state of sinfulness to a state of holiness.

How much virtue would there be in an *involuntary* holiness, a state into which man should be brought independently of his own consent, in which he has no agency? Certainly none at all. Regeneration, then, must take place when man's will is something more than passive. It is true that in regeneration man is a recipient—and a passive recipient, if you will, in a certain sense—of the divine influence. But this divine influence, instead of superseding man's own agency, is only employed in bringing about that change *by* his agency, which constitutes regeneration.

The Bible represents regeneration as consisting in a change of character, as the beginning of a new and holy life. Regeneration is often spoken of as a new creation. But this does not mean the creation, literally, of a new nature. The new birth is a change of character, and not a change in the substance of the soul or body. The new birth is only a change in *the use* of the soul or body.

How did Adam and Eve pass from a state of holiness into a state of sinfulness? It is commonly believed that Adam and Eve were holy before they sinned, but when they sinned, they passed from a state of holiness to a state of sinfulness. Now this was certainly a change of heart in them. They could not have sinned without their hearts being changed, without a total change of moral character. Now, how was this change produced? What power brought them from a state of holiness to a state of sinfulness? Did their conduct produce in them a change of substance, a change of nature, or was it a voluntary change?

The Bible gives us a very clear and plain account of the Fall. When they were holy, they regarded God as supreme, and yielded themselves up to Him in a voluntary obedience. God had, for certain good reasons, prohibited their eating of a certain fruit. He had given them an appetite for fruit, and there was nothing sinful in their gratifying that appetite with any other kind of fruit. But they should not eat the fruit that was forbidden. They had indulged this appetite many times before with fruits they were allowed to eat, without sin.

They also had a constitutional desire for knowledge. Under certain circumstances and upon certain conditions, it was lawful for them to gratify this desire and to seek knowledge.

Now Satan suggested to Eve that God was selfish in having prohibited them from eating the forbidden fruit. "For," said he, "God doth know that in the day ye eat thereof, then your eyes shall be opened, and ye shall be as gods knowing good and evil" (Gen. 3:5). And when Eve saw that the fruit was pleasant to the eyes, and calculated to make one wise, she took and ate of it, and gave some also to her husband, and he ate.

Now, by this act did they change their constitutions or their natures? Or, did they simply withdraw their allegiance from God, and in spite of His requirements give themselves up to their own appetites in a prohibited manner? They placed more practical stress upon the gratification of their appetites than in obeying God. They esteemed the gratification of their appetites as the highest good.

Observe, their appetites were not sinful in and of themselves. If they had regulated their appetites by the will of God, all would have been well. But they changed their own hearts. This was a change in relation to the disposition of their minds. Instead of preferring God's command to their own gratification, they came to prefer their own gratification to God's authority and the interests of His kingdom.

What would have been regeneration in Adam and Eve? Suppose God had come to them immediately after they had sinned and required this: "You must be born again, or you cannot see the kingdom of God." If they had inquired, "What is it to be born again?" What would have been God's natural response? Would He have said that they must have some new faculty, some newly implanted appetites, and undergo a change of nature? What was the matter with their nature? Just a moment before they were living in holiness and in obedience to God. Now they had withdrawn their obedience from Him and yielded themselves to the obedience of their own gratification and appetites.

Now, what does God require of them? Why, that they come back again to the state in which they had been previously and consecrate themselves again to God. Instead of committing themselves to their own gratification in spite of God's authority, as they had done by this act, they should reverse this state of things and devote themselves again once and forever to the authority and service of God.

Regeneration, then, must consist in a change of the disposition of the mind and a voluntary consecration to God. Observe, when they withdrew allegiance from God, and in spite of God's authority committed themselves to the gratification of their appetites, this constituted a fundamental change in their characters. They could not do the thing they did without deliberately preferring their own gratification to obeying God. Committing themselves to sin, then, must have constituted in them an entire change in character.

Regeneration consists in a change in the ultimate intention or purpose of an individual's life. In regeneration, the mind withdraws itself from self-seeking and chooses a higher end. The disposition is changed from supreme selfishness to a devotion of the whole being to the great end for which God lives and for which He made man to live. Regeneration, then, consists in ceasing to live for sin and selfishness, and beginning to live for God.

The Implications of Regeneration

First, in regeneration the mind receives new and more impressive views of truth through the Holy Spirit. In this way, the regenerated receive a clear and vastly more impressive view of their relationship to God, as well as a clearer picture of the real nature of sin and holiness, of their duty to God and of other great truths that are indispensably associated with regeneration. By the influence of the Holy Spirit, they gain a new and more impressive perception of these truths.

This, I suppose, is implied in the new birth as a *condition of it*.

Second, new views of truth and Christianity are implied as *resulting from regeneration*. For example, when people have withdrawn from devotion to themselves and selfish objects, and have devoted themselves to God, they naturally become different people. Before, they viewed everything in a selfish light, and so they acquired a liking for nothing but that which, according to their own views, furthered their selfish ends. They cared for God only so far as they thought He might be useful to them.

All their views were selfish. If they feared God at all, it was only because they feared being made miserable by Him. Or, if they obeyed Him, such obedience was the result of some selfish principle: they hoped to gain some sort of gratification by it.

Every unregenerate person looks at all things in a selfish light. Whatever he imagines will promote his interests, he seeks and loves.

But, when a person is born again, he withdraws himself from seeking his own interests as the supreme good. He has consecrated himself to God; and, as a necessary result of this, he will sympathize with everything that is calculated to promote the interests of God's kingdom. The change that has taken place in his mind causes him to have new views and feelings concerning his relationship to God.

He now strives to promote God's glory and extend His kingdom by making known His will. Before, selfish interests ruled his conduct, and self-gratification was his law; nothing but self interested him. But now, he has come into an entirely different state of mind. He has devoted himself to another end, and he looks upon all things from another point of view, and estimates their value differently.

What constitutes the particular difference between an unregenerate and a regenerated person? There is no change in his physical structure, either of body or mind. So far as substance is concerned, there is no change: but the attitude of his mind is entirely and radically changed. This change of mind will manifest itself in his life; for the *will* controls the *actions* of the body. If I *will* to move my arms they must move, unless there is some opposing force stronger than my will. A change in the will necessarily produces a change in the life.

Third, it follows that a new life results from regeneration. A new outward life is not regeneration, but it results from the new birth, as an effect from a cause. A person devoted to God is engaged in pursuits different from what he did before. Or if engaged in the same pursuits, he acts from a different spirit and motive.

Is he a merchant? When he was a sinner his ruling motive in trade was selfishness: the spirit of self-gratification was supreme in all that he did. But now, his merchandise is God's. The things that he possesses are not his own. He is God's clerk, or steward, and he will not cheat anyone, for he knows that God does not want his servants to cheat. He transacts business for God; and, as he knows in his heart that God hates cheating, he will naturally be honest. If he is not honest, he is not a regenerate man. If his heart is honest, his life will be honest. And so, when regeneration occurs a person's whole life will be marked by honesty.

Fourth, implied in regeneration is a new sort of sympathy and feelings. Before, the sympathies and feelings were all enlisted in one direction, the direction of self. You see a person in this state, and you try to excite him to the performance of some generous action, but you cannot do it unless you can employ selfish motives as a means to accomplish your object. His self-interests are easily excited. Show him how much he can get by acting in the way you desire, and you may succeed, but in no other way. All appeals to higher motives will fail. It is remarkable to what an extent this feeling of selfishness will develop itself.

Make an appeal to an unregenerate person's benevolence, and your appeal has no effect, because his interests, he thinks, are not concerned in it. But make an appeal to his selfishness, and you can excite the deepest foundation of his being. Talk to him about God and Christ, and the Christian faith, and his relations to God, and his sensibilities are not at all excited: his sympathies do not lie in that direction at all. If you tell him of his sins, he does not feel them, and can listen to the enumeration of them without emotion. But at length his mind is changed, and now he lives for other interests.

Now, instead of being devoted to *self*, he is devoted to *God*, and everything relating to God and His kingdom reaches his sensibilities and stirs up the fountains of feeling in him. Talk to him now about God's glory and the interests of souls, spread out the world before him and show him the condition of mankind, and be assured you will move him!

Before, if you expected to get any money from him you must show him how he would benefit by it; now he has made God's interests his own interests, and he sympathizes with God, and with Christ, and he has set his heart upon promoting those interests which shall glorify God and benefit man. Now, only show him the great field of Christian enterprise, and you fire his soul with love to men, and fill him with a desire to promote the kingdom and glory of God in the world. He has consecrated himself and all that he has to these things.

I have often been struck with the beautiful process that goes on in the soul as the Christian grows in grace. Sometimes I have looked upon an old saint, who for many years has been thinking of, and bathing his mind in, the great truths of the gospel. He has had so much communion and sympathy with God that he has become beautifully and sweetly mellow. So delicate, so kind, and so Christlike were the feelings he would manifest, that I have many times been charmed and cheered with the character of a fully developed Christian.

Fifth, in regeneration a great change takes place in the joys and sorrows, and hopes and fears of the soul that has experienced the change. The joys of such a one are of a new sort. Before, he would rejoice greatly in the prospect of earthly good. Now, he rejoices chiefly in seeing and hearing that the work of God is progressing in the land.

He will rejoice to be told that God is pouring out His Spirit, and that souls are brought to Christ. This to him is an entirely new sort of joy. Before, he could take up a newspaper, and if it contained any account of a revival of Christianity, he did not read it. But now when he finds such an article in a newspaper, instead of passing it by, he will eagerly run his eye over the page, producing in him inexpressible joy and delight: his whole being will be moved.

So with sorrow, new objects call it forth. He was accustomed to sorrow chiefly when some worldly loss had been sustained, because it stood closely connected with his own interests. But now let him know that some professing Christian has backslidden, and he is more grieved at that than at all the earthly losses that he ever met with. He is now deeply sorry when he sees professing Christians live in sin, more so than at the worldly troubles and losses that he has ever endured.

Sixth, regeneration implies repentance for past sin and implicit confidence in the Lord Jesus Christ. The new birth implies peace of mind, which cannot be obtained without repentance and faith in Christ; because the elements of discord are always stirring within the minds of the unregenerate. But when they withdraw from the course that their consciences disprove, and devote themselves to the end for which they were made, all the workings of their minds harmoniously blend together and produce peace. There are no stirrings of conscience against their present course: all the powers and faculties within are in harmony. In addition, there is fellowship with God and communion with the Holy Ghost.

Seventh, regeneration implies a state of self-denial. Now, when I say self-denial I do not mean the breaking off from some outward customs and habits in which you have been accustomed to indulge, that you take off some showy articles of dress and wear plainer attire; or that you be a little more temperate, or a good deal more temperate. Self-denial does not belong to the outward selfish appetites.

It is right to eat and drink, but we are to do both to the glory of God, that we may have strength to serve Him. So with respect to all our appetites and propensities, they are to be properly employed to serve the purposes for which they were bestowed, but we are not to make their gratification the business and goal of life.

Eighth, regeneration implies that the mind has new motives of action. I use the term *motive* in the sense of design or intention. We sometimes ask what a person's *motives* are for doing such and such, when we mean his *reasons* for doing them. Sometimes we mean by the question, what is his *design* or *aim*? I use the term *motive* in the second sense of the word. I say, therefore, that the regenerate man now acts from motives opposite to what he did before. This is the great radical change that has taken place, and he is now pursuing a radically different course and end.

Before, his own personal gratification and interests, and those of his family, were the ends for which he lived, moved and had his being. Whatever he did, it was with a view to this end; because of this, everything was radically wrong. Whether he went to prayer meeting or read his Bible, the end in view was the promotion of his own interests. No matter what he did, it was sin and only sin continually. But now he has become regenerated: the design of his mind is to promote other interests and to pursue a radically different end. He gives himself to God, and lives, moves, breathes, and has his being for God and godliness.

Suppose we took an opposite view and affirmed that regeneration consists in a change of nature. Now, I know that the Bible sometimes speaks of regeneration as a change of nature, but we suppose that such language is figurative. We sometimes say of people, how natural it is for them to do certain things. By saying this we mean that they are devoted to this end whatever it may be. Now when a person is pursuing a new end, we say he is a new man; that is, his way of life is changed, his end of being is changed.

But, suppose that we should say that regeneration is a change of nature or of substance; that something new is infused into the person that becomes united with the substance of either his mind or body; what must be the consequence? Is this a change in the moral character? If it is something that God has created within man, and with which man has nothing to do, it cannot imply a change of moral character.

Furthermore, does it imply the power of backsliding from God? Can a man, in such a condition, be a backslider? Can he fall from grace if God has changed his nature? I am astonished to hear people contend that this is the case; that individuals undergo a change of nature in regeneration, and yet they can alter their course and fall from grace. But how is it possible? Who has changed their nature back again? Did God or Satan change it?

It is true, no doubt, of all sinners, that when they have once given themselves up to pursue certain ends, their sympathies, feelings and dispositions become so corrupted that they are naturally led to live sinful and selfish lives. And so when a man is regenerated, it becomes a kind of second nature for him to do right. But still, literally, man has not received a change of nature.

Regeneration Is Necessary for Salvation

Regeneration is very strongly insisted on in the text. When Christ taught Nicodemus the necessity of the new birth, the Pharisee was greatly surprised, and Christ said, "Marvel not that I said unto thee, Ye must be born again." It is no new doctrine that I teach, and you ought, as a doctor in Israel, to know that it is not. No man should marvel at such a plain doctrine, and you least of all.

In considering the necessity for this change, I remark, in the first place, that the unregenerate part of mankind is first of all selfish. No one could *practically* deny this. If someone should proceed to do business upon the assumption that people are not selfish, a commission on lunacy would no doubt be appointed to examine him. And if they did that, who would hesitate to bring the verdict that he was not fit to manage his own affairs? The fact is, all the arrangements of society proceed upon the assumption, which is a fact, that people are devoted to their own interests, and quite regardless of the interests of others.

Now, do you ask how it came to pass that people are selfish? Why, the principle grows up with us almost from our birth. As soon as the appetites and passions of children are sufficiently developed, they employ their wills to seek the gratification of their appetites and passions. They become devoted to the gratification of self.

I suppose you will admit that God is not selfish. A selfish mind is not at rest within itself. People were not made to be selfish, and no one can be satisfied and happy while he is selfish. No one can be at peace with himself while he is pursuing solely his own interests. We were created so that when our minds are selfish we cannot be happy.

Now, suppose that the inhabitants of heaven were selfish. All their interests would be conflicting. Laws would be needed to restrain them from encroaching upon each other's rights, because their sympathies would not blend. The same difficulties would exist there as here, only in a much higher degree. There would be striving and crushing and overreaching. Everyone would be at war with his brother.

Such a community as that can never possess heaven. In order to be saved, then, in order to be happy in heaven, people must really experience a radical change in the end for which they live. They must renounce self-interest, and they must recognize God's authority and interests as supreme. They must love their brother as they do themselves. They must set up a common interest and a common love. Heaven is a place where all is unity and harmony, where there is no selfishness, where God's will is the universal law, and where the interest of one is the interest of all. Now it is easy to see that regeneration would counteract the selfishness of man's being.

Just look at a world of selfish beings with all the restraints of law, and with ten thousand pulpits preaching against selfishness, the press groaning with articles against selfishness, and large numbers of colporteurs running hither and thither with Bibles protesting selfishness; and yet, there is still an immense amount of selfishness that exists in the world, after all. And now, when people are told that they must be born again, they don't understand it.

They have the same false conception of it that Nicodemus had. They do not consider that unless there is a radical change of character, they cannot possess and enjoy heaven. Put a selfish person into heaven, and what will he do there? Why, he will ask if there is any way of making money, any way of making a speculation to his advantage. Heaven, then, is no place for selfish beings.

So, how are people to get to heaven? You tell them they need a change of heart, and they agree that they may need some change, but they do not see the necessity of a radical change of disposition and character. Nevertheless, it is a great truth: unless people cease to be selfish and become benevolent in their dispositions, there is no place for them in heaven. If the selfish person could get there, the holiness and benevolence of heaven would be intolerable to him. His selfish nature would cry out against it, for God is not selfish, the angels are not selfish, the saints in glory are not selfish.

Now, do let me ask you, are you selfish? Have you always lived to please yourself? If so, is it not the most self-evident truth in the universe that unless a change takes place in the end for which you live, you never can sympathize with the inhabitants of heaven?

Suppose that it were possible for you, with a selfish heart, to join in the worship of heaven, to live among those that were not selfish, but perfectly benevolent. What sympathy would you have there? Would it be the delight of your heart to mingle your song with theirs? Could you mingle in their joys, and find pleasure in their pursuits? Never! Your sensibilities do not lie in that direction: your mind is not there! Your heart is not there! You would need to be restrained, or you would spring over the battlements of heaven and go down to hell in order to get out of such holy and benevolent company.

You can see what an infinite mistake those persons have made who make Christianity hard and grievous, for it is never grievous to pursue that upon which your heart is set. Yet a great many religious adherents find it very hard to attend to the duties of the Christian faith. *I have no heart*, they say, *to go to church, but I must not stay away, I must not omit this duty!* And so they do it, but find no satisfaction in it.

Why, friend, you have made a mistake! You have attempted to serve God without giving Him your heart! You have attempted to serve the Lord without consecrating yourself to the great end for which you ought to live! Just let your heart go first, and your life will follow without all this great effort and trouble. If your heart is right, you will not need to put a strong rein upon yourself to keep you from cheating your neighbor. Your aim will then be to do him good. You will love him as you love yourself.

What people need to do is this: turn their minds to God and begin a new life. They must retrace their steps and reverse their minds completely with respect to the great call for which they ought to live.

Those who call in question the necessity of the change, which the Bible says is essential, are entirely unreasonable. Regeneration is as truly a doctrine of natural religion as it is a doctrine of revealed religion. By rejecting the Bible, people need not suppose that they can reject the doctrine of regeneration, for they must either deny the natural state of man, or they must deny that the inhabitants of heaven are holy before they can reject this.

Natural religion itself teaches that some great and radical change is needed—hence the everlasting restlessness of man. Do we not know that all the pains that people take to engross themselves with worldly objects indicate that they are ill at ease with their moral character and conduct? The fact is, they admit the necessity of a radical change in their characters. They never can rest where they are; hence, the Bible represents them as like "the troubled sea, when it cannot rest, whose waters cast up mire and dirt" (Isa. 57:20).

Many have got such ideas of regeneration that when God calls upon them to become new creatures, they wait for God to change their hearts. They expect to have something done to them, resembling an electric shock. So they wait, instead of breaking away at once from their selfishness and coming to Christ.

How divine influence is communicated to man is, by the nature of it, a mystery. The influence is felt, though it remains unseen. Every Christian knows that he has been born again. He knows that he gave himself up to the influence of certain truths when the Spirit began to operate upon his mind, revealing the truth to him. And he was so influenced that his desires and disposition were changed, and he gave himself up wholly to God.

Where the truth is apprehended, people have no cause to wait for anything. God requires them to act: "Turn ye, turn ye, why will ye die?" When they are waiting for something else, they overlook the fact that God is doing the very thing they need.

The mind is highly involved in regeneration. It must be so, or regeneration is not a virtuous action. After regeneration, the mind acts more intelligently than it ever did before, for the decision regarding regeneration was the first truly rational act it can make. The soul now comes to act in view of God's truth and in harmony with God's will, His interests, and His authority. Is regeneration, then, to be called fanaticism or mysticism; and to be branded as something unintelligible? I trust that you will say, No!

Have you been born again? Do you see the necessity if it? Do you see what you are to do? You must cease to live for self and begin living for God's glory, recognizing solely His authority and set your heart upon Him. You must not cleave for salvation to any works of your own, but when God draws you, as He is doing now, you are to say, "Speak, Lord; for thy servant heareth" (1 Sam. 3:9). You are to answer the invitation of God as Paul answered, "Lord, what wilt thou have me to do?" (Acts 9:6). You must recognize Christ's authority, and you must do whatever Christ tells you to do.

Why not make up your mind and come to God at once? There will never be a better time! Why not renounce self now, and make a new heart and a new spirit? Do you ask, "Can I do that?" Certainly, you can. Suppose Adam and Eve had asked, "Can we make ourselves new hearts?" Why, God might have said, "Did you not just do it? But a little while ago, you had holy hearts that were consecrated to me. Now you have withdrawn your allegiance. Have you not, by that act, just created *wicked* hearts? This was your own act, and I only require you to undo what you have just done."

And now, I may safely promise you, if you consecrate yourself to Him, God will not condemn you for your lack of regeneration. If you make up your mind to renounce all your self-interests as the end of life, and freely devote your powers to God, you are safe in a state of regeneration. Remember I am not denying that God has something to do with your regeneration and salvation. God draws you, and your duty is, when He draws, to say, "Yes, Lord, I consent to take thy dear, easy yoke and do thy will. I will do it, Lord, and do it now. I do it once for all and forever. Thy will shall be my everlasting and universal law."

PART 2

The Call of God; the Capacity of Man

"I have set before you life and death . . ."
(Deut. 30:19).

13

THE SINNER'S NATURAL POWER AND MORAL WEAKNESS*

". . . of whom a man is overcome, of the same is he brought in bondage" (2 Peter 2:19).

All people are naturally free, and none the less so for being sinners. They naturally have freedom of will.

By natural freedom I do *not* mean that they have a *right* to do as they please; for this is by no means true. Nor do I mean that they are free agents merely in the sense of being able to *do* as they will to do. In fact, people sometimes can and sometimes cannot execute their purposes of will; be this as it may, moral liberty does not consist in the *power* to accomplish one's own purposes. You are aware that some old philosophers defined liberty of will as "the power to do what you will to do." For many reasons, this cannot be the true idea of freedom of the will.

Consider the department of *doing* that is demonstrated in muscular action. The simple fact is that some of our muscles respond involuntarily, while others are controlled by the will by a law of the sternest necessity.

In regard to this latter class, all the freedom of the muscles is controlled by the will—not by the muscles themselves. It is then a sheer mistake to deny the location of the source of freedom, and to credit it to another source. If there is any such thing as *necessity* in the universe, it is found in the absolute control held by the will over those physical muscles that are placed under its control. The obedience of the muscles is absolute—not free or voluntary in any sense what-

---

Sermons on Gospel Themes, 192–203.

ever. Hence, we may draw a parallel concerning human freedom as well.

This freedom is in the will itself, and consists in its power of free choice. To do, or not to do, this is its option. It has by its own nature the function to determine its own volitions. The soul wills to do or not to do, and thus is a moral sovereign over its own activities. This fact is foundational to *moral agency*. A being so constituted that he can will to do or not to do, and moreover has knowledge and appreciation of his moral obligations, is a moral agent. None other can be.

Every person knows that he has a conscience that tells him how he ought to act; he can either heed or repel the admonitions of this moral power. Furthermore, that a person is free in the sense of determining his own activities is proved by each person's own consciousness. This proof requires no chain of reasoning. It is strong as need be without any reasoning at all. A person is just as much aware of originating his own acts as he is of acting at all. Does he really act himself? Yes. And does he *know* that he acts himself? Yes. *How* does he know these things? By his consciousness. He has the same evidence of being free: for this is equally proved by his own consciousness.

People can distinguish between those acts in which they are free, and those in which they are acted upon by influences independent of their own choice. A person knows that in some things he is a recipient of influences and actions exerted upon himself, while in other things he is not a recipient in the same sense, but a voluntary actor. The fact he is able to discriminate between these things proves the possession of free agency.

The difference between these two sources of influence is one of everyday consciousness. Sometimes a person cannot tell where his thoughts come from. Impressions are made upon his mind, the origin of which he cannot trace. They may be from above or beneath: he knows but little of their source, and little about them, except that they are not his own free volitions. Of his own acts of will there can be no such uncertainty. He knows their origin. He knows that they are the product of an original power in himself, for the exercise of which he is compelled to hold himself primarily responsible.

Not only does he have this direct consciousness, but he has, as already suggested, the testimony of his own conscience. This faculty, by its very nature, takes cognizance of his moral acts, requiring certain acts of will and forbidding others. This faculty is an essential condition of free moral agency. Possessing it, and also his other mental powers, he must be free to act upon them, though he is under moral obligation.

It is inconceivable that a person should be under moral law and government without the power of free moral action. The logical condition of the existence of a conscience in a person is that he should be free to act upon it.

That man is free is evident from the fact that he is conscious of praise or blameworthiness. He could not reasonably blame himself unless it were a first truth that he is free. By a first truth, I mean one that is known to all by a necessity of their own nature. There are such truths—those that none can help knowing, however much they may desire to ignore them. Now unless it were a first truth, necessarily known to all, that man is free, he could not praise or blame himself.

As conscience implies moral agency, so, where there is a conscience, it is impossible for people really to deny moral responsibility. People cannot help but blame themselves for wrongdoing. Conscious of the pangs of conscience against the act, how can they evade the conviction that the act is wrong?

Again, the Bible always treats people as free agents, commanding them to do or not to do as if they had all the power required to obey such commands. A young minister once said to me, "I preach that men *ought* to repent, but never that they *can*."

"Why not preach also that they can?" I said.

He replied, "The Bible does not affirm that they *can*."

To this I said that even human legislatures, having required certain acts, do not proceed to affirm that its subjects have the *power to obey*. The very fact that the requirement has been fixed is the strongest possible affirmation in the belief that the subjects are *able* to do the things required. If the lawmakers did not think so, how could they reasonably require it? The very first assumption to be made concerning good rulers is that they have common sense and common honesty. To assert, virtually, that God lacks these qualities, is blasphemous.

Freedom of will lies among the earliest and most resistless convictions. Probably no one living can remember his first idea of *oughtness*; that is, his first convictions of right and wrong. It is also among our most irresistible convictions.

We assume the freedom of our own will from the very first. The little child affirms it in his first infantile efforts to accomplish his purposes. Watch him reach forth to get his food or his playthings. The little machinery of a freely acting agent begins to play long before he can understand it. He begins to act on his own responsibility long before he can estimate what or how great this responsibility is. The fact of personal responsibility is fastened on us; we might as well escape from ourselves as from this conviction.

Sinners Are in Moral Bondage

While it is true that people have the attribute of moral liberty, it is equally true that they are morally *enslaved*; that is, in moral bondage. Moral liberty was created in them; their bondage comes by voluntary perversion and abuse of this liberty.

The Bible represents people as being in bondage—as having the power to resist the temptation to sin, yet yielding to those temptations voluntarily. As our dough-faced politicians might, but will not, resist the demands of those running the slave trade, so is the bondage of sinners under temptation. The Bible represents Satan as ruling the hearts of people at his will, just as the men who wield the slave power of the South rule the North, dictating the choice of our presidents as well as the entire legislation of the federal government. As Satan ruled Eve in the garden; so he now "worketh in the children of disobedience" (Eph. 2:2).

What the Bible thus represents, experience proves to be true. Wicked people *know* that they are in bondage to Satan. Who do you think puts it into the heart of young people to plot iniquity and drink it in like water? Is it not the devil? Many young people, when tempted, seem to have no moral stamina to resist, but are swept away by the first gust of temptation.

People are in bondage to their appetites. Excited appetites lead them away, as they led Eve and Adam. What can be the reason that some people find it so hard to give up the use of tobacco? They know the habit is filthy and disgusting. They know it must injure their health. But appetite craves, and the devil enforces its demands. The poor victim makes a feeble effort to deliver himself, but the devil turns the screw again and holds him the tighter, and then drags him back to a harder bondage.

It is the same when a person is in bondage to alcohol, and with every form of sensual indulgence. Satan helps on the influence of sensuality, and does not care much what the particular form it takes, provided its power is strong enough to ruin the soul. It all plays into his hand and promotes his main purpose.

Some people are in bondage to the love of money, or to the fashions of the world, or to the opinions of mankind. By these they are enslaved and led on in the face of the demands of duty. Every person who is enslaved is led to abandon his convictions of duty. He is free only when he acts in accordance with those convictions. This is the true idea of liberty.

Only when reason and conscience control the will is a man free— for God made people intelligent and moral beings to act normally; that is, under the influence of their own enlightened conscience and reason. This is the freedom God exercises and enjoys; none can be higher or nobler. But when a moral agent is in bondage to his low appetites and passions, and is induced by them to disregard the dictates of his conscience and reason, he is simply a galley slave to a very hard and cruel master.

God made people to be free, giving them just such mental powers as they need in order to control their own activities, as a rational being should wish to. Their bondage, then, is altogether voluntary. They *choose* to resist the control of reason, and submit to the control of appetite and passion.

Every unrepentant sinner is conscious of being in bondage to temptation. What person, not saved from sin through grace, does not know that he is an enigma to himself? I have little respect for anyone who says he was never ashamed of himself, and never found himself doing things he could not well account for.

Especially I should be ashamed and afraid, too, if I were to hear a student say he had never been impressed with a sense of his moral weakness. Such ignorance would only show his utter lack of reflection, and his consequent failure to notice the most obvious moral phenomena of his inner life. What! Does he not know that his weakest desires carry his will in spite of the strongest convictions of his reason and conscience.

Being in bondage to sin and temptation is a most guilty state, because it is so altogether voluntary, so needless, and so opposed to the dictates of a person's reason and understanding, and so opposed to his own understanding of God's righteous demands. To go counter to such convictions, he must be supremely guilty.

Of course such conduct is detrimental to a person's welfare, for the sinner acts in a manner most decidedly opposed to his own best interests. He will ruin himself, because the course he is pursuing is of all others best adapted to destroy both body and soul. How, then, can it be considered anything but suicidal? He practically denies all moral obligation. And yet he knows the fact of his moral obligation, and denies it in the face of his clearest convictions.

Many times I have asked sinners how they could account for their own conduct. The honest ones answer, "I cannot at all; I am an enigma to myself." The real explanation is, while they were created as free moral agents; yet, by the infatuation of sin they have sold themselves into moral bondage, and are really slaves to Satan and their own lusts.

Bondage to sin and temptation is a state of deep moral degradation. Intrinsically it is most disgraceful. Everybody feels this in regard to certain forms of sin and classes of sinners. We all feel that drunkenness is beastly. We regard a drunkard with revulsion as we see him reeling about, mentally besotted and reeking in his own filth. Surely we must ask pardon of all beasts for this comparison, for none of them are so mean and so vile as this drunkard—not one excites in our bosom such a sense of voluntary degradation. Compared with the self-besotted drunkard, from our human standpoint, any beast is a noble creature.

But there is another and a better standpoint. How do *angels* look upon this self-made drunkard? They see in him one made only a little lower than themselves, and one who might have aspired to companionship with them; yet he chose rather to sink himself down to a level with swine! Oh, how their souls must recoil from the sight of such self-induced degradation! To see the noble intellect discarded; and yet nobler moral qualities disowned and trodden underfoot, as if they were only an incumbrance. This is too much for angels to bear. How they must feel!

Nor is the drunkard alone in the contempt that his sensual degradation entails. See the tobacco-smoker. The correct taste of community demands that by conventional laws he be excluded from parlors, steamboat-cabins, first-class rail-cars, churches, and indeed all really decent places. Yet, for the sake of this low indulgence, the smoker is willing to descend to the indecent places.

See him leave his place among respectable people in the rail-car, and herd with rowdies in the smoking-car, for the sake of his filthy indulgence. If he were only obliged to ride all day in the lower society, to which he sinks himself by this indulgence, it might admonish him of the cost of his sensuality! It might help to open his eyes!

I have taken these forms of sensual indulgence as illustrations of the real degradation of sin. In these cases, those who practice such sins are consigned to places that bespeak the low form of self-indulgence to which they are attached.

If we only saw things in their right light, we should take the same view of the moralist who said, "How can I act from regard to God or to the right? How can I go to meetings from the high motive of pleasing God? I can go from a desire to promote my own selfish ends, but how can I go for the sake of pleasing God?" Yes, that is precisely his difficulty and his guilt. He does not care how little he pleases God! That is the least of his concern. The very lowest class of motives sways his will and his life. He stands far from the reach of the highest and noblest. In this consists his self-made degradation, and his exceeding great guilt.

It is the same of the miser when he gets beyond all motives but the love of hoarding—when his practical question is not, "How shall I honor my race, or bless my generation, or glorify my Maker," but, "How can I make a few dollars?" Even when urged to pray, he would ask, "What profit shall I have if I do pray unto Him?" When you find a man thus incapable of being moved by noble motives, what a wretch he is! How ineffably mean!

So I might bring before you the ambitious scholar, who is too low in his aims to be influenced by the exalted motive of doing good, and who feels only that which touches his reputation. Is not this exceedingly low and mean? What would you think of the preacher who should lose all regard for the welfare of souls, and think only of fishing for his reputation? What would you say of him? You would declare that he was too mean and too wicked to *live*, and fit only for hell!

What would you think of one who might shine like Lucifer among the morning stars of intellect and genius, but who should debase himself to the low and miserable vocation of rooting around for applause, and fishing for compliments? Would you not say that such self-seeking is unutterably contemptible? With all heaven above beckoning them on to lofty purposes and efforts, there they are, working their "muck-rake," and nosing after some little advantage to their small selves!

Watch that ambitious man who so longs to please everybody that he conforms his own ambitions to everyone else's, and never has one that is really his own! He allows himself to be dragged down by those who only aspire to dive and sink—never to soar; whose impulses all tend downward, and never up.

All this comes of bondage to base selfishness. Alas, that there should be so much of this in our world that public sentiment rarely sees it according to its real nature!

Our subject reveals the case of those who are convicted of the right, but cannot be persuaded to do it. For example, on the subject of *temperance*, he is convicted as to duty, knows he ought to reform absolutely, but yet he will not change. Every temperance lecture carries conviction, but the next temptation sweeps it aside, and he returns like the dog to his vomit. But notice this: every successive process of temperance conviction and temptation's triumph leaves him weaker than before, and very soon you will find him utterly prostrate. Miserable man! How certainly he will die in his sins!

No matter what the form of temptation, the person who is convinced of his duty, yet takes no corresponding action, is on the high-road to perdition. Inevitably this bondage grows stronger and stronger with every fresh trial of its strength. Every time you are convinced of duty, and yet resist that conviction and refuse to act in accordance with it, you become more and more helpless; you commit yourself more and more to the control of your iron-hearted master. Every fresh case renders you only the more fully a helpless slave.

You may be a young person who has already made himself a moral wreck. There may be some not yet sixteen who have already put their conscience effectually beneath their feet. Already you have learned, perhaps, to go against all your convictions of duty.

How horrible! Every day your bands are growing stronger. With each day's resistance, your soul is more deeply and hopelessly lost. Poor, miserable, dying sinner! "He, that being often reproved hardeneth his neck, shall suddenly be destroyed, and that without remedy" (Prov. 29:1). Suddenly, you dash upon the breakers and are gone! Your friends move solemnly along the shore, and look out upon those rocks of damnation on which your soul is wrecked. Weeping as they go, they mournfully say, "There is the wreck of one who knew his duty, but did it not. Thousands of times the appeals of conviction came home to his heart, but he learned to resist them: he made it his business to resist; and alas, he was only too successful!"

How insane is the delusion that the sinner's case grows better, while he is yet in his sins. As well might the drunkard fancy he is growing better because every temperance lecture convicts him of his sin and shame, while yet every next day's temptation leaves him drunk as ever! Growing better! There can be no delusion so false and so fatal as this!

You see the force of this delusion yet more clearly when you notice how slight are the considerations that sway the soul against all the vast motives of God's character and kingdom. Must not that be a strong and fearful delusion that can make considerations so slight outweigh motives so vast and momentous?

The guilt of this state is to be estimated by the insignificance of the motives that control the mind. What would you think of the youth who could murder his father for a dollar? "What!" you would exclaim, "for so little a pittance be bribed to murder his father!" You would account his guilt the greater by how little it took to tempt him.

Our subject shows the need of the Holy Spirit to impress the truth on the hearts of sinners. You may also see how certainly sinners will be lost if they grieve the Spirit of God away. Your earthly friends might discourage you, and yet you might be saved. But, if the Spirit of God becomes discouraged and leaves you, your doom is sealed forever. "Woe unto them when I depart from them!" This departure of God from the sinner gives the signal for tolling the knell of his lost soul. Then the mighty angel begins to *toll, toll, toll*! the great bell of eternity: one more soul going to its eternal doom!

14

HARDENING THE HEART*

"Again, He limiteth a certain day, saying in David, To day, after so long a time; as it is said, To day, if ye will hear his voice, harden not your hearts" (Hebrews 4:7).

This text refers to David, as he is quoted in the ninety-fifth Psalm. The writer of Hebrews was addressing Jewish Christians, and was speaking to them of the manner in which their forefathers tempted God in the wilderness, the result of which was that they were not allowed to enter into the Promised Land. Warning the Jews against unbelief, he says to them, "Today, if ye will hear His voice, harden not your hearts."

The Meaning of "Heart"

This term, like many other common words in the Bible, is employed in a variety of senses. Here, however, it obviously means the "will." To harden the heart, in the sense in which the phrase is used here, is doubtless to gather up the energies of the will and to resist, to become stubborn and obstinate. When the Bible commands or exhorts people not to harden their hearts, it is equivalent to saying, "Do not resist and strengthen yourselves against the voice of God. Do not become stubborn and rebellious, and set yourselves against the voice of mercy; but, today, after *so long a time*, if you will hear His voice, harden not your hearts." That is, if you are inclined to listen to what He says, do not harden your hearts and become stubborn.

Parents sometimes have the mortification of seeing their own children become stubborn against parental authority, and of seeing their

---

The Penny Pulpit, delivered on Sunday, December 1, 1850, at the Tabernacle, Moorfields, London.

requirements resisted and their advice unheeded. Parents often see children wax stubborn and rebellious when they are pressed to do anything, refusing to obey. They stand and resist, manifesting a cool determination to persevere in their disobedience, to persist in resisting the claims of their parents. As far as the philosophy of the act is concerned, resistance to God is just the same. The mental process is precisely similar. The mind resisting truth "is hardening the heart," in the sense of the text.

How Sinners Harden Their Hearts

When people resist the truth, they have to make some apology for their conduct. The natural tendency of the truth, when it is presented to the mind, is to convince it, to compel that individual to choose, to yield himself up to its influence. The mind and truth sustain such relations to each other that the former is naturally and necessarily influenced by the latter. And, unless the individual resists the truth, its natural tendency is to lead the will into the state of obedience to it.

When people harden their hearts, there must be some reason for their doing so. In the case of the Jews, the writer to the Hebrews called on them not to harden their hearts because he knew they were in danger of doing so. He knew their prejudices of education, their Jewish notions, and peculiar views of things. He knew the course they had taken with Christ previous to His crucifixion; now He had been crucified, had risen from the dead, and was proclaimed to the world as a risen Savior.

He was writing this epistle to the Jews, and therefore he reverts to a passage of their former national history. And, when he had strongly fixed their minds upon the course their fathers pursued, and its results—knowing well to whom he was addressing himself, being well versed in their prejudices against Christ, knowing their self-righteous spirit, and that they were prepared to resist Christ—knowing all these things, he warned them solemnly not to harden their hearts.

It is easy to see that they could assign themselves multitudes of reasons for resistance. He knew that they were in error—in great error—on the subject of Christianity, and therefore he called on them not to harden themselves, not to react out of their prejudices, and not to fly to their Jewish errors and peculiar notions and strengthen themselves in opposition to the truth.

People are very much in danger of hardening themselves by holding fast to some erroneous opinion or improper practice to which they are committed. All their prejudices are in favor of it, and they are very jealous lest anything should disturb it. They hold on to some particular error, and whenever they are pressed to yield to the claims of God, unless it is done in a peculiar way so as to be consistent with their prejudices, they are apt to rise up and strengthen themselves against it. What danger such people are in of resisting the truth, for the simple reason that it clashes with some of their favorite notions! Even when they see the practical results of the revealed truth contradict some pet theory of theirs, they will strengthen themselves against it.

One evening, in the city of New York, I found among the inquirers a very anxious lady who was exceedingly convicted of her sins. I pressed her strongly to submit to God.

"Ah!" she said, "if I were sure I am in the right church, I would."

"The right church!" I said, "I care not what church you are in, if you will only submit yourself to Christ."

"But," she replied, "this is not the Catholic Church, I am not in the right church; if I were, I would yield."

Her anxiety about the "right church" prevented her yielding at all, and she continued to harden her heart against Christ. This is often the case whether persons are Catholics, or any other denomination. When pressed strongly to submit, they flee to some prejudice, and immediately hide themselves behind it. Although they cannot deny the truth of what they resist, still there is some error or prejudice to which they betake themselves by way of present resistance to the truth that is pressing their consciences.

Others harden themselves by indulging in a spirit of procrastination. "I will follow Christ," they insist, "but not *now*." They say, "I intend to be religious," but when God presses them to yield, they are not quite ready. They say, "This is not exactly the time," assigning to themselves some reason for the present delay, in order to harden themselves. They have something, perhaps, which must be attended to first. But let me ask you this: How many times, when thus pressed to yield at once to Christ, have you urged some such reason as this for your own delay?

Why are you not Christian? Is it because your attention has never been called to the subject? Is it because you never intend to be a Christian? No! Well, what is the matter with you? How have you always succeeded in assigning to yourself a reason for another delay? One time, you have one reason, another time, another reason. You have, in fact, as many reasons as occasions, and they come up whenever you have been pressed immediately to surrender your heart to God. Isn't that true? Do you not know that this is true, just as surely as you know that you exist?

Many people strengthen themselves and harden their hearts by refusing, wherever they can, to be convicted of their sins. They have a multitude of ways of avoiding the point, and forcing away the truth, and hardening themselves against it. Be careful, for instance, of the practice of excusing sin. The worst sinner in the world will make some excuse for what he is doing, at least enough to satisfy himself. It is exceedingly difficult to convince a man against his will. It is remarkable to see how a man will evade conviction.

Go to the slaveholder, for instance, and how many excuses he will make! How many things he will conjure up! Sometimes he will even flee to the Bible to defend himself. At other times, he will excuse himself by saying that he knows not what to do with his slaves, that the laws of his state forbid him to emancipate them. You may press him on every point, you may reason with him again and again, but all to no purpose. Men often excuse and defend their sins in this way; and sometimes they actually deny that they are sins at all when pressed to give them up. But God will never receive their apologies, although they suffice, at present, to delude themselves.

Another way in which people harden themselves is by being unwilling to do what is implied in becoming Christians. They reason within themselves: "I must give up such and such things, if I become a Christian, and I must do thus and thus." They are reluctant to make a profession of faith, and knowing that once they do, the eyes of the world will forever be upon them. They see that they must consequently be careful how they conduct themselves. They cannot go to such and such places of amusement. They must discontinue such and such things they have been in the habit of doing, and which are now so dear to them. This is how they reason. They begin to count the cost.

A short time ago, I was pressing an individual to yield up certain forms of sin I knew him to be guilty of. "Ah," he said, "if I begin to yield this and that, where will it all end? I must be consistent," he said, "and where shall I stop?"

Where should he "stop"? It was clear that the cost was too great. He was disposed to harden himself and resist God's claims, because he believed that God required too much. If he were going to become a Christian, he knew that to do his duty he must give up sin as sin, and that it would cost him the sacrifice of his many idols.

This is a very common practice. If you ask people in a general way, they are willing to be Christians; but "what will be expected of them?" Ah! That is quite a different thing! If you tell them what it really is to be a Christian, that is quite another thing. Now you have set them to count the cost, and they will often find it involves too great a sacrifice. They are wholly unwilling to renounce themselves and their idols; and accordingly, they harden their hearts, strengthening their unbelief.

In the case of the individual I just referred to, the conversation concerned a particular form of sin. Now, why did he not yield at once?

Why did he not instantly say, "I will give it up. I know it is wrong and inconsistent with love to God, and I will therefore renounce it"? He knew that the principle on which he yielded this point would compel him to give up others; and, therefore, he said, "If I begin this, where shall I stop?" He gathered up all the reasons he could, and fortified his position. Thus he hardened his heart. This was just what the Jews did when Christ preached.

When people perceive that they must humble themselves before God, and make restitution where they have been fraudulent in their dealings; they see that to become Christians implies that they undo, as far as it lies in their power, the wrong they may have committed, and become honest men. They see that multitudes of things are implied in listening to the voice of God, in becoming followers of Jesus Christ. This causes them to surround themselves with objections, calculated to sustain them in their unbelief and resistance to the authority of God.

The Foolishness of Hardening the Heart

If you do not harden your heart, you will be converted. I have already said that truth is so related to the mind, and vice versa, that when the mind perceives truth, with its practical bearing, this relation acts as a powerful impulse to the mind, tending strongly to induce it to yield and conform. Truth is a natural stimulus to the mind, prompting it to act in a given direction. To be sure, it can be resisted; and it is this resistance that God exhorts you to avoid. You are to let the truth take effect.

In the Epistle to the Romans, God denounces those who restrain the truth, and go on in unrighteousness; that is, those who hold back and prevent the truth from influencing their mind. This is the way the heart is hardened, by refusing to yield to the truth, withholding the mind from going out in obedience to it.

If the truth is yielded to, conversion results. *Conversion is the act of turning the mind from error, selfishness and sin, and yielding to the claims of truth, and obeying the commands of the Almighty.*

As I said, the natural tendency of the truth is to stimulate the mind to embrace and obey it. God has so constituted the mind that truth is a most powerful stimulant that invites and draws the mind in a given direction. Truth induces the mind to act in conformity with its dictates.

To do this, to obey the truth, is conversion. If you do not obey it, it is because you harden yourself against it and resist its influences. It is an utter impossibility to be indifferent to the presentation of truth, and especially impossible to maintain a blank indifference to the great practical truths of Christianity. They are not mere abstractions, in which the mind sees no practical bearing, but they are realities of such a nature that the mind must either resist them or conform to them. The apostles knew that if the Jews did not harden themselves, they would surely be converted.

Another reason you should not harden your heart is that you will not be converted if you do. God will never *force* you to be converted against your will. If He cannot persuade you to embrace the truth, He will not overpower you by a physical act of omnipotence, as, for instance, He did when He created the world. You are a free moral agent, and He can save you only in His own way. In other words, if He cannot gain your own consent to be saved His way, He cannot save you at all. If you wish Him to save you by moving your will, much as one would move a lamp, He will not do it.

It is not a physical operation that can make you willing; that is not the way in which the will is controlled. He must have your consent. When He sends His ministers to reason with you, when His Spirit strives with you, He strives to gain your free consent; hence He says, "To day if ye will hear His voice, harden not your hearts." If conversion could be forced by a mere act of the physical omnipotence of God, He would not address the issue of hard hearts, *for how could you harden your hearts against omnipotence?*

Many who have this conception scoff at the idea of the sinner's hardening himself against God. Some people assume that conversion depends on an act of omnipotence. They seem unable to comprehend that conversion consists in God's securing a person's consent. Did you ever consider this?

Did you ever reflect on the fact that all you need to do is give your consent to be saved? You fancy you are willing; but the fact is, your stubbornness is the only real difficulty to be overcome, to get you to yield yourself up to God's claims. If you harden your heart, surrounding yourself with prejudices, gathering all your energies up to resist, if you do this, you can only expect to remain unconverted—to live, and die, and perish in your sins! While you harden yourself, it is impossible that you should be converted, for conversion is the very opposite of this resistance. Conversion is the yielding yourself up to the claims of God.

Another reason you should not harden your heart is that *you may be given up!* God may give you up to the hardness of your heart. The Bible clearly shows this is common. Whole generations of Jews were thus given up, and there is considerable danger that if you continue to harden your heart, you may be given up as well. The same God of mercy who now governs the world gave up whole generations in that comparatively dark generation; and if so, what reason have we to suppose that He will not do so with your generation?

God, under the gospel, is not more merciful than He was under the law—He is the same God. You may think there is not so much danger of this now; but the fact is, there is more, because there is more light. He gives them up because they resist the light of the truth with regard to His claims. I beg of you to consider this.

Whose Voice Is Speaking to Us?

Is it the voice of a tyrant, who comes out with His omnipotent arm to crush you? "If you will hear His voice, harden not your hearts." Whose voice is it? In the first place, it is the voice of God; but, more than this, it is the voice of your Father!

But is it the voice of your Father pursuing you with the rod of correction, to subdue you by force? Oh, no! It is the voice of His mercy, of His deepest compassion. Hear what He says: "Is Ephraim my dear son? Is he a pleasant child? For since I spake against him, I do earnestly remember him still: therefore my bowels are troubled for him; I will surely have mercy upon him, saith the Lord" (Jer. 31:20–21).

It's like a father who has almost made up his mind to abandon a disobedient and cruel child, whose misconduct he could not endure, and whom he found impossible to reform. His father-heart stirs up in him at the remembrance of that child; the parental heart yearns over him. "For since I spake against him; I do earnestly remember him still."

Just so, God addresses you. He "earnestly remembers" you. He offers to forgive you. He says, "after so long a time." *How* long a time? How old are you? How many long years has God waited for you? Just number them up; eighteen, twenty, twenty-five, thirty years—perhaps more. How many years have you refused to hear the voice of your Father, your Savior? How long have you ignored the voice of mercy, the voice of invitation, the voice of promise, the voice of entreaty? By His providence, the work of the Spirit, the words of the inspired volume, the ministrations of His servants—in how many ways has this voice reached you? And now He says, ". . . after *so long a time!*"

People often mistake the true nature of hardness of heart. Supposing it to be involuntary, they lament it as a misfortune, rather than regret it as a crime. They suppose that the state of apathy which results from the resistance of their will is hardness of heart. It is true that the mind apologizes to itself for resistance to the claims of God; and, as a natural result, there is very little feeling in the mind, because it is under the necessity of making such a use of its powers as to cause great destitution of feeling.

This is hardening the heart: that act of the mind in resisting the claims of God. For people to excuse themselves by complaining that their hearts are hard is only to add insult to injury. They resist God's claims, and then complain of the hardness this resistance induces. They harden themselves in the ways we have stated, rendering themselves obstinate against God, and then they complain of the results of their own actions. Now, is this the way?

The claims, commands, promises and invitations of God are all in the present tense. Turn to the Bible, and from end to end you will find it is, "Today" if you will hear His voice. "Now" is the accepted time. God says nothing of tomorrow. He does not even guarantee that we shall live till then. It is *"Today*, after so long a time, harden not your hearts."

The plea of inability is one of the most paltry, abusive and blasphemous of all. Are men *not able* to refrain from hardening themselves? I have already said that it is the nature of truth to influence the mind it touches. When the Spirit converts a man, it is by so presenting the truth as to gain his consent. Now, if there were not something in the truth itself adapted to influence the mind, He might continue to present the truth forever, without your ever being converted.

Now, when people complain of their inability to embrace the truth, what an infinite mistake! God approaches with offers of mercy, with the cup of salvation in His hand, saying, "Sinner! I am coming! Do not harden yourself. Do not hide behind professors of religion. Do not procrastinate! For I am coming to win you."

Now, what does the sinner do? Why, he falls to hardening his heart, procrastinating, making all manner of excuses, and pleading his inability to hear the truth. Inability! What? Is not a man able to stop dwelling on these considerations that only feed his stubbornness? Is he not able to desist from this soul destroying business of hardening himself? Oh! sinner, you *are* able; that is not the difficulty.

I said this is a most *abusive* way of treating God. Just think. Here is God, endeavoring to gain the sinner's consent—to what? He is not trying to persuade you to harden yourself, to make you consent to lie down in everlasting sorrow. Oh, no! He is not trying to persuade you to do anything or to consent to anything that will injure you.

He is not trying to persuade you to give up anything that is really good, the relinquishment of which will make you wretched, or unhappy. He is not trying to persuade you to give up all joy, and everything that is pleasant, to give up things that tend to peace. He is not endeavoring to persuade you to do any such thing as this. With regard to all such things, He is not only willing that you should have them, but would bring you into a state in which you could really enjoy them.

He cries out, "Sinner! do thyself no harm!" He is trying to prevent you from injuring yourself; He is not endeavoring to play any game upon you that will interfere with your well-being or happiness. He is trying to prevent your ruining yourself, and trying to gain your consent to be blessed. Will it hurt you to give up your sins? God sent Christ to turn you away from such things, which by a natural law must prove your ruin. What is it, then, that God wishes you to do?

What is that sweet voice which falls so sweetly from heaven? It should melt all stubbornness down. It is the voice of His infinite compassion and love. Oh, sinner, destroy not thine own soul! Flee not from the Savior who has come to save you! Harden not yourself against the offered mercy; and, now that the cup of salvation is passed around, do not push it away!

What are you doing? Has God come to injure you? If He had come in wrath, He would not care whether you hardened your heart or not. O sinner! If you place Him in such a relation that His infinite heart is obliged to make the sacrifice, when He enters into judgment He will not prevent you from hardening yourself, but will say to you, "Can thine heart endure, or can thine hands be strong, in the days that I shall deal with thee?" (Ezek. 22:14).

Oh, no! But now it is different. Now He comes and sweetly tries to win you. He comes as a friend, as a father, as a Savior! He is spreading out His broad arms of love to embrace you, drawing you so near to His great, gushing heart as to thrill its tides of eternal love through all your being.

Oh! will you resist? What? ". . . *after so long a time!*" Oh! sinner, is it not infinitely inexcusable? Shall He fail to get your consent? Then, when you sit before Him in solemn judgment, and the universe shall all be gathered together, He will publish the fact of how He tried to spread out His broad, beneficent arms of love over you, how He tried to gather you under the wings of His protection—but ye would not! He could not gain your consent! What! shall it be told of you in the solemn judgment that God could not possibly gain your consent to the only terms on which He could possibly save you? Ah! when He shakes His skirts, as it were, and exclaims, "I am clear of thy blood!" what will you say?

He will have the eternal consolation, knowing that He had taken all the pains to get you to consent that He wisely could take. You will be obliged to say, "The fault was my own, and I have been an infinite fool! I have resisted the claims of Christ, hardened myself against His dying love, and cast away my soul!" Sinners! how many times have you been invited? What if Christ personally put the question, "Do you think I *ought* to allow you to live any longer in your sins? Do you think I *ought* to let you live to remain in rebellion any longer!"

Suppose He should say, "Unless I fan your heaving lungs in sleep tonight, you will be lost. Unless I keep you, you will lie down in hell before the morning. Now, do you think I *ought* to keep you alive to sin against me another day? Do you think that when you lie down in your sins, I *ought* to watch over you, and see that you do not die; and that Satan does not steal away your soul, and drag you down to the depths of hell?"

Dare you look the Eternal in the face and say, "Yes, Lord." Dare you say, "I think I *ought* to be indulged a little longer, and not be hurried in this way?" No, indeed! You know you are without excuse. You could only say that you are "infinitely to blame," and you are in infinite danger if you do not now cease to sin, and yield yourself up.

(When this sermon was originally delivered, Mr. Finney, after a short prayer, dismissed the congregation. Most of the church body remained afterward to celebrate the Lord's Supper; however, seeing that between three and four hundred people kept their seats, as "spectators" in the spacious galleries, Mr. Finney again addressed the assembly.)

Christ has invited you to "do this in remembrance" of Him. To whom was this directed? Did Christ die for you, and not for me? Or for me, and not for you? Or did He give himself up for us all? Surely it is the duty of all to "do this" for whom Christ died.

Is it possible that you have really never done it? How is this? I want to know *why* you have never done it. Is it because you are not a Christian? Why not? When Dr. Campbell (the pastor of the church) announced that the communicants would seat themselves below, while the spectators would retire to the gallery, I said to myself, "Spectators! Non-communicants!" Who are these non-communicants! Are there, then, those of Adam's race for whom Christ has not died? Are there those who will openly acknowledge that they have "no part or lot in the matter?"

Suppose, now, that Christ actually had died only for a part of mankind, and you knew that it had no more reference to you non-communicants in the gallery than to the fallen angels! If you knew this, why, of course, I should expect to see you non-communicants; for why should you celebrate His death if His blood was not shed for you? You might then absent yourselves with some reason. But, if this were the case, how could you sit around that gallery and look on? Now, do take this view of the matter, and consider it for a moment.

But Christ says, "*Every one* that thirsteth, come ye to the waters. . . . Come, buy wine and milk without money and without price" (Isa. 55:1), and also "Look unto me, and be ye saved, all the ends of the earth" (Isa. 45:22). Suppose, then, that the cup were handed round to you; would you say, "Oh! I am not prepared: I am not a Christian"? Why are you not? You shut yourself out by your own consent. "Not prepared!" You are neglecting Christ, and hardening your hearts against Him. That is the reason you are "not prepared."

"Not prepared!" Just think of it! Who is it that requests you to "do this?" It is a friend—a dying friend—a friend dying in your stead. What does He say? He says, "I am just going to offer up My life for you: break this bread, pour out this wine, and partake of them in remembrance of Me ... partake ye *all* of it, and when you do so, remember my struggle, my groans, my agony, and death." Will you obey this dying injunction? Why, then, do you thus turn your backs upon it?

Suppose that a mortal should do you a similar favor? Suppose a fellow-creature should bleed and die in your stead, and in agony of death should take a ring from his finger, and say, "Here, dear friend, take this, wear it, look at it, and as often as you do so, remember me!" How would you regard this love-token presented in the hour of nature's final struggle? Would you throw the ring away lightly?

Suppose anyone should say, "Give me that ring"; or, "How much will you take for it?" How much *would* you take for it? Why you would sooner part with your heart's blood than lose it. And if they inquired why you so prized it, you would tell them your simple story, and assure them that nothing could induce you to part with it.

Now, think of this! Yet when Christ made an effort to save you from endless death, by suffering himself, how indifferent you are! Was it a mere ring? No! He took bread and broke it, saying, "This is My body which was broken for you"; He took wine and poured it out, saying, "This is My blood which was shed for you, do this in remembrance of Me." Who is to "do this?" Why, all of you; seeing that for all of you His blood was shed.

Instead you say, "I will not do this," and turn your back on the ordinance. What must angels think, when they see a number of persons for whom Christ died, and to whom He said, "Do this in remembrance of me," but who will not do it? If there can be amazement in heaven, surely this would be the cause of it.

Now, *will you ever neglect it again?* I recollect an instance of an individual present at a season like this, when the question came up about his long neglect, when he was so impressed by the consideration of the sin and danger of his position he resolved on the spot that he would never neglect it again. At the next communion he was there, and could rejoice in the resolution he had taken, to draw near to that great heart of love. After that, he was always one of the first at the table.

What do *you* say tonight? Now think of this when you lay your head on your pillow tonight. Can you say, "Lord, this night have I rejected Thee publicly before the whole congregation." Try to go to sleep, but say first, "Lord, do not let me die tonight, I have just come away from Thy table and refused to acknowledge Thee; do not let me go to hell tonight."

Would you not blush to talk thus? Would you not rather say, "Oh, my God! I have tonight rejected Jesus, and how dare I sleep in my sins? This night, Lord, in my heart I give Thee a solemn pledge, that, by Thy grace, I will never turn my back on that ordinance again. It shall never be said of me (by Thy grace), that I am not prepared. I will remember Thee; and in the presence of heaven and earth, I will manifest my gratitude to Thee from this time." Just so, let it be written in heaven!

15

QUENCHING THE SPIRIT, PART 1*

"Quench not the Spirit" (1 Thessalonians 5:19).

The Holy Spirit does not influence the mind by physical agency; nor by imposing direct physical power. The action of the will is not influenced this way and cannot be. The very supposition is absurd. That physical agency should produce voluntary mental phenomena just as it does physical phenomena is both absurd and at war with the very idea of free agency. That the same physical agency that moves a planet should move the human will is absurd.

How the Holy Spirit Influences the Mind

The Bible informs us that the Spirit influences the human mind by means of the truth. The Spirit persuades people to act on the truth, as we ourselves influence our fellow men by truth presented to their minds.

I do not mean that God presents truth to the mind in the same manner as we do. Of course, His mode of operation must differ from ours. We use the pen, the lips, the gesture. We use the language of words and the language of nature. God does not employ these means now. Yet, He still reaches the mind with truth. Sometimes His providence suggests it, and then His Holy Spirit gives it efficiency, setting it home upon the heart with great power. Sometimes the Lord makes use of preaching. Indeed, His ways are various. But whatever the mode of operation, the object is always the same: to produce voluntary action in conformity to His law.

Now, if the Bible were entirely silent on this subject, we should still know from the nature of mind, and from the nature of those in-

---

Sermons on Gospel Themes, 245–263.

fluences that move the human mind, that the Spirit must exert not physical but moral influences. Yet, we are not now left to a merely metaphysical inference; we have the plain testimony of the Bible to the fact that the Holy Spirit employs truth in converting and sanctifying us.

Truth Convicts; the Sinner Decides

God is physically omnipotent, and yet His moral influences exerted by the Holy Spirit may be resisted. You will readily see that if the Spirit moved people by physical omnipotence, His power would be irresistible, for what mortal could withstand His omnipotence? But now, we know that people can resist the Holy Spirit; the nature of moral agency implies this and the Bible asserts it.

The nature of moral agency implies the voluntary action of one who can yield to motive and follow light or not, as he pleases. Where this power does not exist, moral agency cannot exist; and at whatever point this power ceases, there at that point moral agency also ceases.

Hence, if we are to act as moral agents, our moral freedom to do or not to do must remain. It cannot be set aside or in any way overruled. If God should in any way set aside our voluntary agency, He would of necessity terminate at once our moral and responsible action. Suppose God should seize a person's arm with physical omnipotence and forcibly use it in deeds of murder or arson. Would not the moral, responsible agency of that person be utterly suspended? Yet not more so than if, in an equally irresistible manner, God himself should seize the person's will and compel it to act as He willed.

The very idea that moral influence can ever be irresistible originates in an entire mistake as to the nature of the will and of moral action. The will of human beings must be free, in view of truth and of the motives it presents for action. Increasing the amount of such influence has no sort of tendency to impair the freedom of the will. Regardless of the intensity of truth perceived, or amount of motive present to the mind, the will has the same changeless power to yield or not to yield—to act or not to act—in accordance with this perceived truth.

Force and moral agency are terms of opposite meaning. They cannot co-exist. The one effectually precludes the other. Hence, to say that if God is physically omnipotent, then He can and will force a moral agent in his moral actions is stark nonsense. Because of this, any work of God carried on by moral and not by physical power not only can be resisted by people, but may be resisted, though it will undoubtedly endanger their souls.

If the Lord carries the work forward by means of revealed truth, there may be most imminent danger that people will neglect to study and understand this truth, or, knowing, they shall refuse to obey it. Surely, it is fearfully within the power of every person to shut out God's truth from his consideration and bar his heart against its influence.

Quenching the Holy Spirit

We all readily understand what the work of the Holy Spirit is: to enlighten the mind regarding the truth of God, ourselves, and our duty. For example, the Holy Spirit enlightens the mind into the meaning and self-application of the Bible. It takes the things of Christ, and shows them to us.

It is possible to refuse this light; you can shut your eyes against it. You have the power to turn your gaze entirely away, or utterly refuse to follow it once you have seen it; in this case, God ceases to hold up the truth before your mind.

Almost everyone knows by personal experience that the Holy Spirit has the power to shed a marvelous light upon revealed truth, so that this truth shall stand before the mind in a new and most impressive form, and shall operate upon it with astonishing energy. But this light of the Spirit may be quenched.

There is, so to speak, a sort of heat, a warmth and vitality attending the truth when enforced by the Holy Spirit. Thus we say, if you have the Spirit of God, then your soul is warm. If you have not the Spirit, your heart is cold.

How the Spirit May Be Quenched

People often quench the Holy Spirit by directly resisting the truth He presents to their minds. Sometimes people set themselves deliberately to resist the truth, determined they will not yield to its power, at least for the present. In such cases it is amazing to see how great the influence of the will is in resisting the truth. Indeed, the will can always resist any moral considerations; as we have seen, there is no such thing as forcing the will to yield to truth.

In those cases where the truth presses strongly on the mind, there is presumptive evidence that the Spirit is present by His power. And it is in precisely these cases that people are especially prone to set themselves against the truth, and thus are in the utmost peril of quenching the Spirit. They hate the truth presented. It crosses their chosen path of self-indulgence. They feel vexed and harassed by its claims. They resist and quench the Spirit of the Lord.

You have doubtless seen such cases. And if so, you have also doubtless noticed this other remarkable fact: after a short struggle in resisting truth, the conflict is over and that particular truth almost utterly ceases to affect the mind. The individual becomes hardened to its power. He seems quite able to overlook it and thrust it from his thoughts. If this fails and the truth is thrown before his mind, still he finds it comparatively easy to resist its claims. He felt greatly annoyed by that truth until he had quenched the Holy Spirit. Then he is annoyed by it no longer.

If you have seen cases like this, you have doubtless witnessed that, as the truth is pressed upon their minds, they become restless, sensitive, then perhaps angry, but still stubborn in resisting until at length the conflict subsides. The truth makes no more impression; henceforth, it is quite dead with regard to them. They apprehend it only with the greatest dimness, and care nothing about it.

Let me ask you this: Have you had this very experience? Have you resisted some truth until it has ceased to affect your mind? If so, then you may conclude that, at that time, you quenched the Spirit of God.

Second, the Holy Spirit is quenched by endeavoring to support error. Sometimes people are foolish enough to attempt by argument to support a position they have good reason to believe is a false one. They argue it until they get committed to it. They indulge in a dishonest state of mind. Thus, they quench the Holy Spirit and are usually left to believe the very lie they so unwisely attempted to advocate. I have seen many cases where someone has begun to defend and maintain a position he knew to be untrue until he had quenched the Spirit of God. In the end, he wound up believing his own lie and, it is to be feared, will die under its delusions.

Third, you can quench the Holy Spirit by making uncharitable judgments. Perhaps nothing more certainly quenches the Holy Spirit than to impeach the motives of others and judge them uncharitably. It is so unlike God, and so hostile to the law of love, no wonder the Holy Spirit is utterly averse to it, and turns away from those who indulge it.

Fourth, the Holy Spirit is grieved by harsh and abusive language. How often do people grieve the Holy Spirit by using such language toward those who differ with them. It is always safe to presume that people who indulge such a temper have already grieved the Holy Spirit utterly away.

Fifth, the Spirit of God is quenched by a bad temper. When a bad temper and spirit are stirred up in individuals or in a community, revivals suddenly cease—the Spirit of God is put down and quenched. There is no more prevailing prayer and no more sinners are converted.

Sixth, the Spirit is often quenched by diverting the attention from the truth. Since the Spirit operates through the truth, it is most obvious that we must attend to this truth that the Spirit keeps before our minds. If we refuse to attend to the truth of God, as we always can if we choose to do so, we shall almost certainly quench the Holy Spirit.

Seventh, we often quench the Spirit by indulging intemperate excitement on any subject. If the subject is apart from practical, divine truth, strong excitement diverts attention from such truth and renders it almost impossible to feel its power. While the mind sees and feels keenly on the subject in which it is excited, it sees dimly and feels but coldly on the vital things of salvation. Hence, the Spirit is quenched.

The intemperate excitement may be on some topic of a religious nature. Sometimes I have seen a burst—a real tornado—of feeling in a revival, but in such cases truth loses its hold on the minds of the people. They are too much excited to take sober views of the truth and of the moral duties it incites. Not all religious excitement, however, is to be condemned. There must be excitement enough to arouse the mind to serious thought—enough to give the truth edge and power. But it is always well to avoid that measure of excitement that throws the mind from its balance and renders its perceptions of truth obscure or fitful.

Eighth, the Spirit is quenched by indulging prejudice. Whenever the mind is made up on any subject prematurely, before the subject is thoroughly canvassed, that mind is shut against the truth, and the Spirit is quenched. When there is great prejudice, it seems impossible for the Spirit to act, and of course His influence is quenched. The mind is so committed that it resists the first efforts of the Spirit. This thousands have done. Thus thousands have ruined their souls for eternity. Therefore, let every person keep his mind open to conviction and be sure to examine carefully all important questions and especially all such as involve great questions of duty to God and man.

I am saying nothing now against being firm in maintaining your position after you thoroughly understand it and are sure it is the truth. But while pursuing your investigations, be sure you are really candid and yield your mind to all the reasonable evidence you can find.

Ninth, the Spirit is often quenched by violating conscience. There are circumstances under which if a conscience is violated, the light of God seems to be quenched in the soul forever. Perhaps you have seen cases of this sort where people have had a very tender conscience on some subject, but all at once they seem to give it up, and have no conscience at all on that subject. I am aware that change of conduct sometimes results from change of views without any violation of conscience. But the case I speak of is where the conscience seems to be killed. All that remains of it seems hard as a stone.

I have sometimes thought the Spirit of God has much more to do with the workings of conscience than we usually suppose. The fact is undeniable that men sometimes experience very great and sudden changes in the amount of sensitivity of conscience that they feel on some subjects. How is this to be accounted for? Only by the supposition that the Spirit has power to arouse the conscience and make it pierce like an arrow. Then when people, ignoring the reproaches of conscience, still sin, the Spirit is quenched and the conscience loses all sensitivity: an entire change takes place and the person goes on sinning as if he never had any conscience.

Sometimes the mind is awakened just on the eve of committing some particular sin. Perhaps something seems to say to him, "If you do this, you will be forsaken by God." A strange presentiment forewarns him to desist. Now if he goes on, the whole mind receives a dreadful shock. The very eyes of the mind seem to be almost put out. The moral perceptions are strangely deranged and beclouded.

A fatal violence is done to the conscience, regarding that particular issue at least. And indeed, the injury to the conscience seems to affect all departments of moral action. In such circumstances, the Spirit of God seems to turn away and say, "I can do no more for you. I have warned you faithfully and can warn you no more."

All these things sometimes result from neglect of plainly revealed duty.

People shrink from known duty through fear of the opinions of others or through dislike of some self-restraint. In this crisis of trial, the Holy Spirit does not leave them in a state of doubt or inattention regarding duty, but keeps the truth and the claims of God vividly before the mind. If people go on and commit the sin, in spite of the Spirit's warnings, then the soul is left in awful darkness—the light of the Spirit of God is quenched, perhaps forever.

I do not know how many cases I have seen of people in great agony, even despair, who had evidently quenched the Spirit in the manner just described. There was the case of a young man who had undergone a long trial on the question of preparing himself for the ministry. He balanced the question for a long time, the claims of God being clearly set before him. But at last resisting the convictions of duty, he went off and got married and turned away from the work to which God seemed to call him. Then the Spirit left him.

For some years he remained entirely hardened as to what he had done and as to any claims of God upon him. Finally, his wife got sick and died. Then his eyes were opened; he saw what he had done. He sought the Lord, but sought in vain. No light returned to his darkened, desolate soul. It no longer seemed his duty to prepare for the ministry; that call of God had ceased. His cup of wretchedness seemed to be filled to the brim. Often he spent whole nights in most intense agony, groaning, crying for mercy, or musing in anguish upon the dire despair that spread its universe of desolation all around him. I often feared he would take his own life, so perfectly wretched was he under these reproaches of a guilty conscience and these thoughts of deep despair.

When people refuse to do known duty, this refusal does fatal violence to their own moral sense and to the Spirit of the Lord. Consequently, there remains for them only a "certain fearful anticipation of judgment and fiery indignation."

Tenth, people often quench the Spirit by indulging their appetites and passions. You would be astonished if you were to know how often the Holy Spirit is grieved by this means until a crisis is formed of such a nature that they seem to quench the light of God at once from their souls. Some people indulge their appetite for food to the injury of their health, and though they know they are injuring themselves, and though the Spirit of God remonstrates and presses them hard to desist from ruinous self-indulgence, yet they persist in their course, are given up of God, and henceforth their appetites lord it over them to the ruin of their spirituality and of their souls. The same may be true of any form of sensual indulgence.

Eleventh, the Holy Spirit is often quenched by indulging in dishonesty. People engaged in business will take little advantages in buying and selling. Sometimes they are powerfully convinced of the great selfishness of this, and see that this is by no means loving their neighbor as themselves.

It may happen that a person about to drive a good bargain will raise the question to himself, "Is this right?" He will balance it long in his mind and say, "Now this neighbor of mine needs this article very much, and will suffer if he does not get it. This will give me a grand chance to put up the price. But then, would this be doing as I would be done by?"

He looks and thinks. He sees duty, but finally decides in favor of his selfishness. Eternity alone will disclose the consequences of such a decision. When the Holy Spirit has followed such people a long time, has made them see their danger, has kept the truth before them, and finally seizing the favorable moment makes a *last effort* and this proves unavailing, then the die is cast. Thereafter all restraints are gone and the selfish person is abandoned by God, goes on worse and worse, goes to prison perhaps, and certainly to hell.

Twelfth, people often quench the Spirit by unbelief and faithless, restrained prayer. Indeed, restrained praying always quenches the Spirit. It is amazing to see how naturally and earnestly the Spirit leads us to pray. If we were really led by the Holy Spirit, we would be drawn many times a day to secret prayer, and would be continually lifting up our hearts in silent requests whenever the mind unbent itself for even a short time from its other pressing occupations. The Spirit in the hearts of Christians is pre-eminently a spirit of prayer, and so to restrain prayer must always quench the Holy Spirit.

Perhaps you have been in this very case. You once had the spirit of prayer, but now it is gone. You had access to God, but now you have it no longer. You have no enjoyment in prayer, neither do you feel constrained to groan and agonize over the state of the church and of sinners. And if this spirit of prayer is gone, where are you now? Alas, you have quenched the Spirit of God. You have put out His light and repelled His influences from your soul.

Thirteenth, the Spirit of God is quenched by idle conversation. Few seem to be aware how wicked this is, and how effectively it quenches the Holy Spirit. Christ said "that every idle word that men shall speak, they shall give account thereof in the day of judgment" (Matt. 12:36).

Fourteenth, people quench the Holy Spirit with levity and trifling, by indulging in a peevish and fretful spirit, by a spirit of laziness. Many are so lazy that they drive away the Holy Spirit altogether. Habits of procrastination and excuse-making for neglecting duty are sure ways to quench the Spirit of God in the soul.

Fifteenth, many have quenched the Spirit by resisting the doctrine and duty of sanctification. Sanctification has been extensively discussed for the past few years.* Several ecclesiastical bodies have taken ground against the doctrine of sanctification, and sometimes members have said and done in public what they would not by any means have said or done in their own prayer closets or pulpits.

Is it not also probable that many ministers and laymen have been influenced by this ecclesiastical action to oppose this doctrine—and the fear of man thus becomes a snare to their souls? It is also possible that some have opposed the doctrine of sanctification simply because it raises a higher standard of personal holiness than they would like— too high to permit them to hope as Christians, too high for their experience, and too high to suit their tastes and habits for future life.

Now, who does not see that opposition to the doctrine and duty of sanctification on any such grounds must certainly and fatally quench the Holy Spirit? No work can lie more near the heart of Jesus than the sanctification of His people. Hence, nothing can so greatly grieve Him as to see this work impeded—much more to see it opposed and frustrated.

A solemn and awful emphasis is given to these considerations when you contemplate the facts respecting the prevalent state of piety in very many churches throughout the land. You need not ask, "Are re-

---

*Several books in the "Principles Series" discuss sanctification. Particularly, I refer you to *Principles of Sanctification, Principles of Discipleship, Principles of Holiness,* and *Principles of Union With Christ.*

vivals enjoyed, are Christians prayerful, self-denying, alive in faith and responding in love to God and to man?" You need not ask if the work of sanctifying the church is moving forward, manifesting itself by abounding fruits of righteousness. The answer meets you before you can well frame the question.

Woe to us, when the Holy Spirit is quenched under the diffusion of the very truth that ought to sanctify the church! What can save us if the gospel promise in all its fullness is so perverted in the hearts of men, or resisted to the extent that it quenches the Spirit and thus serves only to harden the heart?

Consequences of Quenching the Holy Spirit

Great darkness of mind will result from quenching the Spirit of God; for, abandoned by God, the mind sees truth so dimly that it makes no useful impression whatsoever. Such people read the Bible without interest or profit. It becomes to them a dead letter, and they generally lay it aside unless some controversy leads them to search it. They take no such spiritual interest in it that makes its perusal delightful. Have you never been in this very state of mind? This is that darkness of nature common to people when the Spirit is withdrawn.

There usually results great coldness and stupidity with regard to Christianity in general when the Spirit has been quenched. It leaves the mind without even the same interest in spiritual things as people normally take in worldly things.

People get into such a state that they are greatly interested in some worldly matters, but not in Christianity. Their souls are all awake while worldly things are the subject, but suggest some spiritual subject, and their interest is gone at once. You can scarcely get them to attend a prayer meeting. They are in a worldly state of mind, because if the Spirit of the Lord were with them, they would be more deeply interested in religious services than in anything else.

Now observe these people. Organize a political meeting or a theatrical exhibition and their souls are all on fire. But go and appoint a prayer meeting or a meeting to promote a revival, and they are not there; or if they are, they feel no interest in spiritual things as such.

When a person has quenched the Spirit of God, his Christianity is all outside. His vital, heart-affecting interest in spiritual things disappears. A spiritual person, on the other hand, will take some interest in worldly things, but only to the extent that he regards them as a part of his duty to God; for this reason, to him they are spiritual things, not worldly.

The mind falls very easily into diverse errors in religion. The heart wanders from God, loses its hold on the truth, and perhaps the person insists that he now takes a much more liberal and enlightened view of the subject than before.

A short time ago, I had a conversation with a man who had given up the idea that the Old Testament was inspired, had given up the doctrine of the atonement, and indeed every distinctive doctrine of the Bible. He remarked to me, "I used to think as you do, but I have now come to take a more liberal and enlightened view of the subject."

Indeed! He is so blinded, he does not see that Christ sanctioned the Old Testament as the oracles of God; and yet he flatters himself to think that he now possesses a more liberal and enlightened view! There can be nothing stronger than Christ's affirmations regarding the inspiration of the Old Testament. And yet, this man admits Christ's teachings to be true—including these affirmations, one must suppose—while he denies the very thing they affirm! A most liberal and enlightened view, truly!

How can you possibly account for such views except on the ground that for some reason the person has fallen into a strange, unnatural state of mind—a sort of mental stupidity in which moral truths are beclouded or distorted.

There cannot be a greater absurdity than to admit the divine authority of the teachings of Christ and yet reject the Old Testament. The language of Christ affirms and implies the authority of the Old Testament in all those ways in which, were the inspiration of the Old Testament supposed, He might expect to affirm and imply this fact. The Old Testament does not indeed exhaust divine revelation. It left more things to be revealed. Christ taught much, but nothing more clearly than the divine authority of the Old Testament.

Quenching the Spirit May Result in Infidelity

What can account for such a case as that I have just mentioned, unless it is this: God has allowed the human mind to fall into very great darkness?

Another result is great hardness of heart. The mind becomes calloused to that class of truth that ought to make it yielding and tender. The mobility of the heart under truth depends entirely upon its moral hardness. If very hard, truth makes no impression. If soft, then it is yielding as air and moves quick to the touch of truth in any direction.

Another result is deep delusion with regard to their spiritual state. How remarkable that people will claim to be Christians, having rejected every distinctive doctrine of Christianity. Indeed, such people do sometimes claim that by thus rejecting almost the whole of the Bible, and all its great scheme of salvation by an atonement, they have become "real" Christians. Now they have got the true light! Indeed!

How can such a delusion be accounted for, except on the ground that the Spirit of God has abandoned the person to his own ways and left him to utter and perfect delusion?

People in this state often justify themselves in the most blatant error, because they confuse darkness for light, and light for darkness. They entrench themselves in perfectly false principles, as if those principles were true and could amply justify their misdeeds.

Often people are not aware of what is going on in their minds when they are quenching the Spirit of God. Duty is presented and pressed upon them, but they do not realize that this is the work of the Spirit of God. They are not aware of the present voice of the Lord to their hearts, nor do they see that this solemn impression of the truth is nothing other than the effect of the Holy Spirit on their minds.

When people come to take different views from those of the Bible and abandon their former beliefs, they seem unconscious of the fact that God has departed from them. They flatter themselves that they have become very liberal and very much enlightened overall, and have only given up their former errors. Alas, they do not see that the light they now walk in is darkness—all sheer darkness! "Woe unto them . . . that put darkness for light, and light for darkness!" (Isa. 5:20). Do you see how to account for the spiritual state of some people?

I have good reason to know how people become Unitarians and Universalists, having seen at least hundreds of instances. It is not by becoming more and more people of prayer and real spirituality—not by getting nearer and nearer to God. They do not go on progressing in holiness, prayer, and communion with God until in their high attainments they reach a point where they deny the inspiration of the Bible, give up public worship, the ordinances of the Gospel, and probably secret prayer as well.

Those who give up these things are not led away while wrestling in prayer and while walking humbly and closely with God. No one ever got away from orthodox Christian faith while in this state of mind. But people first get away from God and quench His Spirit, *then* embrace one error after another. Truth falls out of their minds. We might almost say that truthfulness itself, or those qualities of moral attributes that enable the mind to discern and apprehend the truth leave their minds as well. Then darkness becomes so universal and so deceptive that such people suppose themselves to be wholly in the light.

Such a state of mind is most deplorable and often hopeless. What can be done when a person has grieved the Spirit of God away? When an individual or a group of people has quenched the Holy Spirit, they are in the utmost danger of being given up to some delusion that will bring them shortly to destruction.

Those who maintain that a genuine Christian movement—one that is truly the work of God—cannot be resisted are in serious error. For example, I have often seen cases where people would stop a revival and then say, "It was not a real revival, for if it had been it would not have stopped." If a person adopts the opinion that he cannot stop the work of God in his own soul, then he is in a perilous position.

Let a people adopt the notion that revivals come and go without our agency, and by the agency of God only, and it will bring perfect ruin upon them. There never was a revival that could exist three days under such a delusion. The solemn truth is that the Holy Spirit is most easily quenched. There is no moral work of His that cannot be resisted. An immense responsibility pertains to revivals. There is always fearful danger that the Holy Spirit will be resisted. The Spirit often labors with sinners, but many have grieved Him away.

Many people do not seem to realize the nature of the Holy Spirit's operations, the possibility of resisting, and the great danger of quenching that light of God in the soul.

How many young people could I name who were once thoughtful, but are now stupid? Where are those young men who were so serious and who attended the inquiry meeting so long in our last revival? Alas, have they quenched the Holy Spirit?

Have *you* quenched the Spirit until now your mind is darkened and your heart is woefully hardened? How long before the death-knell shall toll over you and your soul go down to hell? How long before you will lose your hold on all truth and the Spirit will have left you utterly?

But let me bring this appeal home to the hearts of those who have not yet utterly quenched the light of God in their souls. Do you find that truth still takes hold of your conscience, that God's Word flashes on your mind, that heaven's light is not yet utterly extinguished— that there is still a faint quivering of conscience? When you hear of someone's sudden death, does your soul tremble, knowing that another blow may single out *you*. By all the mercies of God, I beseech you to take care what you do. *Quench not the Holy Spirit, lest your soul go down in everlasting darkness.*

Just as you may have seen the sun set when it dipped into a dark, terrific, portentous thundercloud, so an unrepentant sinner dies! Have you ever seen such a death? Dying, he seems to sink into an awful cloud of fire and storm and darkness. The scene is fearful, like a sunsetting of storms and rolling thunders and forked lightnings. The clouds gather low in the west; the fury of the storm rides on them, belching thunders seem as if they would cleave the solid earth. Behind such a fearful cloud the sun drops and all is darkness. So have I seen a sinner give up the ghost and drop into a world of storms and howling tempests and flashing fire.

Oh, how unlike the setting sun of a mild summer evening. All nature seems to put on her sweetest smile as she bids the king of day adieu. So dies the saint of God. There may be paleness on his lip and cold sweat upon his brow, but there is beauty in that eye and glory in that soul. I think of a woman just converted.

When she was taken sick, brought down to the gates of death, still her soul was full of heaven. Her voice was the music of angels. Her countenance shone, her eye sparkled as if the forms of heavenly glory were embodied in her dying features. When the moment of death had come, she stretched out her dying hands and hailed the waiting spirit-throng. "Glory to God!" she cried. "I am coming! I am coming!" Observe, she did not say, "I am going!" but, "I am *coming!*"

Compare this woman to the dying sinner. A frightful glare is on his countenance, as if he sees ten thousand demons! As if the setting sun should go down into an ocean of storms—to be lost in a world charged with tornadoes, storms, and death.

You will die like the sinner if you quench the Spirit of God. Jesus himself said, "If ye believe not that I am he, ye shall die in your sins" (John 8:24). Beyond such a death there is an awful hell.

16

QUENCHING THE SPIRIT, PART 2*

"Quench not the Spirit" (1 Thessalonians 5:19).
" . . . and grieve not the Holy Spirit of God, whereby ye are sealed unto the day of redemption" (Ephesians 4:30).

The Holy Spirit is the Author of spiritual life—of all its energy and warmth in man—and of all those states of mind that result from His influences. He is the Author of all spiritual joy and peace in the soul. His influences create that life and energy which belong to true spirituality.

He also employs himself in producing that joy and peace of mind that are peculiar to Christians. To "quench" Him is to extinguish His light and energy—that peculiar light which He brings to the mind, and the energy which naturally results from it. The language used here is figurative, of course. He is said to be like a refiner's fire; to "quench" Him, therefore, would be to put out that fire.

To "grieve" Him is to destroy that spiritual peace of mind in the human soul of which He is the Author. When this is destroyed by anything we do, when the agency of the Spirit of God is resisted, He is represented as being grieved. Undoubtedly, there is a sense in which the Spirit of God himself is grieved: He is a moral agent. He can and does feel, and so there is a sense in which He is himself grieved.

The Spirit Convicts; He Does Not Coerce

The injunction not to quench the Spirit clearly implies that it may be done. And there is a probability of its being done. If it were impossible or improbable, we should not find such an urgent warning in

---

*The Penny Pulpit, July 14, 1850, delivered at the Tabernacle, Moorfields.

Holy Scripture, implying not only a danger of its being done, but the wickedness of it as well.

The Holy Spirit is represented in the Bible as a moral agent. Feelings peculiar to a moral agent are ascribed to Him. He is represented, too, as being infinitely interested in giving himself up to the great work of saving us from sin and death. He is infinitely holy, and therefore opposed to iniquity in every form or degree.

His influences are described as teaching and enlightening, but not by a physical, irresistible agency, in the sense that He overrules the freedom of the human mind. He enlightens, warns, and sanctifies through the truth. He operates by the presentation of such considerations as will most persuade a moral agent. For if holiness is to be the result of His operations, this must be the way in which He operates.

In substance, holiness cannot be created by any creative power. Holiness is love. The Holy Spirit's influence, therefore, must be by truth, and prevails not by setting aside a person's liberty, but by teaching him how to use his liberty rightly, and by presenting such considerations as will induce him to do this. This is done, not by a physical, but by a persuasive and enlightening agency.

How the Spirit May Be Grieved

The Spirit of God is grieved and quenched in all cases where the mind is unwilling to see the truth on any subject. Often people are unwilling to be convinced on certain points, and will avoid coming under the pressure of the truth on certain given points. Whenever this is done, the Spirit of God is resisted, quenched, and grieved.

The Spirit of God is grieved whenever the mind assents to the truth, and yet continues in unbelief. Multitudes confound conviction of the truth with faith. They do not know any better than to suppose that once they are convinced of the truth, they have faith, but there is not a greater error in existence. Being convinced of the truth of a statement is infinitely far from faith. Faith is the mind's voluntary act in view of what the Spirit of God convinces us of.

Unbelief is the rejection of what the Spirit presents to our minds; a refusal to commit ourselves to truth, and to obey it. Now faith is that committal of the mind to perceived truth. Faith is this committal of the mind to the truths that God urges upon them, distinct from those truths that convicted sinners are willing to acknowledge.

For example, convicted sinners may be convinced of God's claims and character—of the necessity and sufficiency of the atonement of Christ, and many other things. Yet, the sinner may withhold faith because he is unwilling to yield up his sin and become a Christian; therefore, he will not receive Christ, grasp the truth in his own mind, and absorb himself completely in it. Wherever the truth is presented and yet resisted, there is unbelief. Wherever unbelief prevails, there the Spirit of God is grieved, resisted and quenched.

The Spirit is grieved, resisted and quenched by all evasions of the truth on questions of reform involving self-denial. There are a great many truths, the reception of which calls for great self-denial—a breaking off from certain things in which we have been in the habit of indulging ourselves. Suppose a slaveholder, when the question of the moral character of slavery is posed, will not so much as read about, listen to, or even talk with anyone upon the subject. Suppose also that when he does at last chance to read or hear a discussion of the morality of slavery, he still will not yield to the truth and set his slaves free. He resists the Holy Spirit.

It is remarkable to see the extent to which this has been manifested in the United States, particularly as it touches the issue of the liquor trade. Traders in this industry must deal with the question just as the slaveholders do. They selfishly maintain their position and will not give up their traffic.

On any question of reform calling for self-denial, wherever the mind resists, and does not receive and obey the truth, the Spirit of God is quenched. There are a great many customs prevalent in society that the gospel utterly condemns. Whenever these questions come up, and the mind will not receive the truth and make necessary sacrifices, there is a quenching and a grieving of the Spirit who is trying to lead them away from all such practices.

Indulging in resentful or otherwise hostile feelings toward anyone is sure to quench and grieve the Holy Spirit, especially where such feelings are persevered in. Many have known what it was to indulge in such feelings till, at length, they have ceased to commune with their God.

To indulge in a judgmental spirit, finding fault and putting a bad interpretation on everything, is another example of transgressing the law laid down in our text. Sometimes you will see a person who puts a bad construction on things unnecessarily, making out that certain people have wrong motives and bad dispositions—even where the motives may be good, for all they know. Now, all such conduct as this no doubt grieves and quenches the Spirit of God.

Likewise, unnecessary, unbenevolent, or unbrotherly publications of the *real* failings of people is another way in which this sin may be committed. People may commit this crime by telling the truth unnecessarily, and thus injuring a person. You have no right to speak of the faults of others unnecessarily. You will not do so if *you* are as careful of his failings as you wish him to be of yours.

If you took to heart the injunction "love your neighbor as yourself," how careful you would be of your neighbor's faults. Wherever this is not the case, wherever the tale-bearer is heeded, wherever you treat your brother or neighbor in a manner different from that in which you desire to be treated yourself, there you undoubtedly grieve the Spirit of God. Never do or withhold that which you would not like done to or withheld from you.

This sin is committed where people make self-justifying, thus God-condemning, excuses for their sins. Some grope on in darkness, error, and distress of mind from year to year, making excuses that virtually throw the blame for their behavior upon God, instead of taking the blame of sin on themselves. This grieves the Holy Spirit. Every selfish person, everyone who is set upon the promotion of his own interests instead of the promotion of God's glory, grieves the Spirit of God.

Such an act is virtual apostasy from God, for once a person has professed his commitment to God, he has no right to do anything except for Him. A person can never enjoy communion with God while in pursuit of any selfish goals—while he seeks things merely for his own pleasure, and not for God. If you do this, you virtually take back your consecration to God and devote yourself to your own interests. It matters not at all in what manner you may excuse yourself for doing so. You have no excuse. Especially is this the case where light has been poured upon the subject.

Now, who can suppose that in this light such a person as John Newton could, even for a time, continue in the slave trade without some compunctions of conscience? But suppose he should take recourse to the Bible and ask, "Were there not slaves in the days of the New Testament? Why did not Christ denounce it? Slavery was known to the apostles, why did not they denounce it if it were so wicked?" This is easily enough answered, though people justify the slave trade in this way; this is particularly true in the southern states of America.

They forget that Christ had a previous question to settle before He could make any direct attack on the several sorts of sin. When Christ came into the world, His mission was not acknowledged immediately; He had to debate every inch of ground. And so, proof of His divinity and divine mission demanded primary attention. By necessity, the world needed to first recognize His *authority* to lay down regulations and prohibit practices. It would have been utterly out of place for Him to have attempted to set right social questions before He had established His authority to intervene in such matters.

Some argue that the apostles did not denounce slavery. But they, too, had a great question that demanded their first attention. They had to establish the fact of Christ's resurrection, of His divinity and messiahship, as well as the divine authority of their own commission. Once this was accomplished, they would naturally commend to the world the truth of Scripture, and let them discern what things are right and what are wrong on the basis of its truths.

It would have been absurd for the apostles to denounce any particular sins without establishing their authority to denounce sin at all. It is a selfish evasion for a slaveholder to talk thus! No man should thus attempt to justify slavery; it is a heinous offense, and no one can pursue it without forfeiting his right to be called or treated as a Christian.

I can recall the time when everyone thought the consumption of alcohol was necessary. We all thought no one could do without it. But by and by, the question was taken up, and it became a point of some debate. Many rose up in resistance, and sin quenched the Holy Spirit—and where are they now? A desolation has come over some of their churches through taking wrong grounds on this question.

But let me say again: if any person allows himself to pursue a branch of business that promotes a great evil to society, he is guilty of the sin spoken of here. Suppose a pirate prides himself on his intention to make a good use of his money; suppose, when apprehended, he were to plead that he was going to give his money to the Bible Society. Would that clear his crime? No, indeed.

There was a rich man who, upon his profession of conversion, made up his mind to give all that he had to the Lord. I saw nothing of him for a time, but after some years he called at our house. After a time, he told me that he had left his former place of residence, and was moving to another part of the country. I asked him where he was going to, and he replied that he was going west, to St. Louis. The man had failed in business.

"Failed in business!" I exclaimed, "How is that?" It turned out that he had speculated in the provision line in order to get money to send evangelists. To do this, he bought up all the provisions along a certain road, put a high price upon them, and thus raised the funds he needed from among the poor that lived along this great thoroughfare. He had, according to his notions, been speculating for God.

I asked him what business he had to do such a thing as that. And I informed him that I was not the least surprised that he had failed. Did God want him to *punish the poor* in order that he might *spread the gospel*? No indeed.

Look again at the liquor trade. There are many who will resist light on this subject. They will talk just as men who are determined not to forsake a business they know is an abomination to the Lord and a curse to society. Yes! If all the tears could be collected together, which this business has caused to be shed, they would make enough, perhaps, for them to swim in.

It has broken hearts, ruined families, dethroned reason, desolated firesides—everything is laid waste. All this, and more, has resulted from the sale of these deadly drinks. Some say it is *necessary*. For the sake of the argument I will admit that, in certain instances, it may be beneficial; but mark this, it will be vastly more abused than it is really needed! Is not the business, therefore, utterly undesirable?

Suppose no more were used than the comparatively small quantity that is actually necessary. Suppose it were not abused, and that there was no probability that it would be abused. How many liquor dealers, think you, would there be in London? How many of them would think of living by the business, if they presumed no more than necessary would be used! In fact, it is the assumption that it will be abused that renders it so desirable an object of business. Everyone engaged in it presumes this, or he would not be in business. Who, then, can pursue such a trade as this, and enjoy communion with the Holy Spirit at the same time!

Drinking and slavery and everything of the kind might go on without its wickedness being dreamt of. But when light is poured upon the subject, and men still refuse to see, it is utterly inexcusable.

Remarkably, those who have resisted this reformation—ministers who have refused to yield after they have been shown the sinfulness of their position—have withered. This has been particularly evident in America, amongst those who have continued to submit to the slave power, after seeing the sinfulness of the traffic. The frown of God has been upon them as manifestly as it could be; they have quenched the Spirit. It would be impossible to calculate the good that has been effected where holy men of God in the ministry have taken the lead in these reforms.

There are multitudes of business practices by which the Spirit of God is grieved. When they see the error, some will still struggle with the Spirit of God. Many men are uneasy and restless from resistance to the Spirit of God in such matters. There is some lack of candor, and consequently there is a fetter upon their spirit. There is a strife, and an agonizing in their souls.

They know there is something wrong. They have not the joy and peace belonging to a Christian. The fact is, they are engaged in a struggle with their Maker. They are quenching and grieving His Spirit in the presentation of the truth on some question that has come before them. Liquor dealers, and all who use drink, are in danger of falling into this state.

I would not apply my remarks so generally in this country as in America, because public opinion is not so far advanced here as it is there. Therefore, I would not assert that those of you who use these drinks cannot enjoy communion with God. Even Newton, Whitefield, and the Countess of Huntingdon, were slaveholders. But if they were alive today, would they be slaveholders! No, indeed!

God is on the way to reform mankind on these points. The state of the world is coming right square up to them. God is turning the attention both of the church and the world to these great evils. Light is blazing forth on every hand. For this reason, it is impossible to pretend that Whitefield or Lady Huntingdon would be slaveholders if they were alive now!

It is the duty of every Christian in the world to take up whatever self-denial these reforms may involve! I have known multitudes who have poured their liquors into the street; and who, when urged to consume it for medical purposes, have replied, "No, we will not touch, nor taste, nor handle the unclean thing."

All jealousy, envying, and party feeling are ways of quenching and grieving the Spirit of God. I have seen the piety of churches decline rapidly and fearfully from such things in great cities, and yet they could not understand the problem. Yet if you question them individually, you will find numbers of them with such attitudes toward one another, that the Holy Spirit, who loves them both, must, in some measure, withdraw His influence.

Who, in this age of the world, thinks to preach against gluttony! Yet it is one of the most common forms of sin. An individual once confessed to me that he had for years been unable to attend properly to his business because he had indulged in too hearty a dinner. During the whole of that time he had never once heard gluttony preached against, or condemned from the pulpit as sinful. I think that a great deal still needs to be done even among Christians, whatever may already have been said on the subject of excessive eating.

The same may be said of drinking and other evil indulgences, such as the use of tobacco in its various forms. How few like to look at this in the proper light. They surely cannot plead that they smoke, snuff, or chew to the glory of God. In some few diseases, somewhere about one in five thousand, tobacco may be used with benefit.

If professing Christians allow themselves in such self-indulgent habits, how can they expect to enjoy communion with God? Is it reasonable for persons to use such things, wasting God's money to buy them, and covering themselves with the stench of it! I was astonished the other day to be introduced to a minister whose hands and pockets were considerably besmeared with snuff. He talked of Christianity as if he never considered the effect it should have on his personal habits. But most men know that all such habits are contrary to the duty of the Christian.

I have known some who, when told that such were wrong, would get up and leave the house, unwilling to be shown the real nature and tendency of these things. Yet if they are unwilling at least to ascertain by honest investigation whether such things are right or wrong, they must assuredly quench the Spirit.

There is no way in which we can keep a clear medium open between our hearts and God without weighing all our habits in the balances of the Bible. If we would have the fruits of the Spirit—love, joy, peace, and so on—we must ever be ready to listen to reproof, and honestly apply every principle of the gospel to all of life; to everything we do.

I used tobacco once myself, and continued to do so even for some time after I was converted. A brother conversed with me on the subject. I had supposed it beneficial to me for a certain reason.

"Brother," he said to me, "do you think, *now*, that it is right?"

I reflected for a moment. He made a suggestion or two on the subject. At length I put my hand into my pocket, and got out my box, which I had just filled. "There," I said, "take that." I saw him some years after; and I had still not resumed the use of it, and have never felt inclined to do so since. I do not speak boastingly, but I have become quite afraid of doing anything that would tend to quench the Spirit.

I have always tried to be careful of this. If anything gets between my soul and God, I have been in the habit of saying, "O Lord, tell me what is the matter! What am I doing? What stands in the way?" We should act in the same way we would if Jesus were physically present with us, just as He was with the disciples. Let that be the rule. Don't do or say anything that will cause Jesus to say, "I am sorry to see you doing or omitting to do so and so . . ." or, "I am sorry to see you engaged in such and such a business." Let your proceedings be of such a nature that you can say, "Oh Lord, are You sorry to see me do this? Does it grieve You? Does Your heart not approve of my doing it?"

Now, do you for one moment suppose that a slaveholder, for instance, could do this, and go away supposing that God would have him continue his atrocious trade? And do you believe that people engaged in businesses of other kinds, which are injurious to society (the liquor trade, for instance), can go and say, "Lord, is this for thy glory! Wilt thou approve, and add thy blessing!" Can they say, "Help me, oh Lord, to sell as much liquor today as I can. Help me to throw out as much alcohol in all the forms that I can to get people to buy it!"

Can they pray so? No man has any right to engage in any business on which he cannot ask the blessing of God. Who would think, in these days, of praying in that way? Who would think of praying against the multitudes of evils that now exist, while they themselves are among the very persons who engage in them!

I do not know if you are guilty of this, but if you are, I wish to warn you in love. I ask you—can you do these things with the idea that you are honoring God? Can you say when you go to your liquor shops, "Oh, God, bless me in this business, help me to do a great deal of business, and thereby glorify Thee!"

Refusing to receive a brother who calls for self-denial is grieving and quenching the Holy Spirit. Refusing to sympathize with Christ in His self-denying exertions to do good to the world will grieve the Holy Spirit. He has led the way by showing what He is willing to do to save mankind. Now those who hold back, unwilling to unite with Him upon the same principles on which He acted, resist and grieve the Spirit.

Not long ago a person was talking to his pastor about the propriety of setting an example to his flock by abstaining from drink, if only for the sake of others. But the pastor rejoined that their abuse of it was no reason for his abstinence. "They abuse many other things as well as that," said the pastor. Now, was this the principle on which Paul acted? No, indeed, he was ready to give up meat "as long as the world lasted." On the same principle Christ might have said He did not see why He should suffer because mankind had abused the government of the Almighty by making bad use of their moral agency.

Christ acted upon the principle of saving those who had no excuse for their sins—not the unfortunate, but the wicked. Thus missionaries and other Christians deny themselves what they might otherwise have had freedom to partake of, because the good they might receive would be so much less than the evil that might result from their actions. But when we take such astounding ground as in the case of the said minister, what can we expect but darkness of mind and fruitlessness of life?

In order to have the Spirit of God, we must yield to Him. If we do not do this, if we do not go from one degree of self-denial to another, we resist the Spirit, who is trying to lead us up to a higher ground than we have occupied until now. The church has never been on a ground so high as to give herself entirely up to reform the world. But the Holy Spirit is pressing her up and up.

Her business, therefore, is to prepare herself to go the whole length of reforming herself, and those around her, and prepare for any degree of self-denial that may be required in order to accomplish this. But if anyone shall insist upon not giving up this and that, although he knows that the good to be obtained, and the evil to be shunned, will far outweigh all that can be gained from indulgence, what would become of the church and the world should they imitate him!

Suppose, for instance, we admit that alcoholic drinks are, in some cases, useful! Is the use of them a greater good than the evil of their abuse? The same cannot be said of meat and drink, seeing that they are necessities of life, and cannot be done without. Things indispensable to life cannot be done without. We are not called upon, therefore, to give them up. But there are drinks and other things that are working a great injury to society, and which it has been demonstrated again and again that they may safely be dispensed with.

All will admit that the injury that results to mankind from the abuses of these things bears no comparison to the doubtful benefit which we might derive from them, individually. Clearly, we ought to give them up.

That was the principle on which Christ acted! "Because of my relations and character," He said, "it is better that there should be this suffering, on my part, than that the human family should suffer eternal death!" If the suffering He endured had been greater than that which He prevented, the course He adopted would have been neither wise nor benevolent. He gained for the universe an unspeakable benefit, and prevented an inconceivable injury.

His rule should be our guide. Self-denial does us good. *Shall we offer the Lord only that which costs us nothing?* Shall we say that if a thing is a good to us, we cannot give it up? Why not! If doing so will avoid a greater evil, and procure a greater good, you are bound to give it up, if you desire to be benevolent to all.

If you will not sacrifice a small good to yourself for the sake of a great good to others, what kind of a Christian must you be? You go in direct opposition to the Spirit of Christ and of the apostles. If a man speculates about his indulgences, if he " . . . does not see why he should give up" this or that, who can expect him to have a face so clear as to look up to God and say, "Thou knowest, Lord, that I would rather die than scatter evils thus around me by anything I should do!" The fact is, beloved, there is a world to be said on this subject. Now who does not see that shuffling and conniving like this grieves the Spirit!

Some of you are aware of the great and powerful revivals that swept through America, and that, when the slavery question came up, the ministers of the North and South united in one great ecclesiastical connection. Many quarters cried out that we should not disturb this connection; often these Northern ministers would not allow notices of anti-slavery meetings to be announced from their pulpits—not even anti-slavery prayer meetings. Instead, they treated the matter just as many ministers in this country do the temperance question: lightly. Neither would they speak out and denounce the sin of slavery.

The resulting blight of the Almighty came upon the churches, causing revivals to disappear and churches to decline; the Spirit was grieved! The very same course was pursued in America with regard to temperance; if I am not mistaken, you have got some solemn lessons to learn on this subject in England. I would that all the ministers of England were here tonight! But some of them will not hear us on the subject; they are unwilling to broach it, in or out of the pulpit! What will become of them and their churches?

We shall see! If their churches remain silent on these subjects, if this question is to be resisted, I believe you will experience a similar suffering to that which has afflicted the American churches. There are many doleful tales to tell on that subject. But these things must be put away. The chains of the slaves must be snapped asunder; intemperance must be swept away; God will have it so.

Let no one trifle with God on these subjects. These great evils must be removed from the face of society. The poor must no longer be lured to the tippling houses; they must be reasoned with, and entreated. Consider! You do not need it. You are better without it. Do not go!

If you could only see some of the affecting instances of Christians who took it upon themselves to go into the ditches, taking the drunken men out, treating them kindly, and giving the whole force of their influence and example against these drinks. How many tears have thus been wiped away! How many hearths have thus been surrounded with joyous smiles, where desolation once prevailed!

There is much to be done; do not resist these movements. Do not stand in the way, lest you grieve the Spirit of God. At the same time, however, beware of dealing out indiscriminate condemnation. Time was when there was as much darkness in America on this subject as there is here now.

I would say to all, "Be willing to practice what you know, and remain open to further conviction." Go for the whole. Say, "I will wash mine hands in innocency: so will I compass thine altar, O Lord" (Ps. 26:6).

Coldness Is a Consequence

Those who grieve the Holy Spirit develop great blindness of mind. You are probably aware that so great has been the blindness of some that they have undertaken to prove from the Bible that slavery is a divine institution! Here in England, you do not need to be told that this is gross darkness. In America, it began as professing Christians gradually shut their eyes to the truth, begetting a coldness of mind and a hardness of heart. Their whole being was brought under the dominion of their lusts. They were chained and bound fast in the fetters of their sin. They are waxing worse and worse, and becoming more and more confirmed in their sins.

Instead of at once starting a universal reformation, with classes denying themselves and setting an example, as the Church takes the lead, what are they doing? They are falling back, shrinking from their work. There is great wreck of ministerial character, oftentimes, where there is not a thorough walk right up to the work. There cannot be much prevailing prayer where there is so much quenching of the Spirit, so few of the fruits of the Spirit in evidence; so many self-indulgent habits, and so few God-honoring practices.

Many tempt God by praying for the Spirit, while, at the same time, quenching it. There is great danger of the Spirit leaving. Some years back, a minister who was about forty years of age came to me after service, and said, "Brother Finney, I am in a terrible state of mind. I must abandon the ministry. When at the theological seminary, I took the wrong side in a discussion; but, having committed myself, I have defended my position contrary to my convictions even here. My deception has caused me to lose the spirit of prayer, and the curse of God has been on me ever since. I have been many years in the ministry, yet I do not know that I have been instrumental in the conversion of a single soul. What shall I do? My fruitless vine is dry and withered!"

He told me many more things of a similar character; but the case was not new to me. I have seen instances of individuals having taken the wrong side, and of God holding them up as a warning to others, lest they fall under the same condemnation.

And now, let me ask you. Are you prepared to go the full length of doing what you think Christ would ask you to do, should you meet Him? If you are not prepared to do this, you are resisting and quenching the Holy Spirit. Are you holding back? What are you doing? Will you live at this "poor, dying rate," or be filled with the Spirit? If so, do not quench the Spirit; resist and grieve him no longer. Give up all your life, heart, and soul, relying upon Him alone. The fruits of the Spirit will abound in you; and, if you do this, those around you will take notice of you, if, indeed, you exhibit the fruits of the Spirit of Christ.

17

THE SPIRIT WILL NOT ALWAYS STRIVE*

"And the Lord said, My Spirit shall not always strive with man" (Genesis 6:3).

Implications of This Verse

This assertion implies that the Holy Spirit does *sometimes* strive with people. It is nonsense to affirm that He will not strive *always*, if the fact of His striving *sometimes* is not implied. Beyond all question, the text assumes the doctrine that God by His Spirit does sometimes strive with sinners.

The text also implies that people resist the Holy Spirit, for there can be no strife unless there is resistance.

If sinners always yielded at once to the teachings and guidance of the Holy Spirit, then there could be no "striving" on the part of the Spirit in the sense implied here, and it would be altogether improper to use the language employed here. In fact, the language of our text implies long-continued resistance; *so* long continued, that God declares the struggle shall not be kept up on His part forever.

I am well aware that sinners are prone to think that they do not resist God. They often think that they really want the Spirit of God to be with them, and to strive with them. Indeed! Think of that! If a sinner really wanted the Spirit of God to convert or lead him, how could he resist the Spirit? But in fact, he does resist the Spirit. What Stephen affirmed of the Jews of his time is true in general of all sinners: "Ye do always resist the Holy Ghost" (Acts 7:51).

If there were no resistance on the sinner's part, there would be no striving on the part of the Spirit. It is a mere absurdity to suggest that a sinner in a state of mind to resist the Spirit should yet sincerely

---

*From *Sermons on Gospel Themes*, 264–291.

desire to be led into truth and duty by the Spirit. But sinners are sometimes so deceived about themselves, so blinded to their own true characters, as to suppose that they want God to strive with them. In fact, they are resisting all He is doing, and are ready to resist all He will do.

The Struggling Is Spiritual, Not Physical

The main thing to be observed is that it is not any form of physical struggling or effort whatever. It is not any force applied to our bodies. He does not literally attempt to push us along toward God or heaven. This is not to be thought of at all.

The striving of the Spirit is the energy of God applied to a person's mind, setting truth before his mind, debating, reasoning, convincing, and persuading. The sinner resists God's claims, reasons, and argues against them. And God, by His Spirit, meets the sinner and debates with him, somewhat as two people might debate and argue with each other. You are not, however, to understand that the Holy Spirit does this with an audible voice to the human ear; He speaks to the mind and to the heart. The inner ear of the soul can hear its whispers.

Our Savior taught that when the Comforter came He would "reprove the world of sin, and of righteousness, and of judgment" (John 16:8). The term rendered "reprove" refers in its proper sense to judicial proceedings. When the judge has heard all the testimony and the arguments of counsel, he sums up the whole case and lays it before the jury, bringing out all the strong points and making them decide with all their condensed and accumulated power upon the guilt of the criminal.

This is "reproving" him, in the original and legitimate sense of the word used here by our Savior. Thus the Holy Spirit "reproves" the world of sin, of righteousness, and of judgment. Thus does the Spirit convince or convict the sinner by testimony, by argument, by arraying all the strong points of the case against him under circumstances of affecting solemnity and power.

Discerning the Drawing of the Spirit

You will not directly perceive the Spirit's influence through any of your physical senses, for His presence is not manifested to these organs. Nor directly by our consciousness, for the only proper subjects of consciousness are those in the realm of the awareness of our own minds. But we know the presence and agency of the Spirit by His works, and by the results He produces; both are the legitimate proofs of His presence.

A person under the Spirit's influence finds his attention arrested to the great concerns of his soul. The solemn questions of duty and responsibility to God are continually intruding upon his mind. If he is a student, his mind is unwittingly drawn away continually from his lesson, to think of God and of the judgment to come. He turns his attention back to his books, but soon it is off again. How can he neglect these matters of infinite importance, which will determine his future well-being?

So with people of every calling. The Holy Spirit turns their minds and draws them to God and the concerns of their souls. When such takes place, you may know that the Spirit of God is the cause. This drawing and inclining of the mind toward God is by no means natural to the human heart, and so when it does occur, we know that the special agency of God is in it.

When a person finds himself "convinced of sin," he may know that this is the Spirit's work. Now it is one thing to know one's self to be a sinner, and quite another to realize the awesome implications of the fact, and to have the truth take hold mightily in the deepest feelings of the soul. The latter takes place only under the Spirit's agency. You may see a person's countenance fallen, his eye downcast, his whole bearing is as if he had disgraced himself by some foul crime, or as if he had suddenly lost all the friends he ever had.

I have often met with unrepentant sinners who looked condemned, as if conscious guilt had taken hold of their innermost soul. They would not be aware that they were revealing in their countenances the deep workings of their hearts, but the observing eye could not help seeing it. I have also seen the same among backsliders, from the same cause— the Spirit of God reproving them of sin.

Sometimes this conviction is of a general and sometimes of a more specific nature. It may enforce only the general impression: "I am all wrong. I am utterly odious and hateful to God. My whole heart is a foul abomination in His sight." Or, in other cases, it may seize upon some particular form of sin, and hold it up before the sinner's mind, and cause him to see his sin's infinite odiousness before God. It may be a sin he has never thought of before, or he may have deemed it a very light matter. But now, through the Spirit's striving, the sin will rise up before his mind with such ugliness and loathsomeness that he will abhor himself. He sees sin in a perfectly new light. Many things are sins now which he never deemed sins before.

The Holy Spirit not only convinces an individual of the fact that certain things are sins, but convicts the mind of the great guilt incurred by sin. The sinner is made to feel that his sin deserves the direst damnation.

The case of an infidel of my acquaintance may serve to illustrate this. He had lived with two pious wives in succession, read almost every book available concerning the inspiration of the Scriptures, and had disputed and debated countless believers in the Bible, always considering himself to have triumphed over them.

He was the most subtle infidel I ever saw. It was remarkable that in connection with his infidelity he had no just views of sin. He had indeed heard much about some dreadful depravity that had come down in the current of human blood from Adam, and was itself a physical thing. But as usual, he had no oppressive consciousness of guilt for having his share of this original taint. His mind consequently was quite unmoved with respect to the guilt of his own sin.

But at length a change came over him, and his eyes were opened to see the horrible enormity of his guilt. I saw him one day so borne down with sin and shame that he could not look up. He bowed his head upon his knees, covered his face, and groaned in agony. I left him in this state, and went to the prayer meeting.

Before long he came into the meeting as he had never come before. As he left the meeting, he said to his wife, "You have long known me as a strong-hearted infidel, but my infidelity is all gone. I cannot tell you what has become of it. It all seems to me as the merest nonsense. I cannot conceive of how I could ever have believed and defended it. I seem to myself like a person called to view some glorious and beautiful structure in order to pass his judgment upon it. But who presumes to judge and condemn it after having caught only a dim glimpse of one obscure corner? Just so have I done in condemning the glorious Bible and the glorious government of God."

Now, the secret to all this change in his mind toward the Bible lay in the change of his views with regard to his own sin. Before, he had not been convicted of sin at all. Now, he saw it in some of its true light, and really felt that he deserved the deepest hell. Of course, he now saw the pertinence and beauty and glory of the gospel system. He is now in a position in which he can clearly see one of the strongest proofs of the truth of the Bible; namely, its perfect adaptation to meet the needs of a sinning race.

It is remarkable to see the power there is in conviction to break up and annihilate the delusions of error. For instance, no one can once thoroughly see his own sin and remain a universalist, and deem it unjust for God to send him to hell.

When I hear a person talking in defense of Universalism, I know he does not understand anything about sin. He has not begun to see his own guilt in its true light. It is the most blind of all mental infatuations to think that the little inconveniences of this life are all that sin deserves. Let a person once see his own guilt, and he will be amazed to think that he ever held such a notion. The Spirit of God, pouring light upon the sinner's mind, will soon utterly shatter the precepts of universalism.

I once labored in a village in New York where Universalism prevailed extensively. The leading man among them had a sick wife who sympathized with him in sentiment. Since she was near death, I went to see her and endeavored to expose the utter fallacy of her delusion. After I had left, her husband returned, and his wife, her eyes now being opened, cried out to him as he entered the room, "Oh, my dear husband, you are on the way to hell. Your Universalism will ruin your soul forever!"

He was greatly enraged, and learning that I had been talking with her, his rage was kindled against me. "Where is he now?" he asked.

"Gone to the meeting," she replied.

"I'll go there and shoot him," he cried. Seizing his loaded pistol, he started off.

When he came in I was preaching from the text, "Ye serpents, ye generation of vipers, how can ye escape the damnation of hell?" (Matt. 23:33). At the time, I knew nothing of his purpose—and nothing about his pistol.

He listened awhile, and then all at once, in the midst of the meeting, he fell back on his seat and cried out, "Oh, I am sinking in hell! Oh God, have mercy on me." Away went his Universalism in a twinkling of an eye: *he saw his sin* and began to sink. This change in him was not my work, for I could produce no such effects as these. I was indeed trying to show from the text what sinners deserve, but nothing less than the Spirit of God could have set home conviction of sin like this.

Again, another fruit of the Spirit is developed in those who are conscious of great hardness of heart and insensibility. It frequently happens that people suppose themselves to be Christians because they have so much sensibility on religious subjects. To undeceive them, the Spirit will direct their attention to some truth that dries up all their feelings, and leaves their hopes stranded on the beach, leaving them in great agony. "The more I hear," they say, "the less I feel good. I was never in the world so far from being convicted of sin as when I felt good. I shall certainly go to hell. I have not a particle of feeling. I cannot feel if I die."

The explanation of this singular state is usually this: the Spirit of God sees their danger—sees them deceiving themselves by relying on their feelings, and therefore brings some truths before their minds that arrays the opposition of their hearts against God and dries up the fountains of their feelings. Then they see how perfectly callous their hearts are toward God. This is the work of the Spirit.

The Holy Spirit convicts the soul of unbelief. Sinners are very apt to suppose that they do believe the gospel. They confuse faith with a merely intellectual assent, and so blind themselves as to suppose that they believe God in the sense of gospel faith. But let the Spirit once reveal their own hearts to them and they will see that they do not believe in God as they believe in their fellow men, and that, instead of having confidence in God and resting on His words of promise as they do on men's promises, they do not *rest* on God at all, but are full of trouble and solicitude—and, in fact, *unbelief*. At last they also see the horribly guilty state of their heart: guilty of not resting in His promises—horribly guilty of not believing with the heart every word God ever uttered.

This change is the work of the Holy Spirit. Our Savior mentions it as one of the effects wrought by the Spirit, that He shall "reprove the world of sin, because they believe not on Me." In fact, we find that this is one of the characteristic works of the Spirit.

I was conversing recently with a person who for many years professed Christian faith, but who had of late been living in seventh chapter of the book of Romans.* He remarked, "I have been thinking of the truth that God cares for me and loves me, and has through Jesus Christ offered me eternal life; and now I deserve to be damned if I do not believe." Stretching out his pale hand, he said with great energy, "I *ought* to go to hell, if I will not believe." Now, all this is the work of the Holy Spirit: making a man see his guilt and the fact that he is deserving of hell, and making a sinner see that everything else is only straw, compared with the eternal rock of God's truth.

The Holy Spirit makes people see the danger of dying in their sins. A young man said to me, "I am afraid to go to sleep at night, lest I should wake up in hell." Sinners often know what this feeling is. I recall having this thought once impressed upon my own mind, and so much agonized was I that I almost thought myself to be dying on the spot! Oh, I can never express the terror and the agony of my soul in that hour! Sinner, if you have these feelings, it is a solemn time, indeed.

Moreover, the Spirit makes sinners feel the danger of being given up by God. Often it happens that sinners, convicted by the Holy Spirit, are made to feel that if they are not given up already, they are in the most imminent peril of it, and must rush for the gate of life now or never. They see that they have so sinned and have done so much to provoke God to give them up that their last hope of being accepted by God is fast dying away. Sinner, have you felt this way? Have you ever trembled in your very soul lest you should be given over to a reprobate

---

*For further explanation of what Finney means by "living in the seventh chapter of the book of Romans" see the sermons on Romans in *Principles of Victory* and *Principles of Liberty*, published by Bethany House Publishers.

mind before another Sabbath, or perhaps before another morning? If so, you may ascribe this feeling to the Spirit of God.

The Spirit often convicts sinners of the great blindness of their minds, causing them to feel that their minds are full of darkness. This is really the natural state of the sinner. But he is not sensible of it until enlightened by the Spirit of God. When thus enlightened, he begins to appreciate his own exceeding great blindness. He now becomes aware that the Bible is a sealed book to him; though he reads it, its meaning is an impenetrable darkness to him. Have you ever been conscious of such an experience? Have you never read the Bible with the distressing consciousness that your mind was not affected by its truth; indeed, with the conviction that you did not get hold of its truth to any good purpose at all? Thus are people enlightened by the Spirit to see the real state of their case.

The Spirit of God shows sinners their total alienation from God. I have seen sinners so strongly convicted of this that they would say right out, "I know that I am not in the least disposed to return to God—I am conscious that I don't care whether I have any religion or not."

I have often seen people who professed to be Christians in this state, conscious that their hearts were utterly alienated from God and from all sympathy with His character or government. Their deep backsliding, or their utter lack of all faith, has been so revealed to them by the Spirit that it is impressed on their consciousness most distinctly.

Sinners who are made to see themselves by the Spirit often find that when they pour out their words before God in prayer that their heart won't go to Him. I once said to a sinner, "Come, now, give up your heart to God." "I will," he said, but in a moment he broke out, *"My heart won't go!"* Have you ever been compelled to say the same? Then you know by experience one of the fruits of the Spirit's convicting power.

When the Spirit of God is not with people, they can dole out their long prayers before God and never think or seem to care how prayerless their hearts are all the time, and how utterly far from God. But when the Spirit sheds His light on the soul, the sinner sees what a hypocrite he is. Oh, then he cannot pray so smoothly, so loosely, so self-complacently.

The Spirit of God often convinces people that they are ashamed of Christ, and that in truth they do not wish for Christianity in their lives. It sometimes happens that sinners do not feel ashamed of being thought "religious" until they are convicted of sin.

Such was the case with myself. I bought my first Bible as a law book, and laid it by the side of my Blackstone. I studied it as I would any other law book, my sole object being to find in it the great principles of law. I never once thought of being ashamed of reading it; I read it as freely and as openly as I read any other book. But as soon as I became awakened to the concerns of my soul, I put my Bible out of sight. If it were lying on my table when people came into my office, then I was careful to throw a newspaper over it. Before long, however, the conviction that I was ashamed of God and of His Word came over me with overwhelming force, and showed me the horrible state of my mind toward God. And I suppose that the general course of my experience is by no means uncommon among unrepentant sinners.

The Spirit also convicts people of worldly-mindedness. Sinners are always in this state of mind; but often not fully aware of the fact until the Spirit of God *makes* them see it. I have often seen people pushing their worldly projects most intensely, but when confronted on the subject they would say, "I don't care much about the world; I am pursuing this business chiefly because I desire to be doing something." But when the Holy Spirit shows them their own hearts, they are in agony, lest they should never be able to break away from the dreadful power of the world upon their souls. Now they see that they have been slaves to the passion for worldly good.

The Holy Spirit often makes such a personal application of the truth as to give the impression that the preacher is talking directly to the one under conviction. The person thus convinced of sin may think that the preacher has, in some way, come to a knowledge of his character, and intends to describe it to the world; that the preacher *means* him, and is preaching to *him*. He wonders who has told the preacher so much about him. All this often takes place when the preacher perhaps does not know that such a person is in the assembly, and altogether ignorant of his history. Thus the Holy Spirit who knows his heart and his entire history applies the truth very personally to that individual.

Have you had this experience? Have you ever felt that the preacher meant *you*? Then the Holy Spirit was upon you. I have often seen people drop their heads under preaching, almost as if they were shot through. They were, perhaps, unable to look up again during the whole service. Afterward, I have often heard that they thought I meant them, and that others thought so too; perhaps they imagined that many eyes were turned on them, and that therefore they did not look up—when in fact neither myself nor anyone in the congregation (in all probability) so much as thought of them. Thus, a bow drawn at a venture often lodges an arrow between the joints of the sinner's coat of mail.

The Holy Spirit often convinces sinners of the enmity of their hearts against God. Most unrepentant sinners and perhaps all deceived professors of faith imagine they are on the whole friendly to God, unless convinced otherwise by the Holy Spirit.

They are far from believing that a carnal mind is enmity against God. They think they do not hate, but love God. Now, this delusion must be torn away or they will be lost. To do this, the Holy Spirit so orders it that some truths are presented that develop their real enmity against God.

The moralist who has been the "almost Christian," the deceived professor of faith, begins to doubt, to find fault, and finally to rail, to oppose the preaching and the meetings and the measures and the men. Perhaps the man who has a pious wife and who has thought himself and has been thought by her to be almost a Christian begins to object to the truth, finding fault with the measures and the manners of the preacher; he then refuses to go to meeting. Finally, he forbids his wife and family to go, and frequently his enmity of heart will boil over in a horrible way. Perhaps he has no thought that this boiling up of hell within him is occasioned by the Holy Spirit, revealing to him the true state of his heart.

His Christian friends may also mistake his case, and conclude that something is wrong with the manners or measures of the preacher that is doing this man a great injury. But beware what you say or do. In many such cases that have come under my own observation, it has turned out that the Holy Spirit was at work in those hearts, revealing to them their real enmity against God.

This He does by presenting truth in such a manner as to produce these results. He pushes this process until He compels the soul to see the truth: that it is filled with enmity to God; that it is not man, but God, to whom he is opposed; that it is not error, but truth, that he opposes; not the manner of preaching, but the subject matter; not the measures but the God of truth, whom he hates.

The Spirit often convicts sinners powerfully of the deceitfulness of their own hearts. They are appalled to see that they have been deluding themselves in matters too plain to justify any mistake, and too momentous to admit of any apology for willful blindness. They are confounded with what they see in themselves.

The Holy Spirit will also strip the sinner of his excuses, showing him clearly his great folly. I recall that this was one of the first things I experienced in the process of conviction. I lost all confidence in any of my excuses, for I found them to be so foolish and futile that I could not endure them. This was my state of mind before I had ever heard of the work of the Holy Spirit, or knew at all how to judge whether my own mind was under His influence or not. Whereas I had been very strong in my excuses and objections, I was now utterly weak; it seemed to me that any child could overthrow me.

In fact, I did not need to be overthrown by anybody, for my excuses and evasions had dwindled to nothing; I was deeply ashamed of them.

I had effectually worked myself out of all their mazes, so that they could bewilder me no longer. I have since seen multitudes in the same condition—weak as to their excuses, their old defensive armor all torn off, and their hearts laid bare to the shafts of God's truth.

Now, sinners, have you known what this is—to have all your excuses and apologies fail you—to feel that you have no courage and no defensible reasons for pursuing any longer a course of sin? If so, then you know what it is to be under the convicting power of the Holy Spirit.

The Spirit of God convicts people of the folly of seeking salvation in any other way than through Christ alone. Often, without being aware of it, a sinner will be really seeking salvation in some other way than through Christ, and he will look to his good deeds—to his own prayers, or to the prayers of Christian friends. But if the Spirit will ever save him, He must tear away these delusive schemes and show him the utter vanity of every other way than through Christ alone.

The Spirit will show him that there is but one way possible for a sinner to be saved, and that all other attempts are forever vain, and worse than worthless. All self-righteousness must be rejected entirely, and Christ be sought alone. Have you ever been made to see this? As a professing Christian, has this been your experience?

The Spirit convinces people of the great folly and madness of clinging to an unsanctifying hope. The Bible teaches that everyone who has the genuine gospel hope "purifieth himself, even as he [Christ] is pure" (1 John 3:3). In this passage, the Apostle John plainly means to affirm a universal proposition, a universal characteristic of the Christian hope. Whoever has a Christian hope should ask, "Do I purify myself even as Christ is pure?" If not, then you do not have gospel hope.

Yet thousands of professed Christians have a most inefficient hope. What is it? Does it really lead them to purify themselves as Christ is pure? No. It is not a hope that they shall see Christ as He is, and be forever with Him, and altogether like Him; it is mainly a hope that they shall escape hell and venture into some unknown heaven instead.

Such professed Christians cannot help but know that their experience lacks the witness of their own consciences that they are living for God and bearing His image. If such are ever saved, they must first be convinced of the folly of a hope that leaves them unsanctified.

You who profess to be Christians, have you lived a worldly life so long that you are ashamed of your hope? Have you not good reason to be ashamed of a hope that has no more power than yours does at present? Are there any today who in the honesty of their hearts must say, "Either there is no power in the gospel or I don't know anything about it"? For the gospel affirms as a universal fact of all those who are under grace, *"sin shall not have dominion over you"* (Rom. 6:14).

Will you go before God and say, "Lord, You have said, *Sin shall not have dominion over you,* but, Lord, that is not true, for I believe the gospel and am under grace, but sin still has dominion over *me!*" No doubt in this case there is a mistake somewhere; and it becomes you to ask solemnly, "Shall I charge this mistake and falsehood upon God, or shall I admit that it must be in myself alone?" The Apostle Paul has said, the gospel "is the power of God unto salvation to every one that believeth" (Rom. 1:16). Is it so to you?

Paul has also said, "Being justified by faith, we have peace with God through our Lord Jesus Christ" (Rom. 5:1). Do you know this by your own experience?* He adds also that we "rejoice in hope of the glory of God. And not only *so*, but we glory in tribulations also: knowing that tribulation worketh patience; and patience, experience; and experience, hope; and hope maketh not ashamed, because the love of God is shed abroad in our hearts by the Holy Ghost which is given unto us" (vv. 2–5).

Is all this in accordance with your experience, professed Christian? Is it true that your hope makes not ashamed? Does it produce such glorious fruit unto holiness as is described here? If you were to test your experience by the Word of the living God, and open your heart to be searched by the Spirit, would you be convinced that you have embraced the gospel in reality?

The Holy Spirit convinces sinners that all their goodness is selfish; and that self is the end of all their efforts, of all their prayers and religious exercises. I once spent a little time with the family of a man who was a leading member in a Presbyterian church. He said to me, "What would you think of a man who prays for the Spirit every day, but does not get the blessing?"

I answered, "I should presume that he is praying selfishly."

"But suppose," he replied, "that he is praying for the sake of promoting his own happiness?"

"He may be purely selfish in that," I replied, "for the devil might do the same, if he supposed he could be made happier by it."

I then cited the prayer of David: "Take not thy Holy Spirit from me. Restore unto me the joy of thy salvation . . . *then will I teach transgressors thy ways; and sinners shall be converted unto Thee*" (Ps. 51:11–13). This seemed to be a new doctrine to him, and he turned away, as I found afterward, in great anger and trouble. In the first gush of feeling, he prayed that God would cut him down and send him

---

*See especially Finney's sermon, "The Kingdom of God in Consciousness" in *Principles of Liberty*.

to hell, lest he should have to confess his sin and shame before all the people.

He saw that, in fact, his past religion had been all selfish; but the dread of confessing this was at first appalling. He saw, however, the possibility of his error, that his hopes had been all delusive, and that he had been working his self-deceived course fast down toward the depths of hell.

Finally, the Spirit's work is to make self-deceived people feel that they are now having their last call from the Holy Spirit. When this impression is made, let it by all means be heeded. It is God's own voice to the soul. Out of a great multitude of cases under my observation in which God has distinctly made sinners feel that the present was their last call, I do not recollect one in which it did not prove to be so. This is a moment of solemn truth to the sinner, and ought to make the warning voice of God ring in his ear like the forewarning knell of the second death.

The Spirit's Final Call Is the Sinner's Final Hope

According to my understanding, the Spirit will not withdraw from mankind forever, but He will withdraw from a particular person, or perhaps even (as in the text) from a whole generation of sinners. In its general application now, the principle seems to be that the Holy Spirit will not follow the sinner onward to his grave—that there will be a limit to His efforts in the case of each sinner, and that this limit is reached at some time before death. At some uncertain, awful point, he will reach and pass it; therefore, it is imperative that every sinner understands his peril of grieving the Spirit away forever.

God is compassionate, forbearing, slow to anger and great in mercy. He does not get impatient and act unreasonably. But God's Spirit will not always strive because He knows it will do the sinner no good. By the very laws of mind, conversion must be effected through the influence of truth. But it is a known law of mind that truth that is repeatedly resisted loses its power upon the mind that resists it.

Every successive instance of resistance weakens the power of truth. If the truth does not take hold with energy when fresh, it is not likely to do so ever after. Hence, when the Holy Spirit reveals truth to the sinner, and he hardens himself against it, there remains little hope for him. We may expect God to give him up for lost.

If we ask again why God ceases to strive with sinners, the answer may be because to strive longer would not only do the sinner no good, but greater harm. For guilt is determined according to the light (truth) received; the more light, the greater guilt. Hence, the more light revealed by the Spirit and longer striving, the greater the sinner's guilt—and the more awful his final woe.

It is better, then, for the sinner himself, after all hope of his repentance is gone, that the Spirit should leave him, than His efforts should be prolonged in vain to no other result than to increase the sinner's light and guilt, and consequently his endless curse. It is in this case a real mercy to the sinner that God should withdraw His Spirit and let him alone.

We are often greatly shocked with the bold and daring sins of people who may not after all have much illumination of the Spirit, and of course comparatively little guilt. But when God's ministers nudge the souls of people with His messages of truth, and people despise or neglect them; when God's providence also enforces His truth and people still resist, they are greatly guilty. How much more so when God comes by His Spirit and they resist God under the blazing light of His Spirit's illuminations! How infinitely aggravated is their guilt now!

Never do sinners so grievously tempt the forbearance of God as when they resist His Spirit. You may see this developed in the Jews of Stephen's time. "Ye stiff-necked and uncircumcised in heart and ears, ye do always resist the Holy Ghost: as your fathers did, so do ye" (Acts 7:51). Stephen had been following down the track of their national history, and running fearlessly across their Jewish prejudices, laboring in the deep sincerity and faithfulness of his soul, to set before them their guilt in persecuting and murdering the Son of God.

And what did they do? Enraged at these rebukes, they gnashed their teeth and set upon him with the spirit of demons. They stoned him to death, although they saw the very glory of God beaming in his eye and on his countenance, as if it had been an angel's. And did not this fearful deed of theirs seal up their damnation? Read the history of their nation and see. They had tempted God to the limit of His forbearance; now all that remained for them was swift and awful judgments. The wrath of God arose against them, and there was no remedy. Their resistance of the Holy Spirit pressed the forbearance of God, until it could bear no more.

It is a solemn truth that sinners tempt God's forbearance most dangerously when they resist His Spirit. Think how long you may have resisted the Holy Spirit. The claims of God have been presented and pressed again and again, but you have as often pushed them away. You have said unto God, "Depart from us; we desire not the knowledge of Thy ways." Have you not the utmost reason to expect that God will take you at your word?

There is a point beyond which forbearance is no virtue. This is and must be true in all governments. No government could possibly be maintained that should always indulge a spirit of forbearance toward the guilty. There must be a point beyond which God cannot go, without peril to His government; and over this point we may be assured He will never pass.

Suppose we should see old, gray-headed sinners converted as often and easily as youthful sinners, and this should be the general course of things. Would not this work ruin God's government, bring ruin even to sinners themselves? Would not sinners take encouragement from this, and hold on in their sins till their lusts were worn out, and till they themselves should rot down in their corruptions?

They would say, "We shall be just as likely to be converted in our old age—putrid with long indulged lusts and rank with the unchecked growth of every abomination of the heart of man—as if we were to turn to God in the freshness of our youth. Let us have the pleasures of sin first, and hold off the unwelcomeness of Christianity until such time that we can enjoy the world no more."

God means to have people converted young if at all; one reason for this is that He intends to convert the world, and therefore must have laborers trained for the work in the morning of life. If He were to make no discrimination between the young and the aged, converting from each class alike, or chiefly from the aged, the means of converting the world would utterly fail, withering with age; in the end, no sinners at all would be converted. There is, therefore, a necessity for the general fact that sinners must submit to God in early life.

Eternal Consequences of the Spirit's Ceasing to Strive

One consequence will be a confirmed hardness of heart. It is inevitable that the heart will become much more hardened, more fully set to do evil.

Another consequence will be a confirmed opposition to true Christian faith. This will likely manifest itself in a dislike for everything pertaining to the subject, often with great impatience and peevishness when that individual is pressed to attend to the subject seriously. Perhaps they will refuse to have anything said to themselves personally, so settled is their opposition to God and His claims.

You may also expect to see them opposed to revivals and to gospel ministers, and preeminently to those ministers who are most faithful to their souls. All those means of promoting revivals that are adapted to rouse the conscience will be peculiarly odious to their hearts. Usually such people become sour in their dispositions, misanthropic, despising all Christians, and delighting to heap slander and abuse on those whose piety annoys and disturbs their stupid repose in sin.

Another consequence of being forsaken by the Holy Spirit is that people will betake themselves to some refuge of lies and will settle down in some form of fatal error. From observation of numerous cases, I believe this to be the case with the great majority of Universalists. They are described by Paul: "They received not the love of the truth, that they might be saved. And for this cause God shall send them strong delusion, that they should believe a lie" (2 Thess. 2:10–11). They hate the truth, are more than willing to be deceived, are restive when pressed with gospel claims; therefore they are ready to grasp at any form of delusion that sets aside these claims and boldly asserts: "Ye shall not surely die" (Gen. 3:4).

It has long been an impression on my mind that this is the usual course of feeling and thought that leads to Universalism. There may be exceptions, but the masses enter into this delusion, having already been abandoned by the Spirit. Thus abandoned, they become cross and misanthropic—they hate all Christians and all those truths that God and His people love. This could not be the case if they had the love of God in their hearts. It could not well be the case if they were enlightened and restrained by the present agency of the divine Spirit.

Generally, those who are left by God come to have a seared conscience. They are distinguished by great insensibility of mind. They are by choice blind to the truth and hardened with respect to the nature and guilt of sin. Although their intelligence affirms that sin is wrong, yet they do not really feel it, or care about it. They can know the truth and yet be reckless of its application to their own hearts and lives. God has left them, and of course the natural tendencies of a depraved heart are developed, unrestrained.

This class of sinners will inevitably wax worse and worse. They become loose in habits, lax in their observance of the Sabbath— slide backwards in regard to temperance and all kindred moral subjects— and slip into some of the many forms of sin. If they have been conscientious against the use of tobacco, they may relinquish their conscientiousness and throw a loose rein on their lusts.

In short, they are prone to wax worse and worse in every branch of morals, and often become so changed that you would hardly recognize them. It will be no strange thing if they become profane swearers—they may begin to steal a little now, and a good deal more later on. And if God does not restrain them, they go down by a short and steep descent to the depths of hell.

A consequence of being abandoned by the Spirit will be certain damnation. There can be no mistake about this. It is just as certain as if they were already there. This state is not always attended with apathy of feeling. There may be at times a most intense excitement surrounding their fate. The Bible describes the case of some who "sin willfully" after they have received a knowledge of the truth, and there remains for them only a "certain fearful looking for of judgment and fiery indignation" (Heb. 10:26–27).

I have seen people like this in such agony and such wretchedness I pray God I may never see again. I have seen them, the very pictures of despair and horror. Their eyes fully open to see their ruined state, exclaiming, "I know I am abandoned by God forever. I have sinned away my day of hope and mercy, and I know I never shall repent. I have no heart to repent, although I know I must or be damned." Such language as this they utter with a settled, positive tone, and an air of agony and despair which is enough to break a heart of stone.

Another consequence of grieving the Holy Spirit, so that He ceases to strive to convert the sinner is that Christians find themselves unable to pray in faith for such sinners. There are some in almost every community for whom Christians cannot pray. I believe it is common for many Christians, without being aware of each other's state, to have a similar experience.

For example, several Christians are praying in secret for some one person, and with considerable freedom up to a certain moment, and then they find that they can pray for him no longer. They chance to meet together, and one says, "I have been praying a long time with great interest for _____ , because he is such an unrepentant sinner. However, at a particular time I found myself all shut up. I could not get hold of the Lord again for him, and never have been able to pray for him since." Says another and another, "I have felt just the same myself. I did not know that anyone else felt as I have, but you have described my case precisely."

If you go to the sinner, he will tell you a story that will develop the whole case, and show that he came at that eventful moment to some fatal determination, grieved the Holy Spirit, and was abandoned by God. The Spirit ceased to strive with him, and consequently He ceased to elicit prayer in his behalf in the hearts of God's people.

Finally, when God has ceased to strive with sinners, there are no means whatever to be employed that will be effectual for their salvation. If you, sinner, have passed that dreadful point, you will not profit by my preaching, though I were to preach to you five thousand sermons. No, you could not be profited though an angel of God should come and preach to you, or even if Christ himself should return and preach to you. All would be only in vain. You are left by God to fill up the measure of your iniquities.

Thus, Christians may understand how to account for the fact that there are some for whom they cannot pray. Even while they are walking with God, and trying to pray for particular people, they may find themselves utterly unable to do so. If in praying for sinners you find this to be so, and if it is clear that all is right between you and God; if you have evidence that there is no sin blocking your communication with Him, then you must infer that God has forsaken that sinner and does not wish you to pray any longer for him.

Sinners should be aware that light and guilt keep pace with each other. They are increased and lessened in proportion to each other; hence, the solemn responsibility of being under the light and the striving of the Holy Spirit. While enlightened and pressed into duty by the Holy Spirit, sinners are under the most solemn circumstances that can ever occur in their whole lives. Indeed, no period of the sinner's existence through its eternal duration can be so momentous as this.

Yes, sinner, while the Spirit of God is pleading and striving with you, angels appreciate the solemnity of the hour—they know that the destiny of your soul is being decided for eternity. What an object of infinite interest! An immortal mind on the pivot of its eternal destiny: on one side, God is debating and persuading; on the other, the sinner resists all truth—to his eternal damnation, as the struggle is about to be broken off as hopeless forever! Suppose, sinner, you could set yourself aside and could look on and be a spectator of such a scene.

Were you ever in a court of justice when the question of life and death was about to be decided? The witnesses have all been heard, the counsel has completed their arguments, and it is announced that the jury is ready to deliver their verdict. Now pause and observe the scene. Note the anxiety on every countenance, and how eagerly and yet with what awful solemnity they wait for the pending decision. And with good reason, for a question of momentous interest is to be decided.

But if this question involving only the temporal life is momentous, how much more so is the sinner's case, when the life of the soul for eternity is pending. Oh, how solemn while the question remains, while the Spirit still strives and the sinner still resists, for none can tell how soon the last moment of the Spirit's striving may come! This ought to be the most solemn world in the universe. In all other known worlds, the destinies of the souls are already fixed.

It is so in hell. All there is fixed and changeless forever. It is a solemn thing indeed for a sinner to go to hell, but far more solemn— the most solemn point in the whole duration of his existence—is that one in which the decision is made.

Oh, what a world this is! Throughout all its years and centuries there is no moment but on whose tender point the question of eternal life or eternal death hangs in the balance for some soul! Is this a place to trifle? Is this a place to be mad and foolish and vain? Ah, no! It would be more reasonable to trifle in any other world than this one. The awful destinies of the soul are being determined here. Heaven sees it, and hell as well, and all are filled with solicitude, swelling almost to agony.

But you who are the subjects of all this anxiety, *you* can trifle and play the fool and dance on the brink of everlasting woe. As the poem says:

> I heard the wretch profanely boast,
> Till at Thy frown he fell;
> His honors in a dream were lost,
> And he awoke in hell.

It is as if the sinner were on a slippery steep, and as his feet slide on the very verge of an awful chasm, God holds him up a short moment; how awful indeed if he trifles away even this short moment in mad folly! All hearts in heaven and in hell are beating and throbbing with intense emotion; but he can be reckless! Oh, what madness!

If sinners duly estimated this danger of resisting the Spirit, they would be more afraid of it than of anything else whatever. They would deem no other dangers worthy of a moment's thought or care compared with this. It is very common for sinners to grieve away the Holy Spirit long before their death.

Some do not agree with me on this view, but think of almost the whole Jewish nation given up to unbelief and reprobacy in the time of the Savior. Abandoned by the Spirit of God, they sinned against far less light—and of course incurred much less guilt—than sinners now incur. If God could give them up then, why may He not do so with sinners now?

If He could give up the whole population of the world in Noah's time, when he stood forth as a preacher of righteousness, why may He not give up people now who are incomparably more guilty than they, because they have sinned against greater light than had ever shone then?

It is infinitely cruel to sinners themselves to conceal from them this truth. Let them know that they are in danger of grieving away the Holy Spirit beyond recall long before they die. This truth ought to be proclaimed over all the earth. Let its echo ring out through every valley and over every mountain top the world around. Let every living sinner hear it and take the timely warning!

We see why so few aged sinners are converted. The fact is striking and unquestionable. Consider this: how many cases do you know of those who are converted late in life, perhaps past the age of sixty? The numbers are small indeed. They are few and scattered, like beacons on mountain tops, just barely enough to prevent the aged from utter despair of ever being converted.

I am aware that infidels seize upon this fact to extort from it an argument against Christianity, saying, "How does it happen that those whose minds are developed by thought and experience, and who have passed by the period of warm youthful passion, never embrace the gospel?" By this they infer that none but children and women become Christians; that Christianity rests on its appeal to the feelings and not to the intelligence.

But infidels make a most grievous mistake by this inference. The fact under consideration should be referred to an entirely different class of causes. The reason the aged are rarely converted is because they have grieved away the Holy Spirit, have become entangled in the mazes of some loved and soul-ruinous delusion, and hardened in sin past the moral possibility of being converted. Indeed, it would be unwise on the part of God to convert many sinners in old age. It would be too great a temptation for human nature to bear. At all the earlier periods of life, sinners would be looking forward to old age as the time for conversion.

It is an awful moment when God's Spirit strives with sinners. I have reason to know that the Spirit is striving with some of you. Even within the past week your attention has been solemnly arrested, and God has been calling upon you to repent. And now are you aware that while God is calling, you must listen; that when He speaks you should pause and give Him your attention?

When God calls you away from your lesson, do you reply, "Oh, I must, I *must* study for my lessons"? Ah, your studies! And what *is* your first and chief lesson? *"Prepare to meet thy God"* (Amos 4:12). But you say, "Oh, the bell will toll in a few minutes, and I have not gotten my lesson!" Yes, sinner, soon the great bell *will toll*, unseen spirits will seize hold of the bell-rope and toll the dread death-knell of eternity, echoing the summons, *"Come to judgment."* And the bell will toll, *toll*, TOLL! And where, sinner, will you be then! Are you prepared? Have you gotten that one great lesson: *"Prepare to meet thy God."*

In the long elapsing ages of your lost doom, you will be asked how and why you came into this place of torment; and you will have to answer, "Oh, I was getting my lesson there at Oberlin when God came by His Spirit; and I could not stop to hear His call! So I exchanged my soul for my lesson! Oh, what a fool I was!"

Let me ask the people of God, "Should you not be awake in such an hour as this?" How many sinners during the past week have besought you to pray for their perishing souls? And have you no heart to pray? How full of critical interest and peril are these passing moments? Did you ever see the magnetic needle of the compass vacillate, quiver, *quiver*, and finally settle down in its fixed position?

So with the sinner's destiny today.

Sinners, think of your destiny as being now about to assume its fixed position. Soon you will decide it forever and forever! Do you say, "Let me first go to my room, and there I will give myself up to God"?

No, sinner, *no*! Go not away from here in your sin; for now is your accepted time, now, today, after so long a time, *now* is the only hour of promise. Now is perhaps the last hour of the Holy Spirit's presence and grace to your soul!

18

THE SPIRIT CEASING TO STRIVE*

"And the Lord said, My Spirit shall not always strive with man" (Genesis 6:3).

The text implies that God's Spirit strives with people at least sometimes. Whenever the Spirit is obliged to strive with a person in order to influence him, then resistance is implied. Whenever the Spirit is said to "strive" with a person, that person must be resisting. The Spirit's striving is not a physical striving, but a moral influence, a persuading, reasoning, and convincing influence. The striving is a striving of mind with mind, and not of body with body. The process spoken of in the text is the presentation of the truth on one side, and the resistance of it on the other.

Sensing the Spirit's Striving

We cannot know this by a direct perception of His agency. The mind does not see the Holy Spirit himself, but it perceives the truth that the Spirit presents. The "striving" referred to is the pressing of considerations upon the mind in order to influence it, and the "resistance" spoken of is the mind's resistance to the reception of these truths.

We must see which particular truths are presented that call forth this "resistance." The Bible says that the Spirit of God reproves of sin. Christ promised that the Spirit would do this, and that He would "take of the things of Christ and show them" to people.

One of the signs by which people are made conscious that the Spirit is working within them is the arresting of their attention to the subject of Christian truth. They find biblical truths fermenting in their minds

---

The Penny Pulpit: a sermon delivered on December 15, 1850, at the Tabernacle, Moorfields.

and pressing upon their consciousness. Perhaps when they read or attend to business, some Christian truth is always coming up. If they considered the subject clearly, they could come to no other conclusion than that there was some invisible agency at work within them which kept the matter incessantly before them.

It seems to occupy their minds more than ever before. They feel an internal conviction of its light, a power and reality in a manner of which they had hitherto no conception. This is the striving of the Spirit.

Conviction of the sinfulness of one's conduct is another sign of the operations of the Spirit within. When people feel the sinfulness of their course of life, that marks the striving of the Spirit. People often go on in sin without reflecting on the sinfulness of what they are doing; but, by and by, the wickedness of their ways seems to gain their attention.

Looking back on their general conduct, and especially on particular acts, they see their sinfulness. Things now come up frequently in their minds and trouble them, things unthought of before. Now these things are regarded from a different point of view, and their error is revealed. In some cases there will be a general sense of sinfulness regarding their whole life. In others, particular acts will stand out and display themselves in a new and sinful light. This is an evident sign of the striving of the Spirit.

When people are striven with by the Spirit, they are not always greatly alarmed at the realization of their dangerous position, though this is sometimes the case. Sometimes they think so little of their danger that the Spirit must often give them a distinct and awful glimpse of the danger of their position by absenting himself for a time.

Some people are exceedingly blind to certain forms of sin. When these people are striven with by the Spirit, they may suddenly perceive clearly this blindness under which they have been laboring. Without this striving, these people are very apt to become self-righteous. When they do feel intensely, they are apt to resist and hold out against the Spirit, while all the time they give themselves credit for the possession of these tender feelings.

Often, the Spirit allows them to become so alarmingly hardened that they may find that the tender feelings on which they prided themselves have disappeared. Up to the very hour of their surrendering to God, this hardness sometimes increases, till they begin to perceive that they never had so little feeling on the subject of Christianity. Their hearts are as hard as stone. The Spirit often shows these people that they have been mistaking the mere excitement of their feelings for tenderness of heart.

Sometimes He convicts people of their unbelief, and shows them that they have not in reality placed their reliance upon God. They have actually placed more reliance on what people have said than on what God has said. People are influenced by each other's testimony, and if a man promises to another that he will do thus and thus, his friends believe and trust him and act accordingly. Now, ask this man, "Do you believe the Bible?" "Oh, yes!" he says. But is he influenced by what it promises, as much as he is by what people promise? Not at all.

If someone were to come and warn you of danger, would you not believe and act? If a person should promise you aid, would you not be relieved and comforted by it? If a person with lots of property gave you a promissory note, would you not naturally expect to have it paid?

But you do not believe God in these respects, yet you are apt to think that you do believe in God. The Spirit at length shows you that you are more comforted by men's promises than by God's. In reality, God's promises afford you very little satisfaction. In fact, you are actually not at all influenced by what God says, as compared to what people say. When, therefore, you thus come to see the sin of this unbelief, you may rest assured that the Holy Spirit is striving with you.

The Holy Spirit convinces people of their enmity against God. Few people think themselves *enemies* of God and of religion, especially if they profess themselves to be Christians. Commonly, where people have made a profession of faith only—where they have gotten into the church, and yet are not true Christians—I have observed that if they are not given up of God and reprobate, if God intends to save them, God convinces them that, in reality, they are *enemies* of Christianity.

Now you can see the necessity of this. If people such as these profess to love Christianity, how can they be saved unless they are convinced that they have made a radical mistake? The Spirit often commences by allowing this enmity to develop itself. They begin by complaining, perhaps, of the preaching; it is too severe, too personal, not "comforting" enough, or something of that kind. Either the preaching matter does not suit them, or the manner in which the sermon is presented is disagreeable. They want something that will make them happy— something "comforting."

They say they are Christians, and believe they speak the truth. They feel sure that if the preaching were what it ought to be, it would be sure to edify and "comfort" them. But God does not mean they should feel so, if He ever intends to save them. They are in a state of delusion, and anything that would make them happy, in this state, would only confirm their delusion. Consequently, God always so directs the preaching and everything as to make it set on them in such a manner as to show them clearly what has, by a great mistake, been covered up until now—the enmity of their hearts toward God.

Sometimes I have been struck by the extent to which this has been the case in revivals. Some members of the church, to the astonishment of their ministers, begin to oppose the movement, finding fault with this and with that. They stay away from the services, and go here and there, where they can be "comforted."

But the Spirit of God continues to strive with them, and keeps them uneasy, being determined to root out the enmity of their hearts. They return to the meetings again and again, and go mumbling away with something more unpalatable than ever. They become each time less "comfortable." How strange everything appears to them! This is the very way in which the Spirit works. He is determined to drag them out of their hiding places and unmask them. Often this goes on till everyone but they can see it. The very preaching that is leading sinners to God, they complain, saying, "We are not edified with it at all."

Do you see the divine philosophy in all this? These people are sometimes very numerous in a church, and pastors are often astonished to see so many of their members complain. The more powerfully these truths are driven home to these people, the more they object. By and by the pastor and deacons watch in amazement as their members run hither and thither in confusion. "What's the matter? What's the matter?" Why, the truth does not sit well on their unbroken heart!

They writhe and writhe, finding this fault and that fault, till they see they do not really love the preaching that God loves. They are, in fact, at enmity with God. I have seen them turn pale at such time as the fact comes out. "Oh! I thought I was a Christian! I have been a member of the church so many years, and yet I find that I stand before God condemned! I see that God and I are at issue—that God loves what I hate, and blesses what I oppose!" Now this is exactly the way the Spirit of God would take with such people.

When preaching at various places, I have often heard, "Why, if that is true, then why does such and such a church member oppose it?" But soon you will see evidently that the truth is coming home, and hitting him hard. Pray for him! What's the matter with him? Has any untruth been said? "Oh, no, but he seems to think you are *so* personal." Ah! does he? Pray for him! God has gotten hold of him. He thinks that the minister and all the people are looking right at him; that the pastor is speaking to him personally, and that all the congregation knows it. Now this is just what God does.

If you see a man begin to "squirm," pray for him. Do not be frightened. This is the way the Holy Spirit works; He is very personal, and makes the truth personal. He directs the mind of the preacher in such a manner as to make the truths He wishes to impress stick close to an individual He wishes to move; thus, people get the impression that the preacher knows them and their history, and think somebody must have been telling him about them.

During my thirty years' experience, people have often told me this, whereas it was nothing else than the Almighty directing my thoughts in a certain channel in order to meet their case. God knew them, although I did not. My bow was drawn at a target, but God directed the arrow, and it found its way through the joints of their harness; and they were "not comforted." Not comforted! Why, the gospel was never made to comfort you in your unsanctified state.

This is also very often the case with merely moral men, who help by their means to support religious institutions. Such men are very apt to overlook the fact that they are enemies to God. Therefore, God must in some way show it to them. How is He to do it? They are almost Christians in their own opinion. Their religious wives say, "Oh! I have great hope of him." How often has this been the case. But God sees their real state. They do not come out and acknowledge Christ publicly. God knows of their rotten heart. They are amiable, and their exterior is lovely, but God must make them know themselves by a course of teaching, preaching, providences, or some other method, and thus take off the veil from their hearts.

Once this is accomplished, they begin to writhe and act in the way the professors just spoken of are accustomed to act. "I do not go to church to be preached *at*, not when I do so much to aid religion. To be treated in such a manner is very personal and abusive." It is very hard, they cannot bear it, although they do not, they *cannot* deny its truth. By and by you will see them writhe. This shows that there is a sediment at the bottom of their hearts; stir it up. Do not be afraid. Pray for them.

If you find your unchristian husband begins to *squirm* and threatens not to go to meeting, *do not side with him*, and say you think he has reason to be offended. If you do not want to ruin his soul, do not take his part. "Oh!" say to him, "Is it true? Then you ought to receive it. For if it means you, and you do not receive it, what will become of you? What! You confess it is true, and true of you, and yet refuse to receive it?" Be careful what you do under such circumstances; for wherever people thus quarrel with truth, they are, in reality, quarreling with God. Remember that. But these people often pretend that it is not the truth they quarrel with, but the offensive manner in which it is said. Take care how you respond to truth. *A real lover of truth is willing to receive it, no matter that it is not on a golden dish.*

One way in which God convinces the sinner of the danger of his dying in sin is by impressing him with the fact that he has not long to live. If he feels that others around are dying in their sins, and that he himself has lived a long time in his sin, he will begin to calculate on probabilities, and to apply it to himself. This type of reflection often induces a decision, or at least it greatly deepens previous convictions. The mode in which the Spirit operates is to warn people of the danger of His leaving them.

At other times, He shows them that they are actually ashamed of Christ, ashamed to have it known that they consider themselves Christians; ashamed to talk of it even to their wives or to their minister, ashamed to be seen reading the Bible, or to have it known that their minds are exposed to the subject. People in this state are afraid of being supposed to be "religious", and therefore often laugh and try to conceal it, while at heart they are full of soreness and distress. But this shows them more and more that they are ashamed of Christ. And they begin to perceive their pride of heart and the awful wickedness of the position they occupy in relation to God.

Sometimes the Spirit operates by leaving people wholly without excuse. Every plea they have been accustomed to is swept from under them. They have none left to hide behind, as they used to do. The Spirit follows them in their excuses, and strips them off one by one, till He has silenced them all; and they turn them over and over, one after the other, but cannot find one to rest upon.

The Spirit of God thus strove with me for months before I was aware of it. I fled from one excuse to another; but my mind would answer each as it rose. Thus the Spirit undermined all my fortifications, until I had not a single excuse for my conduct. Now mark. Perhaps this very process is going on with you. If you feel uncomfortable, see if the truth sits well upon you. If you find that any particular truth does not sit well upon you, whatever your character may be in a general way, if you are at war at least with that one truth, you are at war with God.

People are sometimes convinced of their sin by seeing that they have been altogether selfish. Selfishness is sin. All sin is selfishness in some form. People often see that their very religion has hitherto been selfishness. They can see clearly that they are not in sympathy with God and with Christ, that they have not the Spirit of Christ within them, that they are not living to and for God; and that they are utterly selfish in their business, and even in their Christianity. They are fully convinced of this. Ah! are you convinced of it? Do not resist the light of such questions! If you shut down the gate, turn your eyes away, and refuse to be convinced, you will wake up in the blackness and darkness for ever!

Sinners often get the impression on their minds that this is the last call God will ever give them. Doubtless the Spirit of God means what He says. In such cases it would be very natural for the Spirit in taking the last struggle with a man to give him such an impression; it is no doubt common—and certainly very gracious—for Him to do so. At such times, professing Christians have often had great reason to doubt whether they were ever truly converted; this impression has been confirmed by a glimpse at their lives.

Before long, perhaps, the Spirit of God impresses them with the idea that if they now resist, they will die in their sins. Now, sinner, when God insinuates such things, He is in earnest. The devil does not want you to believe any such things. He would not tell you so if he knew it. It comes from one who cannot lie, and who, in His benevolence, forewarns you that, if you now resist, you are a ruined soul for all eternity.

Reasons Why the Spirit Must Cease Striving

When the Spirit ceases striving, it is not meant, of course, that He will leave the earth. It rather means that He will not always follow a man through the whole of his life, and continue to strive with him to the end of his days.

Why not? First, because it will not do them any good. If, after so many strivings, a person will not repent, why should the Spirit continue to follow him? They are enlightened as much as they need to be enlightened, yet they resist and resist. Why then should He continue to strive with them?

The Holy Spirit will not always strive because of His compassion for people. When He has once thrust home the truths that must convert them, if they ever are converted, He knows that, by a natural law of their minds, the longer they resist the more likely they are to continue resisting. Besides, it would only serve to enhance their guilt. There is, therefore, no way consistent with His honor in which He can follow them any longer.

Their guilt is so aggravated from their striving with God face to face, and resisting, from their sinning with full light and tempting God's forbearance, that although they hope God will save them at some future time, it would be inconsistent with God's honor to do so. There is a point beyond which it is inconsistent with God's high sovereignty that people should continue to resist and quarrel with Him face to face.

If the Spirit would always strive, people would take courage and continue in their sins with the idea that they would be just as likely to have the Spirit strive with them when old as when young. To avoid this inference, God's Spirit will not always strive with people.

Once more, God needs young people to be converted, that He may train them up to do good. If they go on until they have well nigh burnt out the lamp of life, God will, indeed, have compassion on them, if they repent—but how seldom *do* they repent under such circumstances! God's compassion does not change the fact that they have wasted their life and can accomplish little good now. And, having served the devil so long, shall they take the stinking snuff of their expiring lamp—the jaded, putrid remnant of mortality which has resisted the Holy Spirit until the grave is open before them—and cast it, as it were, in the face of the Almighty?

It would be bad policy on the part of God's government to convert old people as easily as young ones. It would tend to harden the young in their sins. The general rule, therefore, must be the conversion of the young, while the conversions of the old will occur in just sufficient number to keep the aged sinner from utterly despairing.

The Ceasing of Striving Is a Serious Matter

The first consequence of the Spirit's ceasing to strive is apathy, carelessness, and prayerlessness with regard to sin. This is the general rule. Another consequence is a confirmed opposition to the Spirit of God—this takes place when an individual has resisted strong convictions, and when his conscience has smarted under the force of truth. His very conscience becomes unfeeling. He can commit sins now without compunction, which once would have filled him with agony. He goes on in sin, with very little remorse. This, too, is a general rule; but in some instances there is the reverse—a fearful looking for judgment. They often, however, wax worse and worse, until if they do not openly apostatize, it is only the fear of damaging their reputation that prevents them.

Christians will find themselves losing the spirit of prayer for such people. The wife will lose the power to pray for her husband under such circumstances. She loses her hold on the throne of grace for him, and it is the same in the husband toward the wife, the parent toward the child, and the child toward the parent. The Spirit will not lead a man to pray for those who have grieved Him away. No means that are used will savingly affect them. They will become more and more opposed to the means, until they finally abandon the use of them. The evil habits they formerly indulged in will come back strongly upon them.

Have you been thus striven with? Did the spirit of resistance come upon you? Have you felt, at some time, that the minister meant you? Perhaps you have said, "Now, if that minister had known my history, he could not have told it better." Have you been in this state? Have you felt offended at his being so "personal?" I have often thought that there are multitudes who have thoroughly quenched the Spirit; and the reason I think so is this: they are in the church, and hold themselves up in hope, while everybody who knows them sees that the Spirit of Christ is not within them.

If they are searched, they feel displeased; there is a lack of honesty in their hearts, a lack of that downright sincerity in Christianity. There is a slipperiness, a carnality, a quibbling dishonesty, a putting on of religion. Still there is something that serves to bolster them up. They are careful to appear faithful, by regular attendance at communion services, lest the minister or deacons should uncover the fact of their being in a state of apostasy from God. But try to get them to do anything else, and you cannot secure their cooperation, unless it is where their character is concerned.

If God is now showing you that you ought to be honest with yourself, do not go on with your deceitful game! I do not know you, but God knows you. I beg you not to ruin your soul by cheating yourself on a point so vital. Many get into such a state that they can hear and remain unmoved even when they hear the truths which smite the hearts of infidels and break them in pieces as a potter's vessel.

If such are moved at all, it is only to opposition. They have no sympathy with the work of God—and care nothing about anybody being converted, not even their own children, perhaps. I have known churches where some of the members were the most hardened and reprobate persons I have known in all my life—the most disposed to argue, and the least disposed to cooperate.

Deacons should know whether such people are in their church. Deacons should know whose hearts are in the work, and who are hardened in their sins. The fact is on such subjects as this, it is the most awful cruelty not to deal faithfully with such men. I would sooner cut off both my hands than play a silly game with a man about his soul, his sins—and his eternal destiny! I have often been astonished to find that while professors debate, ungodly men have said, "Ah! that's just what we need, let it come! Let us know the truth, and the worst of our case. Let it come burning and boiling till it melts the icebergs of our hearts!"

One word more. When the Spirit strives, people are in great danger of putting off submission day after day, until at length the Spirit leaves them. While the Spirit is still striving, they think about Christianity, but do not come to the point of decision. Ah! They do not know the infinite danger they are in, of being left amidst all this bargaining. Listen! "While thy servant was busy here and there, behold the Spirit was gone." They excuse themselves, saying they must wait till they have done this thing or that thing. Day after day the Spirit strives with them, until at length He takes His flight. You should reflect that every moment you resist you are in infinite danger of His leaving you. "My Spirit shall not always strive."

When the Spirit strives, it is the most solemn point of the sinner's existence. The Judgment Day will disclose things that were done in time, but the sinner's destiny is settled here. When the Spirit strives with people, He settles with them personally. The work is finished, one way or the other, and becomes a matter of record. The leaf is folded and laid aside until the day of judgment; but here is the time and place in which the thing is done—this is the world on which hangs suspended the eternal life or death of immortal souls. But not only is the matter finally settled in this world, but there must be some turning point at which the settlement takes place.

Christian! Do you realize that when the Spirit is striving with your children, this is the most important moment of their whole existence? Are you asleep over it? Are they genuine in their manner concerning Christian subjects, or do they creep to the house of God, hardly willing to let you know it? Do you see indications that the Spirit of God has been striving with them?

Are you not looking for this? If you see this interest in their countenances, what are you doing? Are you watching on your knees? Do you feel how great their danger is? Do you feel that their crisis is infinitely more solemn than a fever would be, provided they were Christians? Their eternal destinies may hang on that moment, and what are you doing? God is solemn and in earnest, angels are solemn and in earnest, devils are solemn and in earnest, the Holy Spirit is solemn and in earnest—*do you trifle?* Why, you are the very one that heaven and hell are earnest about!

19

SALVATION IS DIFFICULT FOR THE CHRISTIAN, IMPOSSIBLE FOR THE SINNER*

"If the righteous scarcely be saved, where shall the ungodly and the sinner appear?" (1 Peter 4:18).

From the context of this passage, some have inferred that the apostle had his eye immediately upon the destruction of Jerusalem. They suppose this great and fearful event to be alluded to with the words, "For the time is come that judgment must begin at the house of God: and if it first begin at us, what shall the end be of them that obey not the gospel of God?" (1 Pet. 4:17).

This may refer to the destruction of the city and temple of God's ancient people, yet the evidence for this opinion does not seem conclusive. A reference to this event is possible and even probable. We know that when Jerusalem was destroyed, not one Christian perished. They had timely notice from the signs that Christ had given them. Perceiving the fulfillment of those signs, they all fled to Pella, on the east of the Jordan; hence, they were not involved in the general destruction.

But whether Peter refers to this particular event or not, one thing is plain: the righteous will be saved, though with difficulty, *but the wicked will not be saved at all*. It is plain throughout this whole chapter that Peter had his mind upon the broad distinction between the righteous and the wicked—a distinction that was strikingly illustrated in the destruction of Jerusalem, illustrations that were ordered under the moral and providential government of a holy God.

The salvation of the righteous, though certain, is difficult. On this basis rests the argument of the apostle: that if the salvation of the

---

Sermons on the Way of Salvation, 130–146.

righteous is so difficult, the sinner cannot be saved at all. His salvation is utterly impossible. This is plainly the doctrine of the text, and is strikingly exemplified in the destruction of Jerusalem, though the passage may or may not have reference to that event. All students of the Bible know that this great destruction is often held up as a type or model of the final judgment of the world. It was a great event on the page of Jewish history, and certainly had great significance as an illustration of God's dealings toward our sinful race.

The difficulty in the salvation of either the righteous or the wicked does not reflect on any lack of mercy in the heart of God. It is not because God is implacable and hard to be appeased that the salvation of even the sinner is impossible. Nor is it in any lack of provision in the atonement to cover all the needs of sinners, and even to make propitiation for the sins of the world. The Bible nowhere questions the entire sufficiency of the saving work of Christ to do all that an atonement can do, or need do, for the salvation of our race.

But, one difficulty is found in the nature of God's government, and in the nature of free agency in this world. The constitution of man was created so that God must limit himself to one mode of government over him. This restraint must be moral, not physical. God must appeal to the spirit, and act upon mind as mind, not by such force as may be applied legitimately to move matter. If the nature of the case permitted the use of physical force, it would be infinitely easy for God to move and sway such puny creatures as we are. The physical omnipotence that sweeps the heavens and upholds the universe could find no difficulty in moving lumps of clay so small and insignificant as we.

But mind cannot be moved as God moves the planets. Physical force can have no direct influence upon the mind for the purpose of determining its moral action. If it should act upon mind as it does upon matter, we certainly know there could be neither moral choice nor moral character in such beings as we are. We could not have even a conception of moral conduct. How could it possibly exist under these conditions?

People were placed under God's government with such a created constitution and such established relations to it that they must act freely. God has made them capable of controlling their own moral conduct by the free action of their own wills, and now He expects and requires them to choose between His service and rebellion.

Such being the case, the great difficulty is to persuade sinners to choose right. God is infinitely ready to forgive them if they will repent; but the great problem is to persuade them to do so. They are to be prepared for heaven. For this, an entire change of moral character is requisite. This could be done with the utmost ease, if nothing more were needed than to take them into some Jordan stream and wash them, physically, as if from some external pollution. And God would be pleased to employ physical power for this purpose. But since the change needed is moral by nature, the means employed must be moral. All the influence must be of a moral character.

Now a moral agent must be able, in the proper sense of this term, to resist every degree of moral influence, or else he cannot be a moral agent. His action must be responsible action, and therefore must be performed of his own free will and accord; no power can interpose in such measure as to overbear or interfere with his own responsible agency. Hence, there is a necessity on God's part to establish a moral means to convert sinners, to gain their voluntary consent in this great change from sin to holiness, from disobeying to obeying God.

And hence, this change must be wrought, ultimately, by moral means alone. God may and does employ physical agencies to act morally: He may send sickness to reach the heart, but not to purge away any sort of physical sin.

There are a great many difficulties in the way of converting sinners, and in saving them when once converted, many of which people are prone to overlook. Hence we must go into some detail in order to make this matter plain.

One class of these difficulties is the result of an abused constitution. When Adam and Eve were created, their appetites were doubtless mild and moderate. They did not live to please themselves, or gratify their own appetites. Their deep and all-engrossing desire and purpose to please God was the law, regulating all of their activities.

For a time, therefore, they walked in holy obedience, until temptation came in a particular form, and they sinned. Sin introduced another law—the law of self-indulgence. Everyone knows how terrible this law tends to perpetuate and strengthen itself, the fearful sway it gains so rapidly over the whole being once it is enthroned in power. And so, the beautiful order and subordination that had been obtained in holiness throughout all their active powers was broken up and subverted under the reign of sin. Their appetites lost their proper balance.

No longer subordinate to reason or to God, they became sinful: tyrannical, inordinate, and clamorous. Precisely in this does sin consist—in the irrational gratification of the appetites and passions. This is the form in which it appeared in our first parents. Such are its roots in all the race. Now in order to save people, they must be brought back from this, and restored to a state in which God and reason control the free action of the mind, and appetite is held in due subjection.

Please understand me. The lack of balance—the moral disorder of which I speak—is not the result of an enslavement of the will; it has not lost its inherent power of free moral action. The difficulty is that the senses have been enormously developed, and the mind accustoms itself to yield to the demands that are made by the senses for indulgence. Here is the difficulty. Some have formed habits and have confirmed them until they have become immensely strong, and become exceedingly difficult to break. The rescue must be effected by moral, not physical, means; the problem is to make the moral means powerful enough for this purpose.

We must notice, among the difficulties in question, the entanglements of a multitude of circumstances. I have often thought it well if new Christians do not see all their difficulties at first. If they did, its discouraging effect might be disastrous. If these difficulties were to present themselves to the mind as it posed the elements of the great question—a life of sin or a life of holiness; or, after conversion, these problems were to fall in their power upon the mind at the first, while its purpose to serve God is but little confirmed—the result might be not only greatly trying, but perhaps fatal.

But the ways of God in this, as in all things, are admirable. He does not let them see all their future difficulties at first, but permits them to come up from time to time in succession, as the new Christian has strength to meet them and overcome.

The great difficulty is living to please God rather than self. It is amazing to see how much this difficulty is enhanced by the agency Satan and sin have had in the framework of society. It would seem that a bait is held before every man, whatever his position and circumstances may be. One cannot but be astonished at the number of baits provided and laid in the habits and usages, we might perhaps say, in the very construction and constitution of society.

See how people are interlocked in the relations of life—partners in business, associates in pleasure; and attached in the more endearing and permanent relations of life—husbands and wives, lovers and loved, parents and children. How many influences of a moral sort, often tempting to sin, grow out of each; and, how many more out of *all* these complicated and various relations, combined!

Youth of both sexes are educated—perhaps together, perhaps apart—yet in either case, there arises a host of social attractions, and in the history of the race, who does not know that often the resulting influences are evil? The troubles and cares of business, how often do they "like a wild deluge come" and overwhelm the soul that otherwise would "consider its ways and turn its feet unto God's testimonies"!

How complicated are the sources of irritation that provoke men's spirits to ill-temper, and ensnare them thus into sin! Many times we marvel and say, "What amazing grace is needed here! For what power, less than that of the Almighty, could pluck God's children from such a network of snares and toils, and plant them at last on the high ground of established holiness!"

A man may be chained to a wife who is a constant source of temptation and trial to him. Likewise, there may be a wife who has scarce a peaceful moment in all her life with her husband—all is vexation and sorrow of spirit. Many parents have children who are a constant trial to them. They are indolent, or they are reckless, or they are self-willed and obstinate, or their tempers chafe, and they become a sore temptation to a similar state of chafing and fretting temper in their parents.

On the other hand, children may have equal trials in their parents. Where can you find a family in which the several members are not in some way a source of trial to each other! Sometimes the temptation comes in an appeal to their ambition and pride. Their children have some qualities for the parents to be proud of, and this becomes a snare to parents and children both. Oh, how complicated are the temptations that cross and re-cross every pathway of human life! Who but God can save against the hold of such temptations?

Many children have been brought up in error. Their parents have held erroneous opinions, saturating the moral constitution of their children with this influence from the cradle. How terrible such an influence must be in the end! Or, the business of their parents may have wrongly educated them—the business of rum-selling, for example; who does not know how terribly this kind of influence cleaves to a man, even as his skin, and seems to become a part of him, pervading the very tissues of his soul!

When the mind gives itself up to self-indulgence, a host of appetites become clamorous and impetuous; what a labor it must be to bring the soul into harmony with God! How many impulses must be withstood and overcome. How great the change that must be wrought in both the physical and moral state of the person!

No wonder that the devil flatters himself to think that he has trapped the race of depraved men in his snares, that he can lead them captive at his will. Think how many years he has been planning and scheming, studying human nature and the laws of depravity, that he may make himself fully master of the hellish art of seducing moral agents away from God and holiness. The truth is, we scarcely begin to realize how artful a devil we have to encounter. We scarcely begin to see how potent an adversary is he who, "like a roaring lion, walketh about, seeking whom he may devour" (1 Pet. 5:8). He must be resisted and overcome, or we are not saved.

Many are not aware of the effort necessary to rid themselves of the influence of a bad education. I speak of education in the broad comprehensive sense—embracing all that molds the habits, the temper, the affections, and develops the intellect. Often the affections become unwisely attached, yet the attachment is exceedingly strong, and breaking them seems like a sundering of the very heart-strings.

This attachment may fasten upon friends, wives, husbands, or children. A person may make gold his god, and bow down to its image. Sometimes we are quite unable to estimate the strength of this attachment, except as we see what strange and terrible means God is compelled to use to sever it. Oh, how does God look with careful, tearful pity upon His entangled and endangered children, carefully marking the bands and contriving how He can best sunder them, drawing their wandering hearts back to himself!

We know He never afflicts willingly, nor grieves the children of men—His people—but for their profit, that they may partake of His holiness. Yet how often He is compelled to bring tears from their eyes, to wring their hearts with many sorrows, to tear from them many a fond and loved object of their affections—else He could not save them from their propensities toward sin and self-indulgence! Oh, what a work is this, which Christ undertakes that He may save His people from their sins! How strange and how complicated are the difficulties! Who could overcome them but God?

The darkness of nature is so vast and so deep that it must be an exceedingly great work to save people from its influence, and to pour the true light of God through their intelligence. It is by no means sufficient to know all the theories of Christianity, or to know all of Christian faith that the human mind, unenlightened by the Divine Spirit, can know. Indeed, Christians never know themselves, except as they see themselves as revealed in God's own light.

They need to see God's character in its real nature, and then, in view of what God is, they can see and estimate themselves rightly. This is one important part of the truth on this subject; and another point is, that God himself by His Spirit becomes the teacher of the humble and trustful, and so enlightens the understanding that divine truth can be seen in its real colors and just proportions.

And now do you say, "Oh, God, show me what I am, and make me know my own heart thoroughly?" When you have found yourself perplexed about your own state, and cried unto God for help and light, has He not always answered your prayer by first revealing himself and His own character? And in the light reflected from His character, you saw your own; in the light of His principles of action you saw your own; and in the light of His heart—did you not see your own as well?

You do not see your own state of mind by simply inverting your mental eye and looking within, but by being drawn so near to God that you come into real and deep communion with Him. Then, seeing and knowing God, you see and know yourself. You cannot help but see whether your heart responds in sympathy and aid with His, and this very fact reveals your own heart to yourself. It is wonderful how much the Christian learns of himself by truly learning about God. It is no less wonderful that Christians should experience such moral transformation simply by knowing God, and by being drawn more deeply into sympathy with Him the more they know Him.

The great difficulty is that Christians are shy of God; especially as they relapse into the spirit of the world. Then they find within themselves an almost resistless inclination to *keep off*, to hold themselves aloof from close communion with God. Hence, God is compelled to draw them back, to discipline them with afflictions, to spoil their idols, and to dash their graven images to pieces. He is always awake and on the alert—so the Bible represents it: "He that keepeth Israel shall neither slumber nor sleep" (Ps. 121:4). By day and by night He watches, and "keepeth them as the apple of His eye!" How wonderful is such patience and lovingkindness!

Finally, the greatness of the change required to pass from sin to real holiness, from Satan's kingdom into full fitness for Christ's, creates no small difficulty in the way of saving even the converted. It is difficult, no impossible, to make people see this at first. Indeed, if the Christian were to see it from the start, very likely it would overwhelm him in despair. Hence God wisely lets him see enough to impress strongly his need of divine aid, enough to make him cry out, "Who then can be saved?"

We see why the Scriptures are so full of exhortations to Christians to run, and especially to run by *rule*. He that "strives for masteries" must by all means strive "*lawfully*" (2 Tim. 2:5); that is, according to the rules in such cases made and provided. So let the Christian be careful not only that he runs, but that he runs the right way and in the right manner.

In the same way, we see why the Christian is exhorted to fight, grasping the sword, buckling on the shield, putting on the helmet of salvation, preparing himself in all points for a warlike march through an enemy's country, where fighting must be looked for day and night.

Once he is so girded, he must firmly brace himself with all his strength, as if the enemies hosts were about to charge with the bayonet. "Stand fast," their Captain shouts. "Fight like a man, for your king and for yourselves, for the enemy are down upon you in strength and in wrath!"

Prepare also to struggle; for fierce will the conflict be. It is no contemptible foe whom you must face. The Scriptures decree that only the violent take this kingdom of God, and they do it "*by force*" (Matt. 11:12). What could be more expressive of the energy to be put forth by Christ's people if they would win the victory and wear the crown? We see why Christians are represented as *wrestling*, as people in a personal struggle for the mastery. They have a personal enemy to fight and to subdue.

They must, however, work diligently. Lazy people cannot get to heaven; to get there costs toil and labor, for his will must be sanctified. The entire voluntary department of his being must be renovated. It is remarkable how the Christian warfare develops the will. Not an obstinate will, not a self-will, do I mean, but a strong and firm will. The person disciplined in the Christian conflict cries out, "I must and I *will* believe. I will *trust*."

The Christian is also commanded to *watch*. Not to close his eyes for a little more sleep and a little more slumber. His condition is one of hourly peril, and therefore, what Christ says to one He says to all: *watch*. We can see the reason for this in the light revealed from our subject.

We see also why the Christian is to pray always, as well as to agonize and watch. And yet, it is not all to be done by his own unaided exertions. In fact, one of his chief exertions should turn upon this very point: that he pray always, "*watching* thereunto," lest anything draw his heart down from the throne of his Great Helper.

We may also see why Christians are exhorted to separate themselves from the world. They are told they must hang the old man upon the cross. There are no exceptions to this. Whoever would be saved must be crucified; that is, as to "the old man with his deeds" (Col. 3:9). The crucifixion of Christ is an emblem of this, and serves, therefore, to show what this must and should be.

Do you suppose that the whole intent of Christ's crucifixion is to meet the demands of the violated law? Not so. It was also to be an emblem of the work to be wrought upon and within the Christian soul. *Its* old selfish habits must be broken up and its powerful tendencies to evil must be slain.

That is why Christians are exhorted to spend the time of their sojourning here in fear, walking softly and carefully—as before God—through all the meanderings of their pilgrimage. Speaking only in holy conversation, as reads His book of counsel: steadfast, immovable, always abounding in work—the work of the Lord—so that his labor will not be in vain in the Lord's sight (1 Cor. 15:58).

Every weight must he lay aside. He must not encumber himself with many cares. He must not overload himself with gold nor with care and effort to get it. He must be watchful most diligently on this side and on that, remembering—for both his quickening and his comfort—that with His holy angels Christ watches evermore over him, saying, "I am determined to save you if I can, but I cannot unless I can first gain and then retain your attention, and then rouse up your hearts to the utmost diligence, coupled with the most simple-hearted faith."

Oh, what a conflict there must be to rescue each saved sinner from the jaws of Satan and from the grasp of his own lusts, and finally bring him home, washed and holy, to his home in the heavens! No wonder the Bible should speak of the Christian as being saved only through much difficulty.

If sinners will only exercise a little common sense, they can readily account for the faults of Christians. See that husband with a pious wife. He treats her badly and day after day annoys her by his ill temper and little abuses. The children, too, trouble her, and all the more for the example her husband sets before them. Now he may, very likely, in some of his moods of mind and temper, drop some criticisms regarding lapses he has perceived in her piety, and upon the gospel she professes.

But in his more rational moments he will be compelled to admit, "No wonder my wife has these faults. I have never helped her at all. I have only hindered her in all her Christian course. And I know I have been a continual source of vexation and irritation to her. No wonder she has had faults. I am ashamed that I have done so much to create and multiply them, and so very little ever in any way to improve her character."

When candid men come to consider all these things—the human constitution, the tendency to unbelief, the impulses toward self-indulgence and the strength of temptation—they cannot but see that there is abundant occasion for all those faults in Christian character and conduct which they are foolish to criticize so stringently. Yet often, perhaps commonly, wicked people make no allowance for the faults of Christians, but assume that every Christian ought to be spotless, while every sinner may make so many excuses for his sins that he quite shields his conscience from conviction of guilt.

Nothing, therefore, is more common than for unrepentant sinners to triumph, devil-like, over any instance of stumbling in a professed Christian. Why don't they rather sympathize with their difficulties and their great work—as real philanthropists? That brother who has a Christian sister does not help her at all, but, on the contrary, tries to ensnare her into sin. He should rather say, "I will not be a stumbling block to my sister. If I cannot directly help her on in her Christian course, at least I will not hinder her." Let the unrepentant husband say, "My dear Christian wife! I know something about her difficulties. God forbid that I should play into the devil's hands, and try to help the devil on in his devilish work."

Sinner, why don't you abstain from ensnaring your Christian friend? There is One above who cares for him, who patiently toils for his salvation, and watches day and night over his progress—and who is pledged to save him at last. How can you hope to gain the favor of that Holy and Just Being by trying to ensnare and offend any of His little ones?

20

THE SALVATION OF SINNERS IS IMPOSSIBLE*

"If the righteous scarcely be saved, where shall the ungodly and the sinner appear?" (1 Peter 4:18).

By the "righteous" I do not mean those who have never sinned. It could not be difficult to save those who have never sinned against God. They are, in fact, already saved. But these righteous ones are those, who, having been sinners, now come to exercise faith in Christ, and of course become heirs of "the righteousness which is by faith" (Heb. 11:7). Here it is vitally important to remember that the governmental difficulty in the way of saving you—growing out of your having sinned, even greatly—is completely removed by Christ's atonement. No matter now how great your guilt, have faith in Jesus and accept His atonement as the ground of pardon for your sins.

The difficulty in the way of saving sinners is not simply that they have sinned, but that they will not now cease from sinning and begin to believe on the Lord Jesus Christ. The salvation of sinners is therefore impossible. Their salvation is impossible because they are so wicked and so perverse that they abuse God, making their sin greater by resisting the very best means God so wisely employs to bring them to repentance. Hence God cannot wisely save them.

When I say it is *impossible* for God to convert them, I do not imply that God lacks *physical* power to do anything that is the proper subject of such power. On this point there can be no question. But how can physical omnipotence be brought to bear directly upon the mind and heart?

---

*Sermons on the Way of Salvation, 147–164. This sermon completes the train of thought began in the previous sermon.

It may not be wise for God to bring all the moral power of His universe to bear upon the sinner in this world. If this were wise and practicable, it might avail. But since He does not do it, we infer that He refrains for some wise reason.

Certain limitations are fixed in the divine wisdom to the amount of moral influence that God shall employ in the case of a sinner. In view of this fact I say, *God finds it impossible to gain the sinner's consent to the gospel by any means that He can wisely employ.* He goes as far as is really wise and as far as is on the whole good. This is undoubtedly the fact in the case. Yet all this does not avail. Hence it becomes impossible that the sinner should be saved.

The sinner cannot be saved, because salvation *from sin* is an indispensable condition of salvation *from hell.* Being saved from sin must come first. Every sinner knows, and on reflection and self-inspection he must see, that his state of mind is such that he cannot respect himself. Therefore, the elements of blessedness are not in him, and cannot be until he meets the demands of his own moral nature.

He knows, also, that he does not want to have anything to do with God. In fact, he is afraid of God. He both dreads and hates His presence, and is afraid to die and come as near to God as death bears all men. He knows that all his relations to God are unpleasant in the extreme. How certainly, then, may he know that he is utterly unprepared for heaven.

The sinner must be saved from this guilty and abominable state of mind. No change is needed in God—neither in His character, in His government, nor in His position toward sinners. The utmost possible change and all the needed change is required on the part of the sinner. If salvation implies fitness for heaven, and if this implies ceasing from sin, then, of course, it is naturally and forever impossible that any sinner can be saved without holiness.

The peace of heaven forbids that you should go there in your sins. I know you think of going to heaven. You rather expect you shall go there at last. Your parents are there, as you hope and believe, and for this reason you want to go. You want to behold them in their glory. *Do you think you can follow them, as you are now, in your sins?* What could you do in heaven if you were there? What could you say? What kind of songs could you sing there? What sort of happiness, congenial to your heart, could you hope to find there?

Your pious mother in heaven—Oh, how she has changed! You heard her last words on earth, for they were words of prayer for your poor guilty soul. But now she shines and sings above, all holy and pure. What could you possibly have in common with her in heaven in your present condition? Remember what Christ said when someone told Him that His mother and brothers stood without, desiring to see Him.

"Who," He said, "is my mother? Or my brethren? . . . Whosoever shall do the will of God, the same is my brother, and sister, and mother" (Mark 3:33, 35). In heaven, the law of unity turns not on an earthly relationship, but on a oneness of heart—on the mutual spirit of love and obedience toward their great Father they share in common.

On that basis, do you expect that your mother would be glad to see you—that she would spread her mantle over you and take you up to heaven? Oh, if she were told that you were at the gate, she would hasten down to say, "Oh my sinning child! You cannot enter heaven. Not this holy place. Nothing can by any means enter that 'worketh abomination or maketh a lie.' You cannot—no, you cannot come!" Even if it were left solely to your own mother to decide the question of your admission, you could not come in. She would not open heaven's gate for you. She knows you would disturb the bliss of heaven, mar its purity, and be an element of discord in its sympathies and in its songs.

You know it need not have been so. You might have given your heart to God, and then He would have shed His love abroad in your soul, and given you the Holy Spirit, and made you ripe for heaven. But you *would not*. All was done for you that God could wisely do; all that Christ could do, and all that the Spirit of God could consistently do was done. But all was vain! All came to naught and availed nothing, *because you would not forego your sins*. You would not renounce them, even for everlasting life. And now will heaven let you in? No. Nothing that worketh abomination can by any means go in there.

Besides, you would never be comfortable there. You were never quite comfortable in spiritual society on earth; unhappy even in the prayer meeting. As one individual said here: "Oh, what a place this is! I cannot go across the street without being spoken to about my soul. How can I live here?" Let me tell you, it will be much worse for you in heaven. That can be no place for you, sinner, since you hate, worst of all things on earth, those places and scenes that are most like heaven.

The justice of God will not allow you to participate in the joys of the saints. His wisdom in relation to the universe makes it indispensable that He should protect His saints from such influence as yours. They have had their discipline of trial in such society long enough. The scenes of their eternal reward will bring everlasting relief from this torture of their holy sympathies.

God, their Infinite Father, will throw around them the shield of His protection, raise them upon the mountains of paradise and lift their heads eternally under the sunlight of His glory! His sense of propriety forbids Him to place sinners among His pure and trustful children. It would be so unfitting—so unsuitable! It would throw discord into the sweet songs and sympathies of the holy!

Besides, as already hinted, it could be no kindness to you, the sinner. It could not soothe, but only chafe and fret your spirit. Oh, if you were obliged to be there, how would it torment and irritate your soul!

If, then, the sinner cannot be saved and go to heaven, *where shall he appear?* Not among the righteous and the saved. This is a common form of speaking. Nehemiah said, "Shall such a man as I *flee?*" (Neh. 6:11). No, indeed. This sort of rhetorical question is one of the strongest forms of negation that can be expressed in our language.

Where, then, shall the ungodly and the sinner appear? Certainly in no desirable place or position. Not with the righteous in the judgment, for so God's Word has often and most solemnly affirmed. Christ himself affirms that when all nations shall be gathered before Him for judgment, He will separate them, one from another, as a shepherd divides the sheep from the goats.

This separation, as the description shows, brings the righteous on the right hand and the wicked on the left. Consider that this statement is made by Christ himself. He must be the one who is "given authority to execute judgment." He says He will separate them one from another according not to their national relations, or their family connections, but according to their character as friends or enemies of God.

Oh, what a separation must this bring in families and among dear earthly friends! On this side will be a husband and on that a wife; here a brother and there a sister; here one of two friends and there the other—parted forever—*forever!* If this great division were to be drawn today according to your present character, how fearful the line of separation it would draw! Ask yourself where it would pass through your own family and among the friends you love. How would it divide college classes—how would it smite many hearts with terror and consternation!

It is asked, "where shall the ungodly appear?" I answer, *certainly not in heaven,* nor on the heavenly side. But they must be in the judgment, for God has declared that He will bring the human race into judgment, along with every secret thing, whether it be good, or whether it be evil. All are to be there, but some are on the right hand and some on the left.

The ungodly and the sinner will appear in that day among the damned—among lost angels, doomed to the place prepared of old for their eternal abode. So Jesus has told us. The very words of their sentence are on record: "Then shall he say also unto them on the left hand, Depart from me, ye cursed, into everlasting fire, prepared for the devil and his angels" (Matt. 25:41).

This is indeed the only place for which they are prepared. This is the only society to which their hearts are congenial. They have chosen to belong to Satan's government on earth—at least, in the sense of doing precisely what Satan would have them do. Now, after such a training in selfishness and sin, they are manifestly fit for no other, and no better, society than that of Satan and his angels.

Do not be surprised that the amiable sinners of earth are preparing themselves (by remaining enemies to God with radical selfishness) for the society of the arch spirit of evil. Just observe what restraints are thrown around sinners here. See how obviously they *feel* restrained, and show that they are restive and ill at ease. It may be read out of their very hearts that they would be glad to be vastly more wicked and selfish; that is, in their external life—if they might. It is amazing to see in how many ways God's providence has walled around the sinner's pathway and hedged him in from outbreaking sin.

But let these walls be torn away. Let all regard to his reputation among the good perish forever from his soul. Let despair of ever gaining God's favor take full possession of his heart, and rivet its iron grasp upon him, then what will become of him? Take away all the restraints of civil society, of laws and customs, of Christian example and influence. Let there be no more prayer made for him by pitying Christian friends, no more counsel given, nor entreaty used to persuade him toward the good.

Tell me, where is the sinner then? How terribly will sin work out its dreadful power to corrupt and madden the soul! Bring together a multitude of desperate wretches. What madness ensues with their despair, rage and wrath against God and all good; what a fearful world they would make! What can conceivably be more awful? Yet this is the very world for which sinners are now preparing, and the only one for which they will be found in the judgment to be prepared.

Since this is the only world for which the sinner is prepared, it is the only one that is appropriate and fitting, the case being viewed in respect to his influence for mischief. Only in this prison-house of woe and despair can sinners be effectually prevented from doing any further mischief in God's kingdom. Here they are cut off from all possibility of doing any more harm in God's universe.

In this earthly state one sinner destroys much good. Each and every sinner does much evil. God looks on, concerned, but with amazing patience. He allows a great deal of evil to be done for the sake of securing an opportunity to try the power of His forbearance and love upon the sinner's heart. You are abusing His love and defeating all His kind designs, but still God waits, until the point is reached where forbearance ceases to be virtue. Beyond this point, how can God wait longer?

Here on earth you find ample room for doing mischief. Many are around you whom you influence to evil and urge on toward hell. Some of them would be converted, were it not for your influence to hold them back and ensnare their souls. If this were the place, I could name and call out some of you who are exerting a deadly influence upon your associates.

Ah, to think of the souls you may ruin forever! God sees them, and sees how you are playing into the devil's hands to drag them down with you to an eternal hell. But before long He will take you away from this sphere of doing evil. He will forever cut off your connection with those who can be influenced to evil, and leave around you only those associates who are ruined, despairing, and maddened in sin, like yourself. There He will lock you up, throw away the key, and let you rave on, and swear on, and curse on, and madden your guilty soul more and more forever! Oh! what inmates are those in this prison-house of the guilty and the lost! Why should not God fit up a place for such beings, so lost to all good, and so given up to all the madness and guilt of rebellion?

Only there can sinners be made useful. They refused to make themselves useful on earth; now God will make use of them in hell for some good. Do you ask me if I talk about sin being made useful? Yes, I do. God never permits anything to occur in His universe but He extracts some good from it, overruling its influence, or making the correction and punishment of it a means of good. This is a great consolation to the holy, that no sinner can exist from whom God will not bring out some good. This principle is partially developed in society here, under civil government.

The gallows is not the greatest evil in the world, nor the most unmixed evil. Murder is much worse. State prisons are not the greatest earthly evils. Government can make great use of those men who will not obey law, making them examples and lifting them up as a warning, to show the evil of disobeying wholesome laws.

A great many have had strong and useful impressions made on their minds, as when riding through Auburn on the railroad, and seeing those lofty frowning walls and battlements that enclose and guard the culprits within. Many a hard heart has quailed before those walls, and the terrors of those cells behind. If the outside view does not avail to awe the spirit of transgression, give them the inside view and some of its heart-desolating experience. These things do good. They tame the passion for evil-doing, and impress a salutary fear on the hardened and reckless. And if this is so under all the imperfections of human government, how much more under the perfect administration of the divine!

God cannot afford to lose your influence in His universe. He will rejoice to use you for the glory of His mercy, if you will. Oh yes! He will put away your sins far as the East is from the West, and will put a robe of beauty and glory upon you, and a sweet harp in your hands, and a song of praise on your lips, and the melody of heaven's love in your heart—all these, if you will.

But if you will not, then He has other attributes besides mercy that need to be illustrated. Justice will come in for its claim, and to illustrate He will make you an example of the bitter misery of sinning. He will put you deep in hell. And the holy, beholding you there, will see that God's kingdom is safe and pure, and in their everlasting song they will shout, "Great and marvellous are thy works, Lord God Almighty; just and true are thy ways, thou King of saints. Who shall not fear thee, O Lord, and glorify thy name? . . . for thy judgments are made manifest" (Rev. 15:3–4).

This is the only way God can make you useful in His kingdom, if you will not repent. He has tried every means of bringing you to repentance, but all in vain. He cannot get your consent. Of course there is no alternative but to make you an example to deter all other moral agents from sinning.

There is no other way for God to meet the demands of public justice, but to make you an example to show His abhorrence of sin. God is most thoroughly economical of His resources. He uses everything to the very best account. Everything must, under His hand, be made conducive in some way to the general good. Even with your misery, He will be as economical as He can, and will carefully turn it all to the very best account. Every groan and every throb and pang of your agonized soul will be turned to use.

Yes, rely upon it. All this agony, which does you no good, but is to you only unmingled and unalleviated woe, will be a warning beacon, under God's hand, crying out in tones of thunder, "Stand away! Stand away! Lest you come into this place of torment. Stand far from sin. Fear this awful sin and watch against it, for it is an awful thing to sin against Jehovah. I have tried it and here I am in woe unutterable!" Oh, what a testimony when all hell shall roll up one mighty accumulated groan! A groan whose awful voice shall be, "Stand in awe and sin not, for God is terrible in His judgments upon the guilty."

Oh sinner, think of it. God wants you now to cry out to every fellow-sinner, and warn him away from the brink of hell. Will you do it? For what are you preparing yourself now—to go out as a missionary of light and love and mercy to the benighted? Are you preparing, as an angel of mercy, to bear the messages of salvation?

Oh no! You refuse to do this, or anything of the sort. You disdain to preach such a gospel. But God will make you preach it *in another way*; for, as I said, He is thoroughly economical of the resources of His kingdom, and all must do something in some way for His glory. He will have everyone preach—both saints and sinners. Yes, sinners in hell must preach for God and for His truth. He will make your very groans and tears—those "tears that ever fall, but not in Mercy's sight"—preach.

You will tell over and over the dreadful story of mercy abused and sin persisted in, and waxing worse and worse, until the bolts of vengeance broke at last upon your guilty head! Over and over will those groans and tears repeat the fearful story, so that when the angels shall come from the remotest regions of the universe, they shall cry out, "What is here? What do these groans mean? What mean those flames, wreathing around their miserable victims?" The story told then will make them cry aloud, "Why will God's creatures sin against His throne? Can there be such madness in beings gifted with reason's light?"

These angels know that the only thing that can secure public confidence in a ruler is fidelity in the execution of his law. Hence, to them it is no wonder that sin is punished; they expect that God should punish it with most exemplary severity. Seeing its awful demonstrations before their eyes only serves to impress more deeply on their souls the holiness and justice of the great and blessed God.

From this standpoint we can easily see what we are to understand by the doctrine of election—a doctrine often misstated, and often perverted to a stone of stumbling and a rock of offense. The simple and plain view of it is that God, foreseeing your future existence as perfectly as if all were in fact present, is determined to deal with you according to your voluntary course.

God determined to offer you the gospel, and, on your refusal of it, to give you over to the doom of those who deny the Lord that bought them. Election is not a new plan of divine administration, and no different from what the Bible reveals as the plan of saving men through the gospel. It is this very plan of which the Bible is full, only that it contemplates this plan as framed by the divine mind "before the world began."

If you will now consent to give your heart to God, you can be saved. No election will hinder you. The doctrine of election is simply the fact that God sends forth His Spirit to save as many as by the best system of influences He can wisely save. Surely this never can hinder any sinner from repenting and gaining salvation. This plan contemplates saving men—and not damning them—as its object, and is in fact the sinner's only hope. Come then, repent and believe the gospel, if you would be saved. No election will hinder you; neither will it save you without your own repentance unto life.

How then shall the case turn with you? Almost all who are ever converted are brought in early in life. Not one in a hundred is converted after the age of forty. The old among the converts are always few—only one among a host—one in a long space of time; like scattering beacon lights upon the mountaintops, that the aged may not quite despair of salvation.

But God is intensely interested in saving the young, for He needs and loves to use them in His service. Oh, how His heart goes forth after them! How often has my soul been moved as I have thought of His paternal interest for the salvation of this great multitude of youth! Some come from pious homes, frightened with the prayers of pious fathers and mothers—and what shall be the result?

What has been the result of those prayers *with you?* Has the state of your soul yet been secured—fixed and done for eternity? How many times have you been called to decide, but have decided wrong—all wrong? You have been pressed earnestly with God's claims, and many a time prayers and groans have gone forth from the Christian heart of this whole community. But where are you now? Not yet safe; but in greater peril than ever! "Often reproved . . . hardening his neck"; and what next? "Suddenly . . . destroyed, and that *without remedy*" (Prov. 29:1). Suppose even now your life's curtain should drop; *once you are dead, whither goes the deathless, guilty soul?*

How great the mistake made by universalists, that all men will be saved, when the Bible holds that even the salvation of the righteous is difficult, and that of the sinner, impossible. How strangely they misread the whole Bible! Go not in their ways, youth of Oberlin!

But what are you doing? Do you flatter yourselves that the work of salvation is all so easy that it may be safely and surely done during a few of life's last moments? Will you presume, as the man did who said he should need but five minutes to prepare to die? Hear his story. What was the result of his system? Disease came on. It smote him with its strong hand. Delirium set in. Reason tottered and fell from her throne, and so he died!

Go on, thou young man; drive on, headlong and reckless; make a bold business of sinning, with bold front and high hand. *But know that for all these things God will bring you into judgment.* Consider what tidings we hear of our former pupils who once sat as you now sit, and once heard the gospel as you may hear it now. One is dead, and then another—and now still another. In rapid succession they drop from the stage of mortal life—and what next? Soon we shall meet them in the fearful judgment!

Brethren, what will the universe say of us if we neglect to labor for the salvation of these precious youth? What will the parents of these dear youth say to us when we shall meet them at the Savior's throne of judgment?

I have spoken to you of the difficulties and the struggles of the Christian. These are more and far greater than the ungodly are usually aware of: agonies of prayer, and conflicts with temptation, which only great grace can deliver them from, as conqueror and more than conqueror. If the righteous man is saved with so much difficulty, does it not become you to *strive* to enter in at the strait gate? Are you aware that the smooth sea of temptation bears you on to the breakers of death?

Were you ever at Niagara? How smooth and deceitful those waters as they move along quietly above the draft of the suction from below! But lower down, see how those same waters roar, and dash, and foam, and send up their thick mists to the heavens above you. Yet the waters of the upper stream glide gently and noiselessly along; those riding on the current do not dream of any danger, neither do they make any effort to escape. In a moment you are in the awful current, dashing headlong down; and what will you do then?

And what should you do? Like Bunyan's Christian pilgrim, put your fingers in both ears, and run, shouting, "Life! Life! Eternal LIFE!" How many of you are sliding along on the smooth, deceitful stream, yet only just above the awful rapids and the dreadful cataract of death! What if, this night, delirium should seize upon you? Or what if the Spirit should leave you forever, and it should be said of you, "He is joined to his idols, let him alone"?

What will you do? Do I hear you saying, "If salvation is possible for me—if by putting forth the whole energy of my will I can ensure it—Oh, let me do so! Help me, you ministers of Christ's gospel! Help me, you Christians, who pray between the porch and the altar! Help me, oh, heavens, for this is a thing of life and death, and the redemption of the soul is most precious!"

Surely, ye sinners, it is time that you should set down your foot in fixed determination, and say, "*I must and I will have heaven!* How can I ever bear the *doom of the damned!*"

21

THE DOOM OF THOSE WHO NEGLECT THE GREAT SALVATION*

"How shall we escape, if we neglect so great salvation?" (Hebrews 2:3).

What can Universalists say to such a question as the one implied in our text? Their first doctrine proclaims that there can be no danger! "How shall we escape?" asks the inspired author, strongly implying that there *can* be no escape to those who neglect this great salvation.

The very term *salvation* imports safety or deliverance from great impending evil. If there is no evil from which to escape, then there is no meaning to this term; there is no real salvation.

The writer speaks of the salvation published in the gospel. The idea immediately suggested is the greatness of its author and revealer. Because Jesus Christ, by whom this gospel came, is so great, compared with angels, the writer conceives of this salvation as pre-eminently great and glorious.

This second chapter of Hebrews is closely connected with the first, drawing the train of thought to the fact that while God had anciently spoken to their fathers by the prophets, in these last days He has spoken through His Son. Jesus Christ is the very brightness of God's own glory—the Upholder of all things.

He is shown throughout the Bible as higher than angels; through His ministrations, also, the divine word sometimes came to mortals. That word, revealed by angels, carried with it the sternest authority: every sort of transgression and disobedience would receive a just reward—how then shall people escape who neglect a salvation so great that even God's glorious Son is sent from heaven to earth to reveal it!

---

*Sermons on the Way of Salvation, 203–216.

The Exalted Son came down to create and reveal this salvation. By miracles He confirmed His divine mission. Then, He wrought it out in death. Does this not demonstrate a matter of supreme importance?

Yet the Bible has not left us to infer its greatness from the glory of its Author alone. The Bible presents to us the greatness of this salvation in many ways, for it is great in its very *nature*: it is *salvation from death in sin*.

Let people talk as they will, there is one great fact given to us by the human consciousness: *Men are dead in sin*. Everyone knows this. We all know that apart from God's quickening Spirit, we have no heart to love God. Each sinner knows that whatever may be his powers as a moral agent, left to himself there is a moral weakness in him that effectually shuts him off from salvation, unless God interposes with efficient help. Hence the salvation that meets him in this weakness and turns him effectually to love and to please God must be intrinsically great.

Salvation is great because it *delivers from endless sinning and suffering*. Just think of that: *endless suffering*. How long could you bear even the slightest degree of pain, supposing it to continue without intermission? How long before you would find it unendurable? Experiments in this matter often surprise us. For example, the incessant fall of single drops of water upon the head, a kind of torture sometimes inflicted on slaves. The first drops are scarcely noticed; but, before long, the pain becomes excruciating and ultimately unendurable.

Just think of any kind of suffering that goes on, ever increasing! Suppose it were to increase constantly for one year. Would you not think this to be awful? Suppose it to increase without remission for one hundred years. Can you estimate the fearful amount of torment? What, then, must it be if it goes on increasing *forever!*

It does not matter how rapid or how slow this increase. The amount, if its duration is eternal, must be ineffably appalling! Nor does it matter much how great or how little the degree at the outset. Suppose it ever so small, yet eternal growth must make it appalling beyond measure!

You may suppose the amount of woe endured to be represented by one drop for the first thousand years, yet let it increase for the next thousand, and yet more for the next, and, before eternity shall have rolled away, the amount will be an ocean! It would take a great while to fill up such an ocean as the Atlantic by giving it one drop in each thousand years; yet, time would fill it. It would take yet longer to fill the Pacific at the same rate, but time would suffice to fill it. More time would fill up the Indian Ocean; more yet would cover this globe; more would fill all the vast space between us and fixed stars; but even this lapse of time would not exhaust eternity. It would not even begin to measure eternal duration. How fearful then must be that woe that knows no limit except eternity!

Some deny the sufferings of the wicked to be penal inflictions, and insist that they are only the natural consequences of sinning. I shall not stop now to enter upon any argument on this point. But what difference does that make as to how endurable the eternal woe? Penal or not penal, the Bible represents it as eternal, and its very nature shows that it must be forever increasing.

How, then, can it be essentially lessened by the question, whether it is or is not penal infliction? Whether God has so constituted all moral agents so their sin, allowed to work out its legitimate results, will entail misery enough to answer all those fearful descriptions given us in the Bible; or whether, in addition to all that misery, God inflicts yet more, and this enlarged amount constitutes the eternal doom denounced on the finally wicked, surely it can be of small consequence to decide—as far as *amount* of suffering is concerned.

Some deny that the cause of this suffering is material fire. They may even scoff at this, and think that by so doing they have extinguished the flames of hell and have thus annihilated all future punishment. How vain! Can a sinner's scoff frustrate the Almighty? Did the Almighty God ever lack means to execute His Word? What matters whether the immediate agent in the sinner's sufferings is fire or something else of which fire is the fittest emblem? Can your scoffs make it any less fearful?

This fearful woe is the fruit of sinning; and it is inevitable unless you desist from sinning while yet mercy may be found. Once in hell, you will know that while you continue to sin, you must continue to suffer. The language used in the Bible to describe the sinner's future plight is very terrible. This language may be called figurative; I suppose those terms to be figures of speech, but I cannot tell. I have never been there.

It certainly *may* be literal fire. No one can certainly know that it is not. It must be something *equal to* fire. For we cannot suppose that God will deceive us. Whoever else may speak extravagantly, God never does! He never puts forth great swelling words of vanity—sounding much, but meaning little. Take it, then, whichever way you please. It is an awful revelation to die in your sins, to go away into a furnace of fire, to be among those, the smoke of whose torment ascendeth up forever and ever!

How strikingly this doom is symbolized in the smoke of those doomed cities of the plain, "set forth as an example, suffering the vengeance of eternal fire" (Jude 1:7). Their smoke "went up as the smoke of a furnace" (Gen. 19:28). Abraham lifted up his eyes and saw it! What sort of a night did he spend after that appalling scene? He had risen early, had made his way through the morning dew to the hilltop overlooking Sodom, and then he saw the smoke of those doomed cities ascending to heaven. So may the Christian parent wend his way to the hilltops of the heavenly city, and look over into the great pit, where the ungodly weep and wail forevermore! Shall it be that any of your unsaved children will be deep in that pit of woe?

This salvation is not merely *negative*—a salvation from sin and from suffering. This salvation also has a *positive* side, including perfect holiness and endless blessedness. It is not only deliverance from never-ending and ever-accumulating woe. It is also endless and exceeding bliss in both kind and degree, all we can conceive in this life. In this world we do not realize the full bliss of unalloyed purity. There has always been sin around us, and yet who does not sometimes catch a distinct view of that purity and blessedness that we know reigns in heaven? Most blessed views these are, they are no doubt dim and weak, compared with the great reality.

In heaven, bliss shall be perfect. In heaven, nothing more is left us to desire, but every desire of our soul is filled to its utmost capacity. We shall have the full assurance that this blessedness must increase with the expansion of our powers and with our advance in knowledge as we gaze with ever-growing interest into the works of our great God. All this is only one side; the positive side of that blessedness which comes with this great salvation.

Set yourself to balance these two things, one against the other: an ever-growing misery and an ever-growing blessedness. Find some measuring line by which you can compare them.

You may recall the example I have more than once mentioned. An old writer says, "Suppose a little bird is set to remove this globe by taking from it one grain of sand at a time, and to come only once in a thousand years. She takes her first grain, and away she flies on her long and weary course, and long, long, are the days before she returns again. It will doubtless seem to many as if she never would return. But when a thousand years have rolled away, she comes panting back for one more grain of sand, and this globe is again lessened by just one grain of its almost countless sand. So the work goes on. So eternity wears away, only it does not exhaust itself a particle. That little bird will one day have finished her task, and the last grain of sand will have been taken away. But even then eternity will have only begun: its sands are never to be exhausted."

One would suppose the angels would become so old with the weight of centuries that they would be weary of life. But this supposing only shows that we are judging of the effects of time in that eternal state by the effects we observe in this transient world. We fail to consider that God made this world for a transient life—for one that shall never pass away.

Look again at the example of the little bird removing the sands of our globe. We may extend it, and suppose that after she has finished this world, she takes up successively the other planets of our system: Mercury, Venus, Mars, Jupiter, Saturn, each and all at the same rate—one grain each thousand years. When these are all exhausted, then she takes the sun, and then each of the fixed stars; until the hundreds of thousands of those stupendous orbs are all removed and gone. Even then eternity is not yet exhausted. We have not yet even an approximation toward its end.

End? There is no end! That poor old bird makes progress. Though exceedingly slow, she will one day have accomplished her appointed task. But she will not even then have come any nearer to the end of eternity! Eternity! Who can compute it? No finite mind; and yet this idea is not fiction, but sober fact. There is no possible room for mistake—no ground for doubt.

Moreover, no truth can be more entirely and intensely practical than this. Everyone of us—everyone of all our families, every child, every student—is included. It concerns us all. Before each of us lies this eternal state of our being. We are all to live in this eternal state. There awaits us there either woe or bliss, without measure and beyond all our powers of computation. If woe, it will be greater than all finite minds can conceive.

Suppose all the minds ever created were to devote their powers to compute this suffering, to find some adequate measure that shall duly represent it. Alas, they could not even begin! Neither could they any better find measures to contain the *bliss* of those who are truly the children of God. All the most expressive language of our race would say, "It is not in me to measure infinite bliss or infinite woe." All the figures within the grasp of all created imaginations would fade away before the stupendous undertaking.

Yet, this infinite bliss and endless woe are the plain teaching of the Bible, and are in harmony with the decisive affirmations of the human reason. We know that if we continue in sin, the misery must come upon us. If we live and die in holiness, the bliss will come.

Is this the theme, and are these the great facts, which these young men may go abroad to the ends of the world and proclaim to every creature, and which these young women also may speak of everywhere in the society where they move? Truly they have a glorious and sublime message to bear!

Suppose the joy resulting from this salvation to be a mild form of peace and quiet of soul. We may suppose this, although we cannot forget that the Bible represents it as being a "joy unspeakable and full of glory" (1 Pet. 1:8). But suppose it were only a mild, quiet joy. Even then, a prolongation of it during eternal ages (considering, also, that naturally it must forever increase) will amount to an infinite joy. Indeed, it does not matter how small the unit with which you start, yet let there be given an eternal duration, coupled with ceaseless growth and increase: how vast the amount in the end!

According to the Bible, the blessedness of the holy is the full fruition of God's love. Hence, the bliss that it involves can be nothing short of infinite; it can have no limit. A really comprehensive view of what it will be like would be overpowering.

Who could bear the view of your future self? Could you, if you are a saint? Suppose you could see yourself as you will be ten thousand years from now. Suppose you were for a moment endowed with the power to penetrate the future and see yourself as you will be before the throne of God. If you were not aware that it was yourself, you might fall down and worship!

Or suppose the wicked could see themselves as they will be ten thousand years from now. Suppose they could see how full of torment they will be, and what unutterable woe their souls shall bear there. Could they endure the sight?

Do you suppose that I exaggerate to make my point? Nothing can be further from the truth! For, if one considers only the scope of *immortality*, and the implications of it, all that I have said must follow by necessity. Admit that the soul exists forever, and not a word that I have said is too much. Indeed, when you carry out that great fact to its legitimate conclusions, under the influence of the moral government of God, all these descriptions seem exceedingly flat—they fall so very far short of the truth.

Neglecting this great salvation is fatal. So our text most emphatically implies, and the Bible often most unqualifiedly affirms. No sinner need go about to weary himself to commit iniquity, as if he would make sure of his doom, since mere neglect is fatal. No further effort is necessary.

What Is Fatal Neglect?

At some time, everyone has been guilty of neglect. We shall reach the true answer to our question by asking another, "What is *effectual attention*?" Plainly, it is only that which ensures gospel repentance and faith in Christ. Only that which ensures personal holiness and, thus, final salvation. Therefore, *effectual attention* arouses the soul thoroughly to take hold of Jesus Christ as Savior. To fall short of this is fatal neglect. You may have many good things about you. You may make many good resolves and hopeful efforts. Yet, failing in this main thing, you fail utterly.

You need only be a little less than fully in earnest, and you will certainly fall short of salvation. You may have a good deal of feeling and a hopeful earnestness, but if you are only a little less than fully in earnest, you will surely fail. The work will not be done. You are guilty of fatal neglect, for you have never taken the decisive step. Are you a little less than fully in earnest? You are the one who will weary yourself in vain. You must certainly fall short of salvation.

To do anything short of effectual effort is great folly. Many are just enough in earnest to deceive themselves. They pay just enough attention to this subject to misunderstand it, and do only just enough to fall short of salvation, and go down to death with a lie in their right hand. If they were to stay away from all worship, it would shock them. They go to the assemblies of God's people and do many things hopeful, but, they fall short of entering in at the door into Christ's fold.

What folly is this! Why should you do this foolish thing—only just enough to deceive yourself and others. This is the very way to please Satan. Nothing else could so completely serve his ends. He knows very well that where the gospel is generally understood, he must not preach infidelity openly, nor universalism, nor atheism. Neither would do. But if he can just keep you going along, doing a little less than enough, he is sure of his man. He wants to see you holding fast to a false hope. Then he knows you are the greatest possible stumbling block, and that you are doing the utmost you can to ruin the souls of others.

This salvation is life's greatest work. To put it in any other relation is worse than nothing. If you make it second to anything else, your course will surely be ineffectual—a lie, a delusion, a damnation!

Are you giving your attention effectually to this great subject? Have you this testimony in your own conscience, that you seek first the kingdom of God and His righteousness? Have you become acquainted with Christ? Do you know Him as your Life and your Hope? Have you the joy and peace of believing? Can you give to yourself and to others a really satisfactory reason for the hope that is in you?

This is life's greatest work—the greatest work of earth. Is it effectually begun in you? You cannot do it at all without a thorough and right beginning. I am afraid you may have mistaken conviction for conversion. Like some of Bunyan's characters, I fear you may have clambered over the wall into the palace, and did not come in by the gate.

Do you ask me why I fear this? I will answer only by asking a question back. "Don't you think I have reason to fear it? Have you the consciousness of being pure in heart, and of growing purer still? Do you plan everything with reference to His great work of salvation? What are the ways of life that you have marked out for yourself? On what principle have you shaped them? On what subjects are you most sensitive? What most thoroughly awakens your sensibility? If there is a prayer meeting to pray for the salvation of sinners, are you there? Is your heart there?"

To make the matter of personal salvation only a secondary matter is infinite folly! To do so is only to neglect it. Unless it has your whole heart, you virtually neglect it, for nothing less than your whole heart is devotion. To give it less than your whole heart is truly to insult God, and to insult the subject of salvation.

What shall we think of those who seem never to make any progress at all? Is it not very plain that they give much less than their whole hearts to this matter? It is most certain that if they gave their whole hearts intelligently to it, they would make progress—would speedily find their way to Christ. To make no progress is therefore a decisive indication of having no real inclination in this pursuit. How can such escape, seeing they neglect so great salvation?

PART 3

The Charge to the Church

"Look on the fields; for they are white already to harvest" (John 4:35).

22

CONVERTING SINNERS IS A CHRISTIAN DUTY*

"Brethren, if any of you do err from the truth, and one convert him; let him know that he which converteth the sinner from the error of his way shall save a soul from death, and shall hide a multitude of sins" (James 5:19–20).

A subject of present and great practical importance is brought before us in this text. To clearly apprehend it we must inquire into the true idea of a *sinner*. Essentially, a sinner is a moral agent. This much he must be, whatever else he may or may not be. He must have free will in the sense of being able to originate his own activities. He must be the responsible author of his own actions in such a sense that he is not compelled to act one way or another, apart from his own free choice.

He must also have *intellect*, so that he can understand his own moral responsibilities. A person lacking this element of character is not a moral agent, and therefore cannot be a sinner. He must also have sensibility, so that he can be moved to action, (so that there can be inducement to voluntary activity), and a capacity to discern the motive behind his actions.

There are essential elements of mind necessary to constitute a moral agent, yet they may not all develop themselves in a sinner beyond the initial stages. A sinner is a selfish moral agent devoted to his own interests, making himself his own supreme end of action. He looks on his own things, not on the things of others. His own interests, not the interests of others, are his chief concern. Thus every sinner is a moral agent, acting under this law of selfishness, having free will

---

Sermons on Gospel Themes, 335–346.

and all the powers of a moral agent, but making self the great end of all his action. This is a sinner.

Now we have the true idea of *sin*. A sinner is one that "erreth." "He which converteth a sinner from the *error* of his way." Yet, it is not a mere *mistake*; mistakes are made through ignorance or incapacity. Nor is it a mere defect of constitution, which can be blamed on the Creator. It is an "error of his way," missing the mark in his voluntary course of conduct.

It is not an innocent mistake, but a reckless yielding to impulse. It involves a wrong end, a bad intention, the influence of an appetite or passion in opposition to reason and conscience. It is an attempt to secure some present gratification at the expense of resisting convictions of duty. This is most emphatically "missing the mark."

What Is Conversion?

What is it to "convert the sinner from the error of his ways?" Since his error lies in his having a wrong object of life—his own present worldly interests, to convert him from the error of his ways is to turn him from this course to a benevolent consecration of himself to God and the well-being of the human race. This is precisely what is meant by conversion. It is changing the great moral end of action. It supplants selfishness and substitutes benevolence in its place.

In what sense does a person convert a sinner? Our text reads: "If any of you do err from the truth, and *one convert him*." Our text implies that a man may convert a sinner—though of course the change must be a voluntary one on the sinner's part. The change is not a change in the essence of the soul, nor in the essence of the body, nor any change in the created constitutional faculties. It must be a change in which the mind itself, acting under various influences, changes its own voluntary end of action. It is an intelligent change: the mind, acting intelligently and freely, changes its moral course for perceived reasons.

The Bible ascribes conversion to various agencies. First, to God: God is spoken of as converting sinners, and Christians with propriety pray to God to do so. Christians are spoken of as converting sinners. We see this in our text. The truth is also said to convert sinners.*

Remember, no one can convert another without the cooperation and consent of the other. His conversion consists in the yielding up of his will and the voluntary changing of his course. He can never do this *against* his own free will. He may be persuaded and induced to change his voluntary course; but to be persuaded is simply to be led to change

---

*See especially, *Principles of Revival* for a more complete explanation of the truths in this paragraph.

one's chosen course and choose another.

Even God cannot convert a sinner without his own consent. He cannot, for the simple reason that a forced consent is a contradiction. Being converted implies consent, or else it is no conversion at all. God converts sinners, therefore, only as He persuades them to turn from the error of their selfish ways to the rightness of benevolent ways.

In the same way, a person can convert a sinner only in the sense of presenting the reasons that induce the voluntary change, thus persuading him to repent. If he can do this, then he converts a sinner from the error of his ways. But the Bible informs us that a person alone never does nor can convert a sinner. It holds, however, that when man acts humbly, depending on God, God works with him and by him. People are "workers together with Him" (2 Cor. 6:1). They present reasons to the sinner's mind.

When the minister preaches, or when you converse with sinners, you present truth, and God causes the mind to see it with great clearness and to feel its personal application with great power. Man persuades and God persuades. Man speaks to his ear and God speaks to his heart. Man presents truth through the medium of his senses to reach his free mind, and God presses it upon his mind so as to secure his voluntary yielding to its claims. Thus the Bible speaks of sinners as being *persuaded*: "Almost thou persuadest me to be a Christian" (Acts 26:28).

This language of the Bible is entirely natural. Just as if you should say you had turned a man from his purpose, or that your arguments had turned him, or that his own convictions of truth had turned him. So the language of the Bible on this subject is altogether simple, speaking in perfect harmony with the laws of mind.

The "Death" Referred to

A *soul*, not a body, is to be saved from death; consequently, we may dismiss all thought of the death of the body in this connection. However truly converted, his body must nevertheless die. The passage speaks of the death of the soul. The death of the soul is sometimes referred to as *spiritual death*: a state in which the mind is not influenced by truth as it should be. The person is under the dominion of sin and repels the influence of truth.

Or the death of the soul may be *eternal death*: the utter loss of the soul and its final ruin. The sinner is, of course, spiritually dead at the start; if this condition were to continue through eternity, this would become eternal death. Yet the Bible represents the sinner dying unpardoned, as "going away into everlasting punishment," and as being "punished with everlasting destruction from the presence of the Lord, and from the glory of His power" (2 Thess. 1:9).

To always be a sinner is awful enough. This death is a fearful horror. But how terribly compounded is the horror of it when you conceive it as heightened by everlasting punishment, far away "from the presence of the Lord, and from the glory of His power!"

The Importance of Saving a Soul From Death

Our text says, "He which converteth the sinner . . . shall save a soul from death." Consequently, he saves him from all the misery he otherwise must have endured. And this misery is greater in the case of each sinner saved than all that has been experienced in our entire world up to this hour. This may startle you at first; it may seem incredible. Yet you have only to consider the matter attentively and you will see it must be true. That which has no end, that which swells utterly beyond all our capacities for computation must surpass any finite amount, however great.

Yet, the amount of actual misery experienced in this world has been very great. As you go about the great cities in any country you cannot fail to see it. Suppose you could ascend some lofty peak and stretch your vision over a whole continent, just to take in at one glance all its miseries. Suppose you had an eye to see all forms of human woe and measure their magnitude—all the woes of slavery, oppression, intemperance, war, lust, disease, and heart-anguish.

Suppose you could stand above some battlefield and hear as in one ascending volume all its groans and curses, and gauge the dimensions of its unutterable woes. Suppose you could hear the echo of its agonies as they roll up to the very heavens. You must say, "There is indeed an ocean of agony here!" Yet, all this is only a drop in the bucket compared with that vast amount, defying all calculation, which each lost sinner must endure, and from which each converted sinner is saved.

If you were to see cars rush over a dozen men at once, grinding their flesh and bones, you could not bear the sight. Perhaps you would even faint away. But imagine how you would feel if you could see all the agonies of the earth accumulated, and could hear the awful groans ascending in one deafening roar that would shake the very earth. How your nerves would quiver! Yet all this would be merely nothing compared with the eternal sufferings of one lost soul! And this is true, however low may be the degree of this lost soul's suffering, each moment of his existence.

Yet further, the amount of suffering thus saved is greater not only than all that ever has been, but than all that ever will be endured in this world. And this will always be true, even though the number of inhabitants be increased by millions, and their miseries be augmented in like proportion. No matter how low the degree of suffering that the sinner would endure, if the earth's population increased a millionfold, and the magnitude of its miseries augmented in like proportion, it could not begin to measure the agonies of the lost spirit.

Or we may extend our comparison and take in all that has yet been endured in the universe, all the agonies of earth and all the agonies of hell combined up to this hour. Even so, the total is utterly too scanty to measure the amount of suffering saved when one sinner is converted. Nay, more, the amount thus saved is greater than the created universe ever can endure in any finite duration. Aye, it is even greater, myriads of times greater, than all finite minds can ever conceive.

You may embrace the entire conception of all finite minds, of every man and every angel, of all minds but that of God, and still the person who saves one soul from death saves in that single act more misery from being endured than all this immeasurable amount. He saves more misery, by myriads of times, than the entire universe of created minds can conceive.

I am afraid you may have never given yourself the trouble to think of this subject. You are not to escape from this fearful conclusion by saying that suffering is not a natural consequence of sin, and that there is no governmental infliction of pain. It does not matter whether the suffering is governmental or consequential. The amount is all I speak of now. If he continues in his sins, he will be miserable forever by natural law; and, therefore, the man who converts a sinner from his sins saves all this immeasurable amount of suffering.

Here are two methods of studying and of endeavoring to apprehend the infinite: one by the reason, which simply affirms the infinite; and another by the understanding, which only approximates toward it by conceptions and estimates of the finite. Both these modes of conception may be developed by culture. Let a man stand on the deck of a ship and cast his eye abroad upon the shoreless expanse of waters, he may get some idea of the vastness. Or better, let him go out and look at the stars in the dimmed light of evening. He can get some idea of their number and of the vastness of that space in which they are scattered abroad.

On the other hand, his reason tells him at once that this space is limited. His understanding only helps him to approximate this great idea. Let him suppose, as he gazes upon the countless stars, that he has the power of rising into space at pleasure, and that he ascends with the rapidity of lightning for thousands of years. Approaching those glorious orbs, one after another, he takes in more and more clear and grand conceptions of their magnitude, as he soars on past the moon, the sun, and other suns of surpassing splendor and glory. So are the conceptions of the understanding in reference to the great idea of eternity.

But let us look at still another view of the case. He who converts a sinner not only saves more misery, but confers more happiness than all the world has yet enjoyed, or even all the created universe. You have converted a sinner, have you? Indeed! Then think what has been gained! Let the facts of the case give the answer. The time will come when he will say, "In my experience of God and divine things, I have enjoyed more than all the created universe has done up to the general judgment, more than the combined happiness of all creatures, during the whole duration of our world. And yet my happiness is only just begun! Onward, still onward, onward forever rolls the deep tide of my blessedness, and evermore increasing!"

Then look also at the work in which this converted man is engaged. Just look at it. In some sunny hour when you have caught glimpses of God and of His love, and have said, "Oh, if this might only last forever!" You have said, "If this stormy world were not around me! Oh, if my soul had wings like a dove, then would I fly away and be at rest." Those were only aspirations for the rest of heaven. That which the converted person enjoys above *is* heaven. You must add to this the rich and glorious idea of eternal enlargement—perpetual increase. His blessedness not only endures forever, but increases forever. And this is the bliss of every converted sinner.

Converting sinners is the work of the Christian life. It is *the great work* to which we, as Christians, are especially appointed. It is the greatest work of life because it is so much beyond any other work in importance that it cannot be rationally regarded as anything other or less.

It can be made the greatest work of life, because Jesus Christ has made provision for it. His atonement covers the human race and lays the foundation so broad that "whosoever shall call on the name of the Lord shall be saved" (Acts 2:21). The promise of His Spirit to aid each Christian in this work is equally broad, designed to open the way for each one to become a laborer together with God in this work of saving souls.

Benevolence can never stop short of this great work. Where so much good can be done and so much misery can be prevented, how is it possible that benevolence can fail to do its utmost? Living to save others is the condition of saving ourselves; no one is truly converted who does not live to save others. Every truly converted person turns from selfishness to benevolence, and benevolence surely leads him to do all he can to save the souls of his fellow man. This is the changeless law of benevolent action.

The self-deceived are distinguished by this peculiarity: they live to save themselves. This is the chief end of all their religion. All their religious efforts and activities tend toward this sole object. If they can secure their own conversion so as to be pretty sure of it, they are satisfied. Sometimes the ties of natural sympathy embrace those who are especially near to them; but selfishness goes commonly no further, except as a good name may obligate them.

Some persons take no pains to convert sinners, but act as if this were a matter of no consequence whatever. They do not labor to persuade people to be reconciled to God. Some seem to be waiting for a miraculous interposition. They take no pains with their children or friends. Very much as if they felt no interest in the great issue, they wait and wait for God or miracle to move. Alas, they do nothing in this great work of human life!

Many professed Christians have no faith in God's blessings, and no expectation, thereby, of success. Consequently, they make no effort in faith. Their own experience is good for nothing to help them, because never having had faith, they have never enjoyed success in winning the lost. Many ministers preach so as to do no good. Having failed so long, they have lost all faith. They have not gone to work expecting success, and hence they have not succeeded.

Many, professing Christian faith, seem to have lost all confidence. Ask them if they are doing anything, they answer truly—*nothing*. But if their hearts were full of the love of souls or of the love of Christ, they would certainly make a greater effort. They would at least try to convert sinners from the error of their ways. They would live their Christian faith, and would hold up its light as a natural spontaneous thing.

Each person should make it his business to save souls. There are, indeed, many other things to be done; let them have their place. Don't neglect the greatest business of all.

Many professing Christian faith never seem to convert sinners. How is it with you? Can you say, "Under God, I have been the means of saving some souls." Have you ever labored honestly and with all your heart for this object? Do you know that you have ever been the means of converting one sinner? Are you laboring for God? Have you gone to your unrepentant friends, even to their homes, and by personal, affectionate entreaty, brought them to be reconciled to God? By your pen, and by every form of influence you have, have you sought to save souls and do what you can in this work? Have you succeeded?

Suppose all those professing to be Christians in any congregation were to do this, each in their sphere doing all they individually could do. How many would be left unconverted if each one said, "I lay myself on the altar of my God for this work. I confess all my past neglect. Henceforth, God helping me, this shall be the labor of my life."

If each one would begin with removing all the old offenses and occasions of stumbling, and publicly confess and deplore his neglect in this matter, and every other form of public offense, confessing how little he has done for souls, and cried out, "Oh, how wickedly I have lived! But I must reform, must confess, repent, and change altogether the course of my life." If every church member were to do this, and then set himself, each one in his own place, to lay his hand in all earnestness upon his neighbor and pluck him out of the fire, how glorious would be the result!

But to neglect the souls of others and think you shall yet be saved yourself is one of guilt's worst blunders! For unless you live to save others, how can you hope to be saved yourself? "If any man have not the Spirit of Christ, he is none of His" (Rom. 8:9).

23

THE CONVERSION OF CHILDREN*

The family is, without question, the greatest influence in the whole government of God concerning the destinies of the world. The parents' influence is no doubt the supreme influence. God designed it should be so; this was one reason for establishing the family relationship. It was not only to secure among human beings temporal blessings—the care and nurture of the young—but that parents should exert a spiritual influence over their offspring. The great end God had in view was their spiritual well-being. This was one of His great designs, no doubt; but it is not always kept in view by parents; therefore the great object of the Almighty in establishing the family relationship, at least as far as children are concerned, is defeated.

Remember that this influence, whatever it may be, occurs very early in the lives of children, and is generally decisive one way or the other. The decision that is made in later life, in most cases, is merely the development of what has been thus commenced. The mother begins the work. She heads the undertaking and exerts more influence over the child at first than anyone—or anything—else. If she understands her responsibility, if she is a pious woman, and if she avails herself of the facilities God has put into her hands, she will be, under God, the greatest possible blessing to her child. Children naturally have more confidence in their father and mother than in anyone else, and their position gives them an influence over the youthful mind—for good or for evil—with which no other influence in the world can compare. The results of this influence are formed very early in the child's life, and continue to develop ever after.

Parents have a mighty influence over little children. They lead them to their earliest thoughts and give them most of their first ideas.

---

*The Penny Pulpit: a lecture delivered on December 16, 1850, at the Tabernacle, Moorfields. No Scripture text was given in the original.

The spirit of the parent teaches the child a great deal, even before his words can teach him. The example and influence of the parent is not confined to mere verbal teaching. Everything he does has an influence over the child; every word the parent says, even before the child can fully tell the meaning of words, has an influence over him or her. When the child comes to understand language, the little mind weighs all that it hears and thus the child is educated.

Now if the parents' influence is of a worldly character, if there is nothing in the parent that early leads the child to think about its soul and God, and if that child does not see in the parent a concern for his own soul, the child's education has begun in the wrong direction. If the parent neglects to let his child see his concern for that child's salvation in very early life; if the child does not see that the Christian faith is prominent in the parents' mind; if he does not see that finding and doing the will of God is the parents' life, and that glorifying God is the parents' chief end, the child will know the truth of it.

He will understand it, and this truth will have its influence over him, much earlier than parents are in the habit of believing. I have known children whose temperament was such that when very young they talked much about the Christian faith, and were constantly asking questions about it. So thoroughly were their little minds engrossed with the subject that they scarcely seemed to know that there were any other places than those to which their parents were accustomed to go for worship. Even when a stranger comes in, they ask, "Is that person a Christian?"

The early conversion of children depends upon the parents' sowing Christian truth among the earliest thoughts developed in the minds of their children. Curiously, even the smallest children observe when parents pray and recognize God in all their ways. It is remarkable to see the effect of this on their young minds. As they see their parents pray, they get their little chairs, kneel down and try to pray as well. Their mother has been in the habit of taking them and praying with them from their very birth.

As soon as they can understand her, she leads them into her prayer closet, reads the Bible to them, talks about the Savior, and prays with them daily. Sometimes several times a day. Consequently, you will see them get their little chairs, and have their little meetings, and go down on their knees and pray for themselves. One mother recently wrote to me: "Little Willy gets his chair, kneels down, and clasping his little hands, says, 'Oh Lor' (he could not articulate Lord)." Every little child would begin to pray if he had such a mother.

Now the tendency of all this is to keep the little one's thoughts awake. He will perceive, from the spirit and example of the parent, that Christianity is something of supreme importance. God comes to be in all his little thoughts. He sees that Christianity is the great concern of the parents' life.

Where this is the case, unless there is some error in the teaching or conception of the parent that gets in the way and prevents this influence from producing its natural results, I do not believe there is one case in a thousand in which children are not very early converted. I have known pious parents who have trained their children on the subject of Christianity, but who, from holding certain erroneous views, have laid stumbling blocks in their way. The parents told them some things that were false, which consequently proved injurious to them.

Parents should understand that there is only one of two courses open to them with regard to their children. They must either exert a worldly influence (which would give their little minds an entirely wrong direction), or a spiritual one (which will set them after Christian faith). If the proper spiritual influence is exerted, the child's mind will early be caused to ferment on the subject of Christianity. His earliest thoughts will be about God the Father, faith and Jesus Christ. The earliest influences they can remember will be convictions of sin, heaven and hell, Christ and eternity. These thoughts will put their little minds into a state of effervescence. These influences commence before the child has left the lap of his loving mother.

Things Parents Should Avoid

Be sure you don't stumble on the idea that "you can't expect" the early conversion of your children. A worthy deacon from Birmingham called on me a few hours ago at Doctor Campbell's. The members of his family have all been converted and united to the church. His youngest child is only about ten years of age. He told me that he had been introduced to the deacon of one of the city churches, who had a large family, not a single member of whom has been converted.

On being apprized of the happy condition of the Birmingham family, the second deacon said, "Well you know *we* cannot *give* grace to our children."

"Oh, no," replied the Birmingham brother, "but we can use the means in our possession to make them Christians."

When the fact came out that the youngest child was only ten years old, the city deacon shook his head "Ah!" he said, "I don't believe in forcing people into the church."

"Nor do I," was the response. "I did all I dare do, and said all I dare say. But what could anyone do or say, except let her profess her faith in Christ, as other people do?"

One of the greatest stumbling blocks is cast in the way of families by the idea that to expect the early conversion of children is unreasonable. "The idea of a ten-year-old child being converted! Why we cannot believe it!" But suppose I were to preach the funeral sermon of such a child and to say, "He is gone to hell, no doubt."

"What makes you say so?" you would ask. "Why, surely you do not think that the child is a sinner at ten years of age?"

Indeed he is, and to think otherwise is the greatest and most dangerous error that can be entertained. If a child has intelligence enough to sin, has it not intelligence enough to be converted? If not, what becomes of children old enough to sin, but not old enough to be converted? The fact is, it is easier for the Holy Spirit to convert a child, than it is for Him to convert a man.

Now, what is in the way of the child's conversion? When the child's little conscience first wakes up, sin takes such a hold of it, that it goes into the greatest agony at the thought of it. This is natural. For the little conscience has not yet been trifled and tampered with. Now cannot the Spirit of God teach such children? Cannot those who understand the nature of faith in the parent understand the nature of faith in God? Cannot those who understand parental protection and love understand the protection and love of their heavenly Father? Cannot those who know so well how to depend on a parent depend on God?

They can surely do these things more easily then, than if they wait until they have learned to mistrust everybody and everything from contact with the world. Cannot they, whose tender hearts are so ready to trust, be taught to exercise faith in Christ? This is the most likely time in their lives. It is less likely they will be converted later, if you allow them to grow up and form bad habits. Bad habits are more easily corrected if you use the best and earliest means to prevent their formation at the start.

The fact is, the Spirit of God is always ready to cooperate with the judicious use of means—and just as ready to cooperate with children as with adults. But parents who do not believe this to be the case allow their children to grow up and escape from under their influence. I have observed that just as far as parents have intelligently used the best means in their power to secure the early conversion of their children, they have to that same extent been successful in their endeavors. But when the contrary has been the case, when no such influence has been exerted, I have not been surprised to find that the children have grown up to manhood and womanhood unconverted.

Sometimes I have asked parents if they ever made it a great pressing business to secure the early conversion of their children. "Oh, no; we never set ourselves to make it a pressing business to secure them for God." "You don't? Then is it any wonder that they are not converted?" Multitudes must admit that they never in good earnest set about promoting the conversion of their children and securing it under God. I could tell you of numbers of cases where such sons and daughters have turned out badly.

Many entertain ideas of God's sovereignty that are a great stumbling block in the way of the early conversion of their children. The man who said, "We cannot give grace to our children," doubtless had an idea that God's sovereignty was connected with conversion in a way that he associates it with nothing else. Such beliefs are folly, but common nonetheless. In every other matter such people exert themselves as though there were some connection between means and ends in the government of God. But they assume that there is no connection between means and ends in the act of conversion, that God sets aside all the laws by which He invariably operates at other times, exercising a peculiar kind of sovereignty in conversion.

I have been very surprised to find that multitudes have such ideas of God's sovereignty and agency that they can recognize His hand in nothing short of an absolute miracle. For example, when a person goes and talks to a child in such a manner as to make a deep impression on its young mind, the impression is made accordingly; the child awakens to a deep sense of sin and importance of faith in Jesus. But then the parent says, "Let him alone now, and we will see whether you have been merely playing upon the child's feelings, or whether the Spirit has been cooperating." The fact is, the child is talked to in the very way to produce the effect predicted.

If a preacher so discourses as to affect the minds of his audience in a certain way, and accordingly they are so affected, some say, "Ah! God has had nothing to do with it!" They suppose there can be no perceivable relation between the means and the ends in order to have God recognized. But, if there really is any natural and necessary connection between the means and the end, then why is not God recognized—unless He intervenes in such a manner so as to set aside this connection, and causing an effect entirely inconsistent with it?

For example, if you sit down and converse with a child about playing marbles, who could expect that such conversation would be followed by any religious result? And if a minister got into a pulpit and preached about politics, would you expect anybody to be converted? It seems therefore necessary that the subject of the discourse should have a Christian leaning in order to expect a Christian effect. A discourse concerning some historical facts that are in no way relevant to the sinner's duty would not be expected to achieve the desired results. The preacher must press the matter home, till the sinner fully feels that he is virtually saying, "Thou art the man." "Oh!" you say, "you have been playing upon his sympathies."

So where are we to stop? The fact is you do not, you cannot, expect

God to convert anyone when there is no sort of relevant means used. And if some relevancy, even according to your own ideas of divine sovereignty, is necessary in the means employed, pray *how much* relevancy is absolutely indispensable? When God works, He can never be expected to commit any infraction of the laws He has ordained for the government of the universe. If He operates according to His own laws, why should it be doubted that He is operating at all? For my part, I always expect to see God work in accordance with His own established laws, and I recognize Him all the more when I see how nicely He adapts the means to the end.

He created mind and established its relations to truth, and when He presents truth to the mind, and it is received in accordance with principles He has ordained, am I not to recognize the hand of God in them?

Parents do not seem to feel the necessity of applying themselves to secure the early conversion of their children with as much earnestness as they seek their recovery when sick. A little error in nursing will often have a most dangerous influence on the health of the patient, and a little error in instruction may induce a serious turn in the thoughts, and perhaps present a fatal stumbling block. If God allows things to take this course in the physical world, He will permit it in the moral world. If certain laws are violated in the physical world, and God allows the thing to take its natural course, why should He adopt a different policy toward the moral world? This is the very way in which God's sovereignty really manifests itself.

If you look round on the natural world, you will see that God permits immense results to turn on the most trifling violation of natural laws. A ship will sink, though it be filled with devoted missionaries, if the natural law is neglected. In fact, if they have neglected to take compass or chart, or some such necessary precaution on the pretense of trusting the sovereignty of God, they have in reality been tempting God by not taking care to adjust themselves to His physical laws. And that ship, although it is filled with missionaries, will go to the bottom! And in such a case, perhaps, the salvation of thousands of souls might be suspended on that ship's reaching its destination safely.

It is the same in the moral world, let mother or father make a mistake, either moral or physical; in one instance it is death to the body—and in the other, to the soul. This is the teaching of the Bible, and it is borne out by experience. People should know that they can as certainly ruin the soul, as they can kill the body.

Care should be taken not to cause the child to stumble through bad government or no government at all. Some govern their families too much. Others not at all. Often the spirit of the whole family government is such as to make a false impression. It is not the firm spirit of

God's government. It is either despotic, or no government at all. In other cases, there is one half the time too much rigor and the other half too much laxity.

All such impressions affect the children in connection with Christianity. If the general impression of your deportment should suggest that you are "in God's stead" to them, you cannot underestimate the importance of early seizing their little minds and wills, bringing them under proper control. Oh! that little will! If unsubdued, what will it cost that child to be converted, if it ever is converted! When parents permit the will to pass unsubdued, their little ones get into such a habit of self-will, as to render it extremely doubtful whether they will ever bow either to God or man. At the least, it will render it far more difficult for them to do so than it would have been had a contrary course been pursued.

When I see children agonize at their position, unable fully to yield and come into the kingdom, I always suspect they have never been properly taught to yield to parental authority in their childhood. It is of the utmost importance that parents take hold of this will as soon as it develops itself, and to exert the first moral influence on it under God's moral government, as a representative of the Almighty. Take hold of that little will as a sacred trust under God, holding it by parental authority and love so kindly and firmly that it is lost in your will and controlled by it. Even a look or a motion of the hand, when understood, should be immediately and willingly obeyed.

When the time comes that the child can understand about God, give the whole weight of your will to lead the child's will to submit to God. Did you ever think what a powerful influence you possess? Where the little will from the first has been held under control, and the child is old enough to be talked to about God, bring all your powers to bear upon it to induce it to yield itself up to God, and you will find yourself, as it were, almost handing your child over to God.

You are not to suppose that because your influence is used as a means, that God has nothing to do with it. He has placed you where you are in order to use you. He has stationed you there to watch over the development of that little will, and kindly to control it so that in due season you may hand it over to God through the teaching of the Holy Spirit.

This is the great work you are sent to do, Fathers! Let your parental heart draw the little one close, and let your mind draw the little mind into close connection with yours, and let the little will be as far as possible subject to and guided by your will. Do it prayerfully before God, and you need not fear failure. As soon as the little will can be influenced by Christian truth, pour it in with all the weight of your parental authority and carry that will to God.

A Christian lady once informed me that she had found her daughter under conviction of sin. "I have so trained her," she said, "from her infancy, that she regards my will as her law; a look from me is enough. I did not at first understand properly my relation to her with reference to her conversion; but as soon as the thought came before my mind that I could exert a direct and powerful influence in the matter, and that the Spirit of God would use that influence, I took the child with me to my closet and prayed with her. I there showed her that it was her duty to yield up herself to Christ. I talked and prayed with her, and urged the matter in this light: 'Now, my child, you never hesitate to obey your mother in other things, and I want you now at once to renounce yourself, and give yourself fully up to Christ.' "

Before they left the closet, she said she had reason to believe that her child had really given herself up to God. She said, "Never before had I any idea that the Spirit of God would so use this influence."

Now observe; this was *not* any such authority as would *threaten to whip the child!*—that is neither prudent nor necessary here; proper parental influence can carry the little mind with an amazing power. When the whole weight of this parental influence is concentrated upon the single issue: "My child, give your heart this moment to Christ," what human influence can be more powerful? And this, of course, is backed up by the work of God, and seconded by the Spirit of God—in addition to that will to which the child has always been accustomed to yield. I have seen the infinite importance of this not only in my own, but in many other families.

Parents are very apt to stumble their children by their temper. A temper destroys the confidence of the child in their parent's piety, and causes him to doubt their sincerity; and thus the parent loses all hold on him. Few things more surely and speedily destroy the influence of a parent than to scold them peevishly, or even to speak to them snappishly, and call them hard names. Anything that savors of ill temper has a dreadfully powerful influence in leading the child away from Christ and counteracting well meant endeavors.

Parents must be careful to feel and manifest concern for their children's spiritual welfare; if they do not, a young child cannot be expected to feel a concern for himself. Suppose a parent felt truly concerned to keep a child out of bad company, he would remind the child often, keeping it always before the mind of that child. If concerned for his health, he would keep that before the little one, and teach him how to take care of himself. It is just the same with anything else of this kind. Now the parent ought to feel and manifest a supreme interest in the child's salvation.

Let all your conversation plainly indicate that it is so. Let your children see that health, worldly prospects, and everything else must be subordinate to Christian faith. Do these things, and you are beginning right; and by a natural law you can hardly fail to see their early conversion.

Parents often manifest great error in not seeing to it that their children are punctual and regular at public worship. I have been in a great many churches, and have known the history of a great many families. Sometimes I have found households in which the children were both punctual and regular. At chapel pews where some families sat, you would see that all the children, able to come out, were always there. They were where their parents were. They felt that they were no more expected to absent themselves from chapel when their parents went, than from the dinner table. They were not allowed to wander about, their parents not knowing where they went. Where this is allowed parents have little or no Christian influence over them.

Parents must also guard against laxity with reference to the due observance of the Lord's Day. It is not right to throw everything into the hands of the sovereignty of God, assuming that that alone will convert them, whatever influence may be brought to bear upon them; a more damning error never entered the world. Truly, other influences may possibly convert the child, and as other influences may save the child in sickness, but no thanks to the parents in either case.

There is another fault of parents I must notice. They do not take sufficient pains to provide a happy home; the children, not finding friendship and sympathy at home, run about elsewhere in search of it. Their home is not a happy one, and they consequently rove about and come under bad influences. Now a happy home is one of the principal things at which a parent should aim. The home should be rendered so pleasant that the child would rather remain there than go about.

Dear parents! Are you aware how often a child's life is embittered by the neglect of this? They must be made happy, and have something to love at home, or they will naturally seek company and happiness somewhere else. Oh! that parents would see the necessity of using this and every other means they can devise to secure and retain their proper influence over the little minds! They ought to feel toward you so that they would sooner tell you than anybody else their little thoughts.

Fathers are more apt to neglect this than mothers. Children often seem afraid of their fathers, so that they cannot tell him the workings of their little minds. He treats them with a kind of tolerance, and manifests no interest in their little concerns; and as he does not sympathize with them, they therefore turn to someone else, fall under some other influence, and are gone! How many parents who have had to lament the evil conduct of their children, could look back and attribute their children's behavior largely to this! The father has been sharp and has not kept his influence over their little hearts.

Oh! how often Christian people, and even ministers, have been so busy with other matters that they have neglected their own children in this respect, shutting them out from their hearts, so they have fallen into other hands, and under evil influences.

Now, dear parents, one of the first things God wishes you to do is to secure and retain the affections and confidence of your children, and to use your influence over them for Him. In order to keep their hearts open to you, let yours be open to them. You will surely secure your end if you do so. But, on the contrary, if they are afraid to approach you because you keep them at such a distance, then, if they are not ruined, it is no thanks to you.

Instead of telling you all the temptations and trials they fall into— all their plans, and the books they read—instead of feeling that in you they have advisers who can and will sympathize with them, they will manifest the same reserve to you on these matters that you have displayed to them, and you have, therefore, failed in a vital point.

Another point I wish to notice is the evil practice of allowing children to wander about where they will in the evening. As I have said, if you would make the home what it should be, they would *never want* to do this. They would rather be with you than anywhere. But if you allow them to go out and keep late hours, they are sure to go in the way of temptation.

I have often seen the injurious influence of holidays being too numerous and long; parents make a great deal of difference at such times with regard to their control over their children. They are allowed to do things then, *because* it is a holiday, which you would not permit at other times, and this leads them astray. The holidays are near; what will be your influence over them during that period? Parents! think of this.*

---

*For Finney's letters to parents see *Principles of Discipleship.*

BIBLIOGRAPHY

Most of the sermons in this book are taken from *The Oberlin Evangelist*, a newspaper published by Oberlin College, Oberlin, Ohio, from 1839–1862; and from *The Penny Pulpit*, sermons published in tract form from Finney's tours in England.

Additional sermons are from his *Lectures to Professing Christians* (Oberlin, Ohio: E.J. Goodrich, 1880); *Sermons on Gospel Themes* (New York: Fleming H. Revell Company, 1876); *Sermons on the Way of Salvation* (Oberlin, Ohio: E.J. Goodrich, 1891); and *Sermons on Important Subjects* (1836).